Girard and Theology

Girard and Theology

Michael Kirwan

t&t clark

Published by T&T Clark
A Continuum imprint
The Tower Building   80 Maiden Lane
11 York Road   Suite 704
London SE1 7NX   New York, NY 10038

www.continuumbooks.com

All rights reserved. No part of this publication may be reproduced or transmitted in any form or by any means, electronic or mechanical, including photocopying, recording or any information storage or retrieval system, without permission in writing from the publishers.

Copyright © Michael Kirwan, 2009

Michael Kirwan has asserted his right under the Copyright, Designs and Patents Act, 1988, to be identified as the Author of this work.

British Library Cataloguing-in-Publication Data
A catalogue record for this book is available from the British Library

ISBN-10: HB: 0-567-03226-4
               PB: 0-567-03227-2
ISBN-13: HB: 978-0-567-03226-3
               PB: 978-0-567-03227-0

Typeset by Newgen Imaging Systems Pvt Ltd, Chennai, India
Printed and bound in Great Britain by MPG Books Ltd, Bodmin, Cornwall

Contents

1 **Introduction: 'The man on the train'**   1
    Theology's bickering handmaids   4
    Girard: Philosopher or critic?   6
    Repetition and mimesis   9

2 **René Girard: Life and work**   13
    Revelation and conversion:
    From *Things Hidden* to *Evolution and Conversion*   17

3 **The mimetic theory of René Girard**   20
    Thinking on a grand scale   20
    A tripartite theory   21
    Mimesis and conflict   24
    'The Kingdom of God has become scientific'   27
    Conclusion   30

4 **The Innsbruck connection: Dramatic theology**   33
    Raymund Schwager: 1935–2004   33
    Dramatic theology   36

5 **A theological 'anthropophany'**   45
    Naming humanity before god   45
    The turn to the subject   48
    Girard and anthropology   50
    A mimetic anthropology   54

6 **The drama of salvation**   57
    Christ, then salvation   59
    Girard and Anselm   61
    Conclusion: Beyond salvation   67

Contents

7	**'Painting pictures on clouds':**	
	The metaphors of atonement	**70**
	First model: Christ's victory over the devil	70
	Second model: The justice of God	73
	Third model: Sacrifice	75
	The exodus from sacrifice	76
	Conclusion	79
8	**Girard and the Bible**	**81**
	From myth to gospel	81
	The logos of the victim	84
	An exegetical response	86
	Figura and ambivalence	87
9	**Political theology**	**93**
	The violent return of religion	93
	Violence and the sacred in the modern world	94
	The doctrine of the katechon	96
	The 'apocalyptic feeling'	99
10	**Views from the South**	**106**
	Girard and liberation theology	109
	Witchcraze	110
	Conclusion	115
11	**Girard and the religions**	**120**
	The revelation of Holy Week	120
	A stuttering conversation: Boston 2000	123
12	**Girard and the theologians**	**132**
	Epilogue	**143**
	Notes	146
	Bibliography	151
	Index	161

Chapter 1
Introduction: 'The man on the train'

Professor René Girard is 'immortal'. In November 2005 he was admitted to chair number 37 of the Académie Française, whose 40 members have been known since 1651 as *les immortels*. New members are elected by the Académie, so this is in itself a notable and fine achievement; but when we consider that Girard's lifetime work on violence, culture and religion has been highly disputed and largely unfashionable in his native France, such recognition by his peers is astonishing. It seems that, 30 years after Girard first came to widespread attention with the publication of *La violence et le sacré* in 1972, many people are taking a second look.

If René Girard is 'immortal', what does he have to say to theology? Can he help the theologian to speak correctly about God?

The beginnings of an answer to these questions can be found in an event which took place in the winter of 1959. For several months René Girard was commuting once a week on the rickety Pennsylvania Railroad, between colleges in Baltimore and Philadelphia.[1] He was what we would call an 'emerging scholar', having just written his first book, a study of key European novelists. The completion of the final 12th chapter of *Mensonge romantique et vérité romanesque* (English translation *Desire Deceit and the Novel*) was presumably a cause of deep satisfaction, not least because Girard's struggle to establish himself as an academic in the United States had been far from easy. He recalls how the weekly train journey through the downbeat industrial landscape of Delaware and south Philadelphia was transformed by his sense of elation during this time. Girard would watch the sunset in a state of ecstasy.

This elation was in fact the stirring of a religious conversion. Girard's reading of Cervantes, Flaubert, Stendhal, Proust and Dostoyevsky had, surprisingly, shown up common patterns of religious language and symbolism. Although these are five very different writers, each seemed to have undergone a similar transformation of consciousness, which Girard discerned by comparing their earlier work with their more mature writings. This led him back to an interest in the Christianity which he had long ago left behind, and to an identification with his chosen authors. He thinks about the 'analogies between the religious experience and that of the novelists, in which one is systematically revealed as a liar, in favour of the "I", which leads to a thousand lies', which accumulate over a lifetime.

> Then I realised that I had just at the same time had an experience similar to that which I had just wanted to describe. The religious symbolism, which in the novelists is there in embryo, began to work in my own case, spontaneously bursting into flame. (Girard, 1994: 180; my translation from German)

On one level Girard was disconcerted by this, since he was proud of his scepticism, and couldn't imagine genuflecting in church and so on:

> On an intellectual level I was converted, but I was still unready to bring my life into line with my thought. For several months the faith was for me a sensitive pleasure, added to other joys, a sweetener in a life, which was not sinful exactly, more tiresomely self-indulgent . . .

A 'conversion', then, but a rather aesthetic, complacent affair: Girard speaks also of being opened up to music during this time, so that even the *Marriage of Figaro* was infused with a mystical quality. Then he received a health scare, the discovery of a cancerous growth on his forehead. At first the growth was not especially dangerous, but after an operation it returned, and the inefficiency and tactlessness of his doctor left Girard badly shaken. This took place shortly before Lent, the penitential season when Christians commemorate Christ's testing in the wilderness and traditionally make a confession of their sins. Weeks of sleepless nights followed before the doctor gave him the all-clear: it was now the Wednesday of Holy Week.

> Never before had I experienced a feast to compare with this liberation. I saw myself as dead, and suddenly I was risen. The most wonderful aspect of this whole story was for me the fact that my new intellectual and spiritual awakening, my real conversion, had occurred before my huge scare during Lent. If it were down to that, I wouldn't have really believed. As I am a sceptic by nature I would have remained convinced that my faith was due solely to my fear. The scare for its part could not be the result of faith. . . . God had brought me again to awareness, and had thereby allowed a small joke which basically in view of the mediocrity of my case was fully justified. (183)

Introduction

Girard's 'dark night' ended just in time for him to celebrate the Easter Triduum, after which he had his children baptized and his marriage regularized in the Catholic Church. He saw and continues to see such events as signs from God, which the learned and the clever do not notice as objectively significant, but which are unmistakeable to the one who experiences them. The memory has stayed with and supported him ever since.

Clearly, this provides a key to understanding Girard's life: but how is it the key to his work? And how, precisely, does a text of literary criticism turn out to be the catalyst for an encounter with God?

It seems we should look more closely at *Deceit, Desire and the Novel*, and especially its 12th chapter, 'The Conclusion'. As we have seen, Girard found in his chosen novelists a similar patterning of religious symbols and concepts, but one that went well beyond any merely aesthetic or literary effect. This pattern signified nothing less than a transformation in the life and consciousness of each of the authors, a conversion from untruthfulness or inauthenticity which is inseparable from the quality of their finest work. Girard puts it thus: 'The ultimate meaning of desire is death but death is not the novel's ultimate meaning' (1965: 290). Deathbed scenes in Cervantes (*Don Quixote*), Stendhal (Julien Sorel in *The Red and the Black*) and Dostoyevsky (Stephan Trophimovitch in *The Possessed*) are similar, because they each involve a definitive repudiation, couched in religious language of repentance and even resurrection, of a life of illusion and lies.

What is being renounced in each case is a proud but mistaken assertion of autonomy. The mistake consists in the hero failing to recognize that in fact the desires which drove him were not in the least spontaneous; rather, they were mediated by one or more models whom the hero had been obsessively imitating. Such mimicry is nothing more than a pathetic attempt at self-divinization. Only when the false divinity which attaches itself to the desiring hero and to his or her model is renounced can a genuine transcendence be opened up.

This movement from falsehood to truth is the essence of the novel as a genre: 'all novelistic conclusions are conversions' (1965: 294). Girard contrasts this with 'romantic' criticism, which stays on the surface and does not achieve 'breadth and depth of vision', that is, novelistic vision. Here is a paradox. Conversion in the orthodox Christian sense means setting aside one's *self-centredness*. For Girard, this self-centredness betrays itself in our being driven to imitate one another: we in fact live *outside ourselves*. 'Conversion' therefore entails both a turning away from oneself, but also achieving a greater intimacy with oneself and a withdrawal from the baneful influence of others – a renunciation, in other words, of mimetic desire. 'This victory over a self-centredness which is other-centred, this renunciation of fascination and hatred, is the crowning moment of novelistic creation' (299). It is also to be found, argues Girard, in the great works of Marcel Proust and in Fyodor Dostoyevsky, the two novelists whom he cites in his concluding flourish:

> The conclusion of *The Brothers Karamazov* is borne on the highest crest of Dostoyevsky's genius. The last distinctions between novelistic and religious experience are abolished. But the structure of experience has not changed. It is easy to recognize in the words *memory, death, love,* and *resurrection* found in the mouths of the children of this novel the themes and symbols that inspired the creative ardor of the agnostic author of *The Past Remembered.* (1965: 314; original emphasis)

Finally, the triumphant words of Alyosha Karamazov: '"Certainly, we shall all rise again, certainly we shall see each other and shall tell each other with joy and gladness all that has happened!" Alyosha answered, half-laughing, half-enthusiastic.' Two years after *Desire, Deceit and the Novel*, Girard's second book was published: a study of Dostoyevsky, which would later be translated as *Resurrection from the Underground*.

Theology's bickering handmaids

It may be observed that there is nothing inherently 'religious' about the conversion which Girard is describing, nor especially revolutionary. The painful journey from lies to truth, from illusion to *désillusion*, is after all the basic pattern of other intellectual or therapeutic endeavours, such as philosophy (think of Plato's myth of the cave), or psychoanalysis. One can also discern echoes of the existentialist search for authenticity, or of Kierkegaard's progression, which we will look at in more detail below, through different 'stages on life's way': aesthetic, ethical and religious. So there are precedents.

Even so, Girard's is an extraordinary and unsettling approach to reading literature, in which 'the last distinctions between novelistic and religious experience are abolished'. Surely literary criticism is an autonomous discipline, with its own rules and procedures – why is it being mixed up with theology and religion like this?

The plot thickens when we register the surprising fact that Girard is not strictly speaking a literary critic. Trained as a medieval historian, it was only by accident, as it were, that he found himself teaching French language and literature. For academics who like to keep to strict demarcations and specialisms, Girard's cheerful interdisciplinarity (which over his

Introduction

long career has seen him stray into ethnology, anthropology, psychology, philosophy, mythology and theology as well as literary criticism), is something of an irritant.

Here we begin to see the relevance of Girard's work for theology, the particular focus of this study. Theology is less worried by Girard's kind of multidisciplinary promiscuity, and in fact sees it as essential to its own task. This is because theology is a 'second-order discipline', that is to say it proceeds by reflecting upon the insights of ancillary investigations into what is 'really real'. To draw on a quaint traditional image: Christian theology was known during the High Middle Ages as the 'Queen of the Sciences' because it was the culmination and capstone of the various disciplines in the syllabus. The other sciences, and particularly philosophy, played a subordinate role as the Queen's 'handmaidens' (the word *ancillary* comes from the Latin for 'servant'). Theology has always needed help to carry out its exalted and important task, and over the centuries has enlisted the services of many number of philosophical schools and thinkers. Only with the aid of Plato, Aristotle, existentialism, hermeneutics, and even Marx and Freud, have theologians been able to begin to speak, however stutteringly, about the things of God.

The relationship between the Queen and her handmaidens has not always been harmonious, and it so happens that René Girard's academic career coincides with the latest phase in a long-standing crisis between them. First of all, the Queen has for a long time now been 'dethroned': theology is no longer regarded as the most prestigious of the disciplines, and adjusting to her humbler role has not been easy. Secondly, while the deposed Queen is still in need of her servants, they have begun to be stroppy and less inclined to do the tasks traditionally required of them. As its name implies, classical philosophy aimed at the achievement of wisdom or enlightenment, in a way which was analogous to and coherent with theology's own search for truth. More recently, however, philosophers have held back from this grand calling, confining themselves to humbler, more specific goals, such as the clarification of concepts by means of linguistic analysis or hermeneutics. To put this polemically: philosophy is alleged to have 'abdicated' many of its traditional responsibilities, bringing into question its adequacy as a 'handmaid' for the poor Queen.

This is where literary criticism and René Girard come in. One effect of the crisis of philosophy had been a new awareness of the potential of literature: if philosophy finds the 'big' questions about the meaning of life too hot to handle, perhaps we should return to the insights of creative writers and artists to help us frame and even to answer some of these questions. Girard was one of the postwar French generation of thinkers taking inspiration and solace from existentialism, whose proponents such as

Camus and Sartre attempted to construct meaning and purpose in peerless novels such as *La Peste* and *L'Etranger*.

This view of literature, as a vehicle for authenticity and responsibility, stood in polar contrast to an insistence on the autonomy of literature which is to be found in some versions of postwar theory, notably the so-called New Criticism. For New Critics such as Northrop Frye, who sought to establish criticism as a 'scientific' activity, two forms of demarcation were important: first, the existence of the poem or novel independently of its author, and secondly, the proud autonomy of criticism with regard to other, non-literary disciplines, for example, history, ethics, psychology or theology.

A Girardian approach to literature, drawing on the biography of the author and linking up with theology (abolishing 'the last distinctions between novelistic and religious experience') flies in the face of these formalist prescriptions.

In short: as a teacher of literature in postwar American academies, Girard is both observer and participant in a 'mimetic' power struggle between literary studies and philosophy, disciplines whose status and self-confidence had been undermined by complex political and intellectual changes in the postwar era. Debates over the merits of deconstructionism and other postmodern theories are skirmishes in this wider struggle. To return to our regal metaphor, his work is carried out in the context of this palace feud and is inevitably shaped by it.

Girard: Philosopher or critic?

We need to place Girard more precisely within this distinctive cultural and academic context. What kind of thinker is he: a philosopher, or a literary critic? 'Although his work has profitably been taken up by philosophers, Girard is, strictly speaking, not a philosopher' (Fleming, 2004: 3), which means that to understand him requires more than simply an elucidation and clarification of central concepts. Another commentator, Jean-Marie Domenach, makes the same point but negatively, objecting that Girard occupies the position of a scientist and a philosopher, but without accepting the burdens and responsibilities of either.

A conference on 'Girard and Philosophy' in Antwerp in 2001 offers some enlightenment.[2] Guy Vanheeswijck on 'The Place of René Girard in Contemporary Philosophy' begins with the excitement created by Alexandre Kojève's lectures on Hegel in Paris between 1933 and 1939. Kojève's recovery of Hegel, and the reaction against this recovery, together defined the philosophical tenor of a generation of French scholars; it is impossible not to see resonances between 'Hegel à la Kojève' and Girard in the light of

Introduction

Kojève's declaration that '[h]uman history is the history of desires that are desired'. Girard, Jacques Derrida and Michel Foucault, in very different ways, have all explored the problematic of 'difference' in the shadow of Hegel and Martin Heidegger.

Vanheeswijck argues for Girard's rich engagement – arising out of a 'thematic congeniality' – with continental philosophers such as Jacques Derrida and Gianni Vattimo,[3] and Anglo-Saxon philosophers Charles Taylor and A. N. Whitehead.[4] Taylor in particular shares with Girard a post-Hegelian starting-point for questioning the notion of the autonomous, self-sufficient subject; the same literary 'canon' (part three of *Sources of the Self* cites Flaubert, Proust and Dostoyevsky; see Taylor, 1989); and a Catholic Christian commitment, though in Taylor's case this has been more implicit.

In short, Girard's place in contemporary philosophy is relatively assured, though Vanheeswijck acknowledges that '[t]ime and again, Girard has expressed his preference for literature over both humanities and philosophy'. And yet Girard's attitude towards literary theory seems to be similarly offbeat. In 1978 he published *'To double business bound': Essays on Literature, Mimesis and Anthropology* (Girard, 1978), in which he makes clear that 'I am speaking here not of all literary texts, not of literature per se, but of a relatively small group of works . . . [which] reveal the laws of mimetic desire' (vii–viii). In other words, it is the theme of imitation which is always the object of Girard's research – whether this theme manifests itself in anthropology, literature or philosophy. Girard is a 'mimetologist'! In the interview which concludes this volume Girard asserts:[5]

> The writers who interest me are obsessed with conflict as a subtle destroyer of the differential meaning it seems to inflate. I must share somewhat in that obsession . . . I do not claim to be a complete critic, or even a critic at all. I am not really interested in a text unless I feel it understands something I cannot yet understand myself.

For this reason, a 'theory of literature' approach is alien to Girard, as it can only have a deadening effect on the text itself:

> Not literature as such, I believe, but certain literary texts are vital to my whole 'enterprise' as a researcher, much more vital than contemporary theory. Mine is a very selfish and pragmatic use of literary texts. If they cannot serve me, I leave them alone. (1978b: 224)

In a lively and iconoclastic essay titled 'Theory and Its Terrors' (Girard, 1989), Girard argues robustly as to why he finds theory less than helpful, though he is in a mischievous mood and suggests we take what he says with a grain of salt. Under pressure from scientific and philosophical positivism, literary studies had downplayed the importance of content and turned towards formalistic methods – hence the attractiveness of the European schools of structuralism and deconstruction. Lévi-Strauss, Foucault and Derrida are united in declaring war on philosophical texts and systems, while at the same time using these texts to undermine structural linguistics in its turn. Deconstruction originates in a spirit of 'mimetic rivalry' with the social sciences; though poles apart, their destructive effect on the academy is indistinguishable, like matter and antimatter.[6]

What survives intact from all this, says Girard, are the great texts of literature. Formalistic criticism over the past 50 years has sought to empty literature of its content, but it is time to return to that content – not least because literature itself (the example Girard gives is the drama of Molière) is our best guide to the patterns and processes of resentful mimesis which threaten academic life. Refusing to be intimidated by 'linguistic terrorism', Girard insists that 'the most perspicacious texts from the standpoint of human relations are the great texts of Western literature' (1989: 253–4).

So Girard is not really a critic or a theorist, just a reader of texts which he finds intriguing. Although he limits his interest to writers like himself who 'are obsessed with conflict as a subtle destroyer of the differential meaning it seems to inflate', there seems to be no shortage of such obsessives: *To Double Business Bound* has essays on Dante, Camus, Dostoyevsky and Nietzsche; there is his 1963 book on Dostoyevsky; and most significantly, a lifetime's sustained engagement with the drama of Shakespeare, which issues in *A Theatre of Envy* (1991, 2000). In these readings Girard makes clear a particular indebtedness to two plays, *A Midsummer Night's Dream* and *Julius Caesar*. The first of these, he suggests, should be 'compulsory reading for anthropologists', but it is in an essay on the late romance *A Winter's Tale* where Girard moves towards his beatific vision. His analysis of the play's climax, in which Hermione's 'statue' miraculously 'comes to life', takes up where chapter 12 of *Deceit, Desire and the Novel* left off: a pattern of death and resurrection which

> is banal and may signify little, but may also refer to the experience I have just defined, so fundamental to the greatness of great works and so powerful that the creators are irresistably led to allude to it, generally at the place in the work that is best suited to the purpose, the conclusion. (Girard, 1991: 340)

Hermione's restoration is just one such conclusion; it also marks the conversion of her jealously cruel husband, Leontes: '[w]hat makes our hearts turn to stone is the discovery that, in one sense or another, we are

Introduction

all butchers pretending to be sacrificers'. Girard is in no doubt about the template for this remarkable scene:

> His genius, and *more than his genius* [my emphasis] enabled Shakespeare to recapture in this conclusion something that belongs exclusively to the Gospels, the nonmagical and yet nonnaturalistic quality of their resurrection. (342)

Girard is not the first, of course, to note the mood of transcendence in Shakespeare's late plays, and in this marvellous scene in particular. His reading of the climax to *A Winter's Tale* can be read alongside that of the theologian Hans Urs von Balthasar, who is naturally drawn to this scene as part of his project of a 'Theo-Drama'. So once again, and even more dramatically than in *Deceit, Desire and the Novel*, 'a transcendental perspective silently opens up'. The motif of *conversion as resurrection* recurs, and the distinction between 'novelistic' and 'religious' experience is abolished.

Repetition and mimesis

Are there parallels or precedents in other authors? Two come to mind: Søren Kierkegaard, in his short work *Repetition* (1845) and Erich Auerbach's classic text of literary criticism, *Mimesis*. Kierkegaard's description of 'stages on life's way' sees life as operating on three levels or dimensions: the aesthetic, the ethical and the religious. Progression through these is a journey into different modes or degrees of serious engagement with life's possibilities. As is well known, a personal crisis propels Kierkegaard from the 'ethical' to the 'religious'. He believes himself to be providentially barred from the happiness of married life (the 'ethical'), and the shattering news that his beloved Regina Olsen is engaged to someone else triggers his great works of religious existentialism, *Fear and Trembling* and *Either/Or*.

Repetition, published in the same year, deals with the same themes. 'Repetition' is both an aesthetic and a religious concept, intended as a third experiential category between 'recollection' (nostalgia) and 'hope' (revolutionary optimism), a renunciation therefore of both Plato's *anamnesis* and Hegel's mediation.

> Repetition's love is in truth the only happy love. Like recollection's love, it does not have the restlessness of hope, the uneasy adventurousness of discovery, but neither does it have the sadness of recollection – it has the blissful security of the moment. (Kierkegaard, 1983 [1845]: 131–2)

But 'is repetition possible?' The protagonist of this challenging work makes an 'investigative journey', trying to recreate or relive a memorable visit to Berlin in his youth: 'So I arrived in Berlin. I hurried at once to my old lodgings to ascertain whether a repetition is possible.' The experiment is a failure: his lodgings, the atmosphere of the town and above all his visit to the theatrical show which had enthralled him all those years previously, all are inferior to the original experience: 'The only repetition was the impossibility of repetition' (170).

On the spiritual or religious level, however, 'repetition' is indeed possible; in part II of Repetition we encounter a melancholy 'young man' whose crisis, an unrequited romantic involvement, replicates the real-life experience of Søren Kierkegaard. On the discovery that the woman has married, the young man declares: 'I am myself again'. A liberation of poetic creativity – 'ideas spume with elemental fury' – is accompanied by a new sense of answerability:

> I belong to the idea. When it beckons to me I follow; when it makes an appointment, I wait for it day and night . . . when the idea calls I abandon everything, or more correctly, I have nothing to abandon.

Girard refers to Kierkegaard's writing of 1843, 'which seems to suggest a connection between mimesis and repetition' (Girard, 2007a: 111), while Melberg (1995) notes that the author of *Repetition* invites us to move back and forward (repetition and recollection), like Diogenes refuting the sceptics who 'denied movement'. Compare with Girard's own self-commentary:

> We have no choice but to go back and forth, from alpha to omega. And these constant movements, this coming and going, forces us to construct matters in a convoluted, spiralling fashion . . . I think one needs to read [my work] like a thriller. All the elements are given at the beginning, but it is necessary to read to the end for the meaning to become completely apparent. (Girard, 2001b: 87–8)

Another work which has interesting parallels to Girard's mimetic theory is *Mimesis: The Representation of Reality in Western Fiction* by Erich Auerbach; Girard refers also to Auerbach's important essay, *Figura* (1938), which shaped his reading of the Bible. *Mimesis* is an astonishing book, written in Istanbul between 1942 and 1945, when Auerbach was exiled from European libraries. It is an exploration of realism as a perennial possibility in Western literature, one which is only fully realized in the

Introduction

nineteenth-century novel. Auerbach identifies two kinds of realism, summarized thus by Potolsky:

> Homer represents things, Auerbach writes, 'in a fully externalised form, visible and palpable in all their parts, and completely fixed in the spatial and temporal relations' . . . The Bible story of Abraham, by contrast, leaves much in darkness. There are no descriptions of setting or character, we are given little insight into Abraham's thoughts as he contemplates sacrificing his son, and even God does not reveal His intentions in demanding this sacrifice. For Auerbach, the lack of descriptive and psychological detail creates a sense of hidden complexities. The Biblical characters 'have greater depths of time, fate and consciousness' than do the characters in Homer (Auerbach, 1974: 12). They seem embedded in a process of individual, historical and theological change.
>
> Thus Auerbach identifies two kinds of realism, which roughly accord with what we found in Plato and Aristotle: the descriptive and sensory realism of Homer and the interior, psychological realism of the Bible. Whereas the classical tradition following Homer will insist on clarity, order and unity of representation, the Biblical tradition leads to psychological depth, uncertainty of meanings and the need for interpretation. (Potolsky, 2006: 105–6)

This has important social implications. By contrast with classical norms, the Christian imagination renders even a poor and lowly life as the dramatic setting for intense conflicts of religious faith and doubt. The story of Peter's denial of Jesus, for example, a common person in an extraordinary situation, fits none of the genres of antiquity: 'too serious for comedy, too contemporary for tragedy, politically too insignificant for history' (Auerbach, 1974: 45). Auerbach calls this 'creatural realism', a realism of corporeal suffering, and he is clear as to what has made possible such a break with classical theory: 'It was the story of Christ, with its ruthless mixture of everyday reality and the highest and most sublime tragedy, which had conquered the classical rule of style' (555).

The notions of *figura* and figural interpretation are used by Auerbach to specify the concept of reality in late antiquity and the Christian Middle Ages. As we shall see, figural interpretation is, once again, a movement forward and backwards, as seemingly unconnected events prefigure and fulfil one another. Girard's interlocutors in *Evolution and Conversion* draw a parallel, with which Girard agrees, between his 'novelistic truth' and Auerbach's figural interpretation (2007a: 180). As with Kierkegaard on 'repetition', Auerbach's analysis of mimesis offers a parallel to Girard's own experience of literature, where the 'deep structure', as it were, of even apparently secular modern literature is seen to be shaped by the Christian imagination, the logic of incarnation, death and Resurrection. In von Balthasar's words, 'a transcendental perspective silently opens up'.

I have dwelt at length on Girard's conversion which stole upon him during those train journeys in 1959: a meeting with God which Girard recalls in the simplest, most accessible terms. It is this experience which reverberates 'theologically', through the entirety of his work. During his long career Girard has turned to history, anthropology, philosophy and other disciplines in order to articulate his insights. In fact it is none of these but a handful of great novels, which both catalysed and embodied Girard's encounter with the divine.

To begin with, as we have seen, this was a decidedly 'aesthetic' conversion, but did not remain so for long. Girard is excited by Auerbach's work, but his fundamental criticism is the same one which he advances against every theorist on mimesis, from Plato onwards: 'nobody is able to see – neither Auerbach nor anyone else – . . . that in myths the victim is represented as guilty before being divine while in the Bible the victim is shown to be innocent, falsely accused' (209). Auerbach's 'creatural realism' is not realistic enough. Girard is not interested in mimesis for its own sake, but in the connection between mimesis and victimhood, which previous theorists on mimesis had either overlooked or not pressed home.

This brings us, finally, to those aspects of Girard's theory for which he is perhaps best known: the astounding claim that religion and cultural order originate in spontaneous processes of expulsion or extermination, which Girard calls the 'scapegoat mechanism'. This is the thesis of *Violence and the Sacred*, his highly acclaimed work of 1972, that 'violence is the heart and secret soul of the sacred'. It is important to note that this process of expulsion is the outcome of mimetic interaction, and so the investigation of mimetic desire, such as we have begun in this chapter, is logically prior to any discussion of scapegoats. What becomes clearer for Girard is the intimate connection between them; in fact, it is this insistent linking together of two sets of data about human beings – the mimeticism of desire, exclusionary violence – that forms the very core of Girard's mimetic theory.

Chapter 2
René Girard: Life and work

We saw in the first chapter that Girard's reading of Shakespeare is highly significant for his thought, with a high regard being paid to two plays, *A Midsummer Night's Dream* and *The Winters' Tale*. The volume of essays on Shakespeare, titled *A Theatre of Envy*, has a good deal of reflection from Girard on the business of biographical criticism: its legitimacy and usefulness. One essay, titled 'Do You Believe Your Own Theory?: "French Triangles" in the Shakespeare of James Joyce' (Girard, 1991: 256–70), explores a notorious example of biographical criticism, the lecture on Shakespeare given by Stephen Daedalus in James Joyce's novel *Ulysses*. Beneath the playful anarchy of Stephen's speculation into Shakespeare's erotic history is a serious intuition about the mimetic nature of desire, as it happens. The message of this curious episode, for Girard, is that a judicious and even humorous use of biographical enquiry will yield results, and we should not be bullied into abstaining from biographical criticism altogether in the name of some false *cordon sanitaire* between life and art.

In the same way, the intellectual and existential aspects of Girard's thought cannot easily be separated, which the editors of *Evolution and Conversion* (2007a [2004]) recognized in setting up this conversation with Girard as in part an intellectual biography. Just as when Girard reads Proust, or Camus, 'the life and the work are one', so a biographical approach to Girard is required which will do justice to his 'double conversion': first an intellectual, then an authentically faith-based appreciation of the revelatory power of the Christian gospel. So the opening chapter of *Evolution and Conversion*, recounting Girard's early life and career, is titled 'The Life of the Mind'. Despite the aridity of his school and university education in France, Girard speaks warmly of his happy childhood, and is explicitly resistant to any overdramatization of his non-belonging to any one intellectual or cultural ambience:

> [I]t is true that I tend not to belong to specific environments or fields, but on the other hand, I cannot be considered an outsider in the classical sense of the term. I never felt an *outcast*, as many intellectuals like to represent themselves. This is probably because

Girard and Theology

> I had, and still have, a very strong sense of belonging to my childhood . . . that's probably the reason I could never lose my French accent! (Girard, 2007a: 26)

Biographically, there seems little here to attract attention; instead, Girard goes on to locate the sense of 'not belonging' in certain theoretical options or approaches:

> I think there is always an advantage in being what one truly is. My relative marginality can be seen in the books that are most characteristic of me: the first book and the book on Shakespeare. Above all, the parts about mimetic relationship. This is probably the centre of my work, and even the anthropological and religious aspects of it are strongly tied to that key concept. (27)

This would seem to be significant, that the two 'most characteristic' texts are *Deceit, Desire and the Novel*, which we examined in the previous chapter, and *A Theatre of Envy: William Shakespeare*. These works of literary criticism are methodologically similar, in the same shuffling back and forth between writer and works, more specifically between the earlier and later works of the subject, in search of ever clearer hints and indicators of what he has called 'mimetic realism'.

In the light of the fashions and preferences of literary theory during the early years of Girard's career, epitomized in the school called New Criticism, such an approach was like a red rag to a bull. He recounts one especially hostile reaction from a colleague who objected to the mingling of literature and biography in the manuscript of *Deceit, Desire and the Novel* (2007a: 29). Such an approach made Girard an unholy mix of Sainte-Beuve and Freud as far as this colleague was concerned.

René Noel Theophile Girard was born on Christmas Day in Avignon in 1923, the second oldest in a family of six. His father was the curator of the library and Museum of Avignon, as well as of the Castle of the Popes. Girard Sr had little sympathy for Christianity, though his mother was a devout and cultured Catholic. From the age of 12 until his conversion at 36, Girard was himself distanced from the Church, being politically and intellectually a thinker of the left. He decided to follow his father as a medieval researcher, training in Paris at the Ecole des Chartes under difficult conditions of wartime occupation.

Not surprisingly, growing up as a young man in France during the Second World War has been clearly formative on Girard's interests. A recent study has referred to his involvement with the French Resistance; speaking of this period, Girard recalls how impressed he was, even as a young

Rene Girard: Life and Work

agnostic, with the fact that those of his acquaintances who seemed most able to resist being caught up by the contagious attraction of Fascism on the one hand, and of Communism on the other, were the Young Christian Workers – perhaps a pregnant observation in the light of his later religious commitment. Asked to reflect on experiences of personal marginalization which might account for his interest in the theme of scapegoating, Girard has pointed to the feeling of discrimination he felt as a 'southerner' when he arrived in Paris.

He eventually presented his dissertation in 1947, on the theme of 'Private Life in Avignon in the Second Half of the Fifteenth Century', though he is pretty dismissive of his formal education: 'I never learned anything from school and universities. I'm a self-taught man' (2007a: 24), which explains, he surmises, his interest in so many different fields of thought. Although he encountered *avant-garde* artists, writers and actors in Paris and Avignon (Picasso, Braque, Jeanne Moreau: he mentions being in a 'state of mimetic drunkenness'), these seem to have intellectually quite dispiriting years for Girard, and he welcomed the chance to head to the United States when a teaching post at Indiana University became available. Girard has spoken of the impact of his brother's suicide after he had left for America, and the difficult family dynamic created by this sad event (Girard, 1997b). In the same interview in *Der Spiegel*, he describes his own personal experience of violence: when taking a photo of blacks and whites together in a bar in a still-segregated Alabama, a crowd of people turned hostile.

Further studies in history produced a second Ph.D. (which 'wasn't special') at Indiana University, on 'L'opinion americaine et la France 1940–1943'. It is in this period that his intellectual interests started to clarify: Sartre, phenomenology, and above all the European novelists were eventually to feature in his work of criticism. Specifically, however, it is the similarity between two shorter works, *El Curioso Impertinente* (Cervantes) and *The Eternal Husband* (Dostoyevsky) which alert him, once and for all, to 'mimetic realism' (26).

Girard's earliest employment at Indiana was as a teacher of French language and literature, with subsequent posts at Duke University, Bryn Mawr College, and then Johns Hopkins University in Baltimore, where he was Professor of Literature from 1961 to 1968. His output at this stage was very much in the area of literary criticism: *Deceit, Desire and the Novel* (1961), a collection of essays on Proust (1962), and a book on Dostoyevsky (Girard, 1997a; French original 1963), with his work characteristically showing an interest in the relation between creative writers and their intellectual and social contexts (see biographical sketch in Williams, J., 1996).

During this time, of course, the conversion experience which we looked at in the previous chapter took place, which radically altered Girard's self-perception as a puppet of mimetic desire, parallel to the similar discovery by his chosen novelists. In 1966, Girard was one of the organizers of a symposium titled 'The Languages of Criticism and the Sciences of Man'. With Roland Barthes, Jacques Derrida, Jacques Lacan, and other important critical theorists in attendance, the symposium was significant for bringing structuralism onto the American academic scene. Girard found the contact with Jacques Derrida of especial importance for his own theory of the scapegoat.

From 1968 Girard taught at State University of New York before returning to Johns Hopkins in 1976. *La violence et le sacré* appeared in 1972, and a collection of essays, *Critique dans un souterrain* 4 years later (on Albert Camus, Dante, Victor Hugo, Deleuze and Guattari). Some of these essays are included in the 1978 English collection, *'To double business bound': Essays on Literature, Mimesis and Anthropology*, together with essays on Nietzsche, Richard Wagner and Lévi-Strauss. Also in 1978, the French original of *Things Hidden since the Foundation of the World* appeared, in which an explicit Christian interest shows through in Girard's work for the first time.

From 1980 until his retirement in 1995 he was the Andrew Hammond Professor of French Language, Literature and Civilization at Stanford University in California. As Williams (1996) points out, Stanford University was certainly a prestigious location for Girard to find himself, but by the same token it was a centre for the kind of academic political correctness which has been inimical to Girard's intellectual concerns. In his next two books, *The Scapegoat* and *Job: The Victim of His People* (French originals 1982, 1985) Girard continued to develop his biblical hermeneutic, first by using a medieval poem to construct a typology of and criteria for 'the scapegoat'; secondly, by looking at the book of Job as a persecutory text.

Girard's book on Shakespeare, *A Theatre of Envy: William Shakespeare* (1991; reprinted 2000) is the culmination of a lifetime's engagement with Shakespeare, who looms extremely large in Girard's thinking, as we have seen. *Quand ces choses commenceront* (1994) is an important book-length interview with Girard, and the *Girard Reader* edited by James Williams (1996) is a significant resource. Girard returns to biblical and anthropological reflection in *I See Satan Fall like Lightning* (French original 1999) and *Celui par qui le scandale arrive* (2001c; not translated). *Le Sacrifice* appears in 2003, and *Les origines de la culture*, 2004 (English translation, 2007a). His latest writings, as we shall see in chapter 9, have centred on the theme of apocalypse; this includes his most recent book, *Achever Clausewitz* (Girard, 2007b) which uses the life and work of Carl Clausewitz to shed light on our contemporary social crisis. Much of René Girard's writing consists of contributions to collective works, and of articles or interviews in journals.[1] He has also contributed regularly to *Contagion: Journal of Violence, Mimesis and Culture*, which is the refereed journal of the *Colloquium on Violence and Religion*.[2]

Revelation and conversion: From *Things Hidden* to *Evolution and Conversion*

For an unacquainted reader who wishes to make headway with the Girardian 'canon' the options are rather daunting. Girard has said himself that his work needs to be read like a 'thriller', which has the reader turning pages back and forth; his thought moves in spirals rather than straight lines. So where to begin? The most famous of Girard's books, *Violence and the Sacred* is not the most helpful, since it contains nothing of the Christian dimension which was to become so important for Girard. He has himself suggested that *Deceit, Desire and the Novel*, and the collection of essays on Shakespeare may be the most characteristic of his works, which is an interesting observation. Certainly the elegance and lightness of touch of his Shakespeare readings make *A Theatre of Envy* a delightful entry into mimetic theory. Many readers have found *The Scapegoat* a more accessible way in.

The most efficient way to the core of Girard's work, I propose, is to consider two texts, written 20 years apart. If one were allowed only two Girardian books onto a desert island, *Things Hidden since the Foundation of the World* (1987a) and *Evolution and Conversion: Dialogues on the Origin of Culture* (2007a) would be the ones to take.[3] *Things Hidden* is the most extended volume from Girard's hand exploring mimetic theory in its various aspects, with a triptych of sections on Fundamental Anthropology, the Judaeo-Christian scriptures and Interdividual Psychology. Its distinctive format – Girard in a conversation with two interlocutors (both psychiatrists: Guy Lefort and Jean-Michel Oughourlian) – is picked up in the later book (where Girard converses with Pierpaolo Antonello and João Cezar de Castro Rocha). The echo is deliberate: *Evolution and Conversion* offers an important retrospective on the fate of the mimetic theory over the intervening 20 years. The conversations recorded here began as Girard was retiring from teaching at Stanford University, so they are an attempt to take stock of his lifetime's work. It is an opportunity to record corrections, refinements and clarifications, and especially to indicate the new avenues of exploration which are opening up for mimetic theory. Neither of these books are an easy read particularly, yet taken together they provide more than adequate 'snapshots' to the spirit and content of Girard's theory.

Things Hidden since the Foundation of the World takes its title from Mt. 13.35, and is the first indicator in Girard's work of the biblical dimension which is to become so important. The three-way conversation is arranged in three long sections; in the first, Girard sets out his anthropological theory, as a theory of human origins. In the second section, he applies this understanding explicitly to the Old and New Testaments, showing that central texts of the Bible, by contrast with mythical texts, are not the result of the scapegoat mechanism but in fact take the part of the victim and seek to reveal the working of the scapegoat mechanism. The third section looks at psychological questions, with sexuality, especially narcissism, sado-masochism and homosexuality coming to the fore.

In the repetition of this 'Socratic' format in *Les origins de la culture* Girard sat down once again with two interlocutors, who prompted an opening chapter, 'The Life of the Mind', in which Girard speaks of the intellectual and artistic influences which shaped his early career in particular. The chapters which follow set out the mimetic mechanism, as well as some of the criticisms which have been mounted against it, and questions of method. 'The Scandal of Christianity' is the penultimate chapter, followed by 'Modernity, Postmodernity and Beyond'. The opening of *Things Hidden* is an extended justification by Girard of his apparently misguided search for anthropological origins, specifically his protest that any attempt to explore the origin nature and function of 'religion' is ruled out of court before it has begun. What chance would the natural sciences have had, he asks, if people like Charles Darwin had been discouraged from framing their large hypotheses and theories on a grand scale? In the later book the point is emphasized by the quotations from Darwin which precede each chapter; Girard makes clear that he sees mimetic theory as on a par with Darwin's 'one long argument from the beginning to the end'. Such a scientific endeavour has to involve a certain 'brutalization' of data, for which Girard is unrepentant.

'Scientific inquiry is reductive or it is nothing at all', and the valuing of diversity for its own sake which has become a byword in literary studies can only be decadent if allowed to infect the human sciences. An obsessive emphasis on infinite and inexhaustible diversity signifies only 'a huge unionization of failure' (1987a: 40).

So, Girard insists on the right to think in a grand manner, and the evocation of Darwin in the later work reinforces this claim. This is related to his status as a 'hedgehog' thinker, who knows one or a few 'big things': mimetic desire, the scapegoat (2007a: 1).

The reconstruction of his 'long argumentative discourse' around these themes points up areas of revision and expansion. Foremost is the major revision which Girard made regarding the concept of 'sacrifice'. This theme is explored in more detail in Chapter 7, but we need to note here this important corrective to *Things Hidden*, where we find a radically anti-sacrificial interpretation of Christianity which Girard later came to regret. The second area of development is that of mimesis, which is now attracting the attention of scientists in a way that was not the case before. The two areas which are specified here are Richard Dawkins on memetics, and the research of Vittorio Gallese and Giacomo Rizzolati into 'mirror neurons'. A new paradigm seems to be emerging in the behavioural and neurosciences, one which is consonant with Girard's mimetic model of desire. It may be noted that we have in *Evolution and Conversion* a more explicit account of the positive aspects of mimesis and mimetic desire than previously. The latter does not always lead to violence, but can in fact be a means of soothing rivalry (5). In general Girard's interlocutors are keen to reinforce the anthropological theory which Girard first elaborated in *Things Hidden*. This is partly because Girard's own training in the humanities means his formulations are limited, but also because the science since 1978 requires updating, specifically in the areas of ethological and cognitive-symbolical development.

Regarding Girard's religious vision, there is in *Evolution and Conversion* a foregrounding of Girard's biblical-literary style of reading, which is recognized in the earlier work as figural interpretation, but which is explicated more here, largely through the example of Erich Auerbach, whom we considered earlier. The link between literature and anthropology is made explicit by the notion that the remnants and hints of sacral violence and murder which we come across can be read as *figurae Christi*: 'this form of comparativism is actually intrinsic to the historical exegesis of the Bible itself' – whose meaning is revealed in the discernment of repetitive patterns of unjust persecutions. Also foregrounded in the later work is the notion of 'conversion' as an epistemic category, and not just a moral or existential one. This is of course what we found with Girard's own engagement with his novelists in *Deceit, Desire and the Novel*, a painful discovery of the falsity of the 'Romantic Self', undertaken by each of the novelists, and by René Girard.

The overall impression from these two texts, as one might expect, is of a refocusing and refinement. In the process, new and interesting details come to light, but the main parts of the whole, the 'hedgehog' obsession with mimetic desire and exclusionary violence, are dauntingly present. The next chapter will set out in more detail how these phenomena are related, along with the gospel message – 'the Cross is the source of all knowledge of God' (262) to comprise Girard's mimetic theory.

Chapter 3
The mimetic theory of René Girard

Thinking on a grand scale

Mimetic theory grapples with three very simple questions. What causes social groups and societies to come together and cohere successfully? What causes those groups to disintegrate? What is the function of religion in these two processes?

Whether or not we are impressed with the Girardian answers, we should at least stand back and admire the elegance and audacity of a theory which hurls itself upon such impossibly vast themes. As René Girard admits, the idea that a unitary description of 'religion' is even feasible runs counter to the current orthodoxy in anthropology and religious studies. His description of mimetic theory as 'a global theory of religion, at the centre of which stands a hypothesis about the emergence of the victim', is a bold resuscitation of an intellectual tradition which began in 1860, but seemed to have exhausted itself by the middle of the twentieth century. The ethnologist E. Evans-Pritchard declared that the search for a universal theory of religion was and would remain meaningless; Girard, for his part, protests vehemently at this dogmatic and discourteous foreclosure of present and future research possibilities (Girard, 1987a: 4).

Is Girard correct? Can there be any value in this kind of grand theorizing, when most other scholars feel it has been discredited? What Girard is after is the kind of general explanatory principle which transforms understanding and organizes knowledge in a completely new way: what Newton's theory of gravity is to the physical sciences, or Darwin's theories of evolution and natural selection are to biology. The inability of the social and human sciences to arrive at a similar unifying model has been a real limitation on progress, says Girard; a continued prohibition on the kind of large and obvious questions which would enable such a model will only keep these sciences in a state of infancy. He thinks that his elucidation of two anthropological 'discoveries' – mimetic desire, the scapegoating mechanism – amounts to precisely this kind of grand theory which changes everything. The examples of Newton and Darwin are not accidental: his most recent major work *Evolution and Conversion* has very deliberate echoes of Darwin, while a psychologist, Jean-Marie Oughourlian, has resorted to the Newtonian model to explain the significance of mimetic desire:

> Just as in the cosmos, the planets, stars, and galaxies are simultaneously held together and kept apart by gravity, so also mimesis keeps human beings together and apart, assuring at one and the same time the *cohesion* of the social fabric and the relative *autonomy* of the members that make it up. In physics, it is the force of attraction, gravity, that holds bodies together in space. They would be pitilessly hurled against each other into a final fusion if gravity did not also preserve their autonomy, and hence their existence, through motion. In psychology, the movement of mimesis that renders one autonomous and relatively individual is called 'desire'. (Oughourlian, 1991: 11; original emphasis)

A tripartite theory

I have mentioned that Girard offers two anthropological insights, and yet it has become customary to see three broad strands to Girard's thought. First, the mimetic or imitated — and therefore potentially rivalrous and violent — nature of desire, which became evident from Girard's reading of his prized novelists at the time of his conversion; secondly, the scapegoating mechanism as the source of group cohesion and social order, as embodied in religious, cultural and political institutions. The third topic for Girard is the power of the Judaeo-Christian revelation as the vehicle of our enlightenment concerning the first two. We might think of this as 'two bits of bad news, one piece of Good News'; the Good News being: human beings are indeed mimetic scapegoaters, but because of God's action in Christ things can be different. By following the thread of mimesis and of exclusion, Girard finds his way to the Gospels as the source of our anthropological knowledge.

This threefold scheme has the merit of allowing us to see Girard's career evolving through three disciplines, and to align each with a key work: literary criticism (*Deceit, Desire and the Novel*, 1961); cultural anthropology (*Violence and the Sacred*, 1972); and biblical theology (*Things Hidden since the Foundation of the World*, 1978). This is perhaps overschematic: Girard's writing on literature has been a constant throughout his career, not just the early years, and *Things Hidden* contains much more than Girard's thoughts on Christianity, although it is the first place where these are explicitly and systematically set out.

To see how this all links up, I propose we examine a specific theme: the political and cultural crisis triggered by the events of 11 September 2001 and their aftermath. The 'violent return of religion' symbolized by 9/11 coincides with the acknowledged failure of theories of secularization: the confident prediction of such theories, that religion would be a declining force in world affairs, does not appear to have been borne out. His alternative 'take' on religion fills a theoretical vacuum, therefore. A general anxiety about the 'persistence of the theologio-political', together with the poverty of theoretical resources to comprehend it, has no doubt contributed to the new wave of interest in Girard's work, even though the basic theoretical matrix of cultural origins, religion and violence has been present in mimetic theory long before anyone had heard of Al Qaida.

The theme is too vast and too well-trodden to say very much here, but we can specify one or two aspects. First, it is worth noting a contrast between two kinds of judgement on the religious dimension of terrorist atrocities. On the one hand, aggressively secularist thinkers like Richard Dawkins declare that fanatical violence has always been endemic to religion, and should cause us no surprise. The 'faithheads' have learnt new technologies, such as flying planes, but the violence and fanaticism are of the ages. The critical theorist Jürgen Habermas disagrees: the fundamentalist religion which spawns such attacks is entirely a modern phenomenon, the defence mechanism of groups and communities which feel themselves under threat from inappropriate or rapid processes of secularization. Fundamentalism is the flip side of modernity.

For Dawkins, modernity is completely irrelevant to the problem of violent religion; for Habermas, it is crucial. Where does Girard stand? One could say that he has a distinctive point of view which nevertheless contains elements from each of these positions. He sets out his position in an interview in *Le Monde:*[1]

> The error is always to reason within categories of 'difference' when the root of all conflicts is rather 'competition', mimetic rivalry between persons, countries, cultures. Competition is the desire to imitate the other in order to obtain the same thing he or she has, by violence if need be. No doubt terrorism is bound to a world 'different' from ours, but what gives rise to terrorism does not lie in that 'difference' which removes it further from us and makes it inconceivable to us. On the contrary, it lies in an exacerbated desire for convergence and resemblance. Human relations are essentially

The Mimetic Theory of René Girard

relations of imitation, of rivalry. What is experienced now is a form of mimetic rivalry on a planetary scale. (Girard, 2001b)

Here is a dimension that 'transcends Islam, a dimension of the entire planet'. On the one hand the perpetrators are the losers: Third World victims in a relationship of mimetic rivalry with the West. On the other hand, the terrorists are 'American', in their sophistication with regards to means and strategy. As has frequently been pointed out, Osama Bin Laden is hardly one of the 'wretched of the earth', but he is nevertheless consumed by mimetic contagion, imitating the hated West while adopting its values.

Especially disturbing for Westerners, however, is the implication that the contagion works both ways. As well as the immediate and temporary resurgence of churchgoing in response to 9/11, we have a more lasting religious aftermath, namely the creation of a sacred space, 'Ground Zero', and the mobilization of a people for a Holy War, subsequently renamed a 'War on Terror'.[2] It is almost a cliché to point out that the speeches and mentality of President Bush are shot through with religious imagery and purpose, for all that he is the leader of an allegedly secular democratic state. On this account, Bush and Osama bin Laden are mirror images, and the stand-off between the United States and its Islamist opponents is a clash of fundamentalisms.

Insofar as this 'exacerbated desire for convergence and resemblance' is an anthropological constant, then Girard would agree with Dawkins that it certainly predates the modern era; he would even concur that 'religion', as an embodiment and expression of such a desire, has those destructive properties which Dawkins condemns. However, Dawkins is wrong to see religious violence as a purely archaic phenomenon which has somehow arbitrarily resurged in the modern era. Here Girard would agree with Jürgen Habermas: modernity is causally and not accidentally related to fundamentalism. It is modernity itself which has 'exacerbated' and escalated the 'desire for convergence and resemblance'.[3]

Where do we find this in Girard's writings? In his book on the European novel, written all of 40 years ago. *Deceit, Desire and the Novel* considers in almost chronological sequence five key writers, beginning with Cervantes in the seventeenth century and ending with Proust and Dostoyevsky. This sequence also charts the history of mimetic desire in the modern age, according to which the distance between subject and mediator shrinks, and the dangers of mimetic interaction increase. The mimeticism depicted by Cervantes and Flaubert is relatively harmless, because their characters (Don Quixote, Emma Bovary) are imitating fictional mediators. There can be no rivalrous conflict between the fictional Amadis de Gaul and

Don Quixote, or between Emma and the lascivious heroines of her leisure time reading.

Mimesis and conflict

This is what Girard calls 'external mediation' or 'external mimesis'. As long as social or other distinctions are able to canalize mimetic desire, its conflictual dimension is under control. Not so in Stendhal, Proust and Dostoyevsky: these authors portray 'internal mediation', where the mediator unavoidably becomes a rival since he stands on the same ground as the proud imitator. The greater the proximity between subject (imitator) and model (imitated), the greater the risk of rivalry leading to violence. When we come to Dostoyevsky, we are in a seething universe of bitter antagonisms: the 'Underground Man' in *Notes from Underground*; the parricidal jealousies of the Karamazov family; and above all, for present purposes, the fanatical resentment of the anarchist radicals in *The Possessed*.

The history of mimetic desire from Cervantes to Dostoyevsky is the history of the modern world, in which the collapse of hierarchical differentiation under the forces of revolution and democracy has heralded more intense 'internal mediation' – as writers like Thomas Hobbes and Alex de Tocqueville understood very well. We will explore this at greater length in a later chapter, but for now we can begin to see Girard's crucial move. Mimetic desire is not only the morbid affliction of select individuals, it is the motor which powers modernity and its discontents. It should now be clear that Girard rejects any view of great literature as disengaged from real life. By drawing on this literature, from Shakespeare through to Proust, and by a sustained engagement with the key thinkers on desire and modernity, namely Hegel, Freud and Nietzsche, Girard has constructed a powerful critique of modernity and its aftermath.

Which leads us to a fundamental question: if Girard is correct, and rivalrous mimetic interaction poses a constant threat to human cohesion, how do societies form in the first place? To repeat: Girard describes modernity in terms of a revolutionary loosening of the constraints upon mimetic desire. If open aggression and warfare are to be avoided, then this 'difference gone wrong' has to be channelled into 'safe' forms of competition and rivalry – the capitalist market system and parliamentary democracy being obvious examples, as well as various forms of nationalist expression, sporting competitions and so on. It is also of vital importance that judicial and military systems have evolved, in which the state has an official monopoly on violence and punishment.

The Mimetic Theory of René Girard

But all this begs the question: what was there before? How did ordered societies come into being in the first place, if human beings are as volatile and unstable as mimetic theory makes out? 'Man is a wolf unto man', and our natural state seems to be that described by Thomas Hobbes in *Leviathan*: a permanent mobilization for the war of all against all. Just as metaphysical philosophy asks: 'why is there something, why not nothing?', so mimetic theory asks: 'why is there society, why not anarchy?'

Girard's answer to this question forms the core of his best-known book, *La violence et le sacré*. Before examining his argument, we will note that there are two kinds of response which he rejects. The first is to deny Hobbes' pessimistic anthropology, and assert the basic goodness and innocence of human beings in their natural state, as Romantic philosophers do. We are born free, but enfolded by the chains of society and civilization which are the sole cause of disfigurement and misery. This is the 'Romantic Lie', which simply bypasses the mimetic roots of rivalry and violence. The second possibility is Hobbes' own response to the dilemma he has set up, namely to posit a 'Social Contract' by which the warring wolves agree to renounce their aggression and invest sovereignty in one person, a 'mortal god' who will afford order and protection to the community. But this will not do either, says Girard, who cannot see how a group of human beings at each others' throats will, at that precise moment, decide to bury their differences and sign a social contract. Only an Englishman could place this much trust in people's capacity to behave reasonably and calmly in such a bloody crisis!

In one moment, a seething cauldron of chaotic and rivalrous desires; in the next, an ordered and stable society. Just how do humans manage to make the transition from one to the other?

Girard's answer: by mimesis. The crisis which has arisen through the escalation of mimetic desire, and which threatens a war of 'all against all', is resolved by a realignment of the aggression. A chance blow or gesture from one of the antagonists is directed against another, someone weaker, isolated or marginal. His example will be followed – mimetically – by others, so that the universal warfare becomes a 'war of all against one'. The victim is of course innocent, and yet is held to be the one responsible for the strife. This perception is confirmed when the group expels or destroys the victim, and discovers itself to be 'at peace' once more. The cathartic effect of projecting the group's violence reunites the group and reinforces the impression that they have destroyed the original source of the conflict.

In fact this projection is even more complex, being what Girard calls a 'double transference'. He postulates that the victim's death carries an ambivalent significance: he or she is the source of both the original disorder and of its peaceful resolution. A power which is conceived as malevolent

25

and beneficent at the same time: this is the classical description of the primitive sacred as both good and evil. Since his death is seen to have won divine favour, the victim is himself invested with a divine aura; he becomes a god. The community which has been 'saved' from its own violence understands itself to have performed a holy and beneficial action; when the crisis recurs, and the reconciling effects start to wear off, it moves instinctively towards a repeat performance, 'reproducing this event in a controlled and selective fashion' (Fleming, 2004: 61).

> This reproduction of the crisis through ritual prohibition and myth is what Girard invariably calls 'the sacred' [le sacré]. The 'sacred', in Girard's purview, denotes the cultural products and practices of the distorted and selective comprehension of surrogate victimage by those involved in its perpetration. . . . Sacred renderings of (violent) events typically reverse the state of affairs that gave rise to them by a constitutive transcendentalization of mob violence: the sacrificed victim in ritual, for instance, becomes an appeaser of the gods, rather than the actual state of affairs – of the victim/god being the *appeaser of the mob*. (61–2; original emphasis)

The new-found harmony comes to be attributed in a mysterious way to the expelled victim, who thus acquires a 'sacred' numinosity. The violence of the expulsion or immolation is kept at a distance, by replicating both the crisis and its resolution in controlled, ritually legitimate ways. Here, for Girard, is the origin of the practice of religious sacrifice. Rites in which humans are killed as placatory offerings are to be understood as instances of 'scapegoating', channelling a community's aggression onto an arbitrary victim or group, so as to prevent that aggression overwhelming the whole society. 'The sacred' is the means by which a society's mimetic rivalry and its consequent aggression are contained. Mimetic desire breeds violence, and on a society-wide level would engender chaos without the universal tendency of human groups to regulate it in this way. Sacrifice is a momentary reversion to the chaos of an 'acceptable' violence which maintains differences rather than threaten to eradicate them. Myths and theologies, in turn, are typically rationalizations of an original or initial act of violence, which the group needs to conceal from itself.

Girard attributes to this scapegoat mechanism not just all the central elements of every religion, such as myth, ritual and taboo, but also political power (e.g. sacred kingship), juridical violence (the death penalty), the arts, theatre and philosophy. In this way his theory does not remain in isolation from other scientific world-views; on the contrary, in his engagement with Freud (the Oedipus complex, *Totem and Taboo*) and Claude Lévi-Strauss, the similarities to and differences from contemporary psychoanalytical and structuralist models are set out.

How does Girard come to piece together such an extraordinary story? He is still reading texts, only this time he has gone beyond the modern European novel and taken up more ancient texts. Chapter 3 of *Violence and the Sacred* is titled 'Oedipus and the Surrogate Victim'; chapter 5 is on 'Dionysus'. The resonances between the Oedipus tragedies and the Dionysus cycle enable Girard to make the connections, 'from mimetic desire to the monstrous double' (the title of chapter 6). We are still in the realm of 'literature'.

'The Kingdom of God has become scientific'

Girard wanted originally to explore the biblical text in this book, and therefore include Judaism and Christianity in his theory, but for a long time it was not possible for him to systematize the differences and similarities between mythical and biblical texts. It is this neglect of the biblical text that caused some early reviewers of *Violence and the Sacred* to misunderstand what they read as the 'first authentically atheistic theory of religion and the sacred' (Fleming, 2004: 111, citing G. H. de Radkowski). It is in his third major book, *Des Chose Cachées depuis la fondation du monde* (*Things Hidden since the Foundation of the World*) that he finally speaks more explicitly about the significance of the Gospels for mimetic theory. The thesis of the scapegoat mechanism is here broadened into a theory of human relations, but the earlier attribution of the origin of religion to the sacrificial crisis and its origin in mimetic desire is significantly developed in favour of a more positive appraisal of the Judaeo-Christian tradition – one which, in fact, amounts to a new *apologia* for Christian faith.

Despite their surface similarity to persecution texts, the biblical texts, and especially the gospel accounts of the death of Jesus, stand as 'revelation' in opposition to the concealments of 'religion' in that they constitute an exposure of the victimage mechanism and a declaration of God's siding with the innocent victim. The sacrificial mechanism, thus exposed, is seen to have only a temporary and limited efficacy. This is the third strand in Girard's thought, a surprising turn towards the Christian revelation. The scriptures certainly contain mythical elements, but they are singular in their narrative identification with the victim: the condemnation of Cain, the prophetic repudiation of the sacrificial cult, the innocence sufferer of the Servant Songs in Isa. 40–55; the Gospels, above all, disclose the secret of the mythic camouflage of violence and the way of liberation through a love that refuses violence.

Girard and Theology

In *Le bouc émissaire* (1982: Eng., *The Scapegoat*, 1986), Girard attempts to make plausible his thesis of the scapegoat mechanism with a sustained comparison between medieval accounts of persecution and mythical texts. The text Girard uses is the *Judgement of the King of Navarre* by Guillaume de Machaut, a French poet of the mid-fourteenth century. He considers a text which relates the persecution of Jews who are accused of causing a visitation of the plague by poisoning wells. These are charges, he insists, which no present-day historian or reader would take seriously: we recognize this as a persecution text and the role of the Jews as scapegoats. But Girard argues that we can and should read myths in the same way as we read such texts. Just as the medieval text narrates, from the perspective of the persecutor, the actual and bloody punishment of human victims, so myths are no more than reports of collective violence against an innocent victim, from the perspective of the lynchers.

Behind myth, therefore, lie real acts of violence, described in a way that tries to convince us that the victims are the cause of the crisis and are therefore justly condemned to death. Myths differ from persecution texts only insofar as the religious justification of the collective violence is much stronger, and its decoding therefore much harder. In the second half of this book, Girard is concerned with central texts of the New Testament (the Passion, the beheading of John the Baptist, the denial of Peter, the Gerasene demoniac, Satan, the Holy Ghost), showing how these must be radically distinguished from mythical texts, as here the perspective of the victim, not that of the persecutor, is upheld: a stress which is maintained in *La route antique des hommes pervers* (1985; Eng., *Job, the Victim of His People*, 1987b).

We have discussed Girard's account of 'novelistic conversion' in the opening chapter, according to which 'the distinction between "novelistic" and "religious" experience is abolished'. This curious and discomforting mixture of sacred and secular styles is here seen to characterize Girard's work as a whole, as we see the Bible being privileged as an epistemological source. As one critic puts it, with Girard 'the Kingdom of God has become scientific'.

Chapters 6–10 of this book will seek to explore the religious implications, in terms of theological anthropology, the doctrine of salvation (soteriology), biblical criticism political theology and the theology of religions. What concerns us here is the 'scientific' respectability of Girard's insights, which are sometimes referred to as a hypothesis, but generally go by the name of 'mimetic theory'. We have seen that Girard himself acknowledged the huge resistance this kind of thinking encounters, and has continually appealed to figures such as Charles Darwin as a counter-example.

Two challenges seem to stand in the way of this being 'science' in any recognizable sense of the word, however. First of all, Girard's appeal to

The Mimetic Theory of René Girard

the uniquely revelatory power of the biblical texts surely runs completely counter to scientific investigation. Secondly, a fairly obvious difficulty: where on earth is the evidence? The dilemma is that the evidence is not there, or at least is very difficult to find. That is why the intriguing comparison which Girard makes with the detective story is extremely apt; like all good crime stories, 'in the beginning was the corpse', and the various clues as to what might have happened have to be sifted. But the bodies are well-hidden, the clues are desperately hard to come by.

Robert Hamerton-Kelly responds to this last challenge when he argues for mimetic theory as a form of 'scientific realism',[4] which incorporates the view that 'it is in principle proper to posit the existence of unobservables by "abductive" or "retroductive" inference from observables', provided the posited entity can be seen to produce observable effects. This approach (unlike empiricism) 'gives permission' to posit causal mechanisms of the kind put forward by mimetic theory. The procedure of abduction of unobservable structures is equivalent to the proposal and testing of hypotheses and the formulation of laws: it is a legitimate procedure which ensures that 'the scientific status of the theory of sacred violence is secure within the context of responsible debate within the philosophy of science' (Hamerton-Kelly, 1992: 44).

The term 'theory' is understood here as a moment of creative insight which guides our looking. The movement 'from law to theory, from the fashioning of hypotheses to the development of explanations of them' is not induction, but a leap or break in consciousness. Hypotheses are proposed and tested in the search for laws, but:

> [t]heories are tested differently, not by the reliability of correlations but by their power and elegance. According to Waltz, the power of a theory is its ability to guide our attention to the important phenomena in the field, to enable us to ask the right questions, formulate fruitful hypotheses, stimulate and guide research, and provoke countertheories. The elegance of a theory is the ratio between its complexity and its range of explanation. An elegant theory is a simple one with a wide range. So a critique of theory is a questioning of the power and elegance of the whole theory in its capacity to guide the decision to focus on this or that item in the field and to control the formation of hypotheses for testing. Theory, therefore, orients research and facilitates understanding. (1992: 2)

Understanding consists in the integration of new knowledge into old, guided by theory, since theory is a series of generalizations based on a wide range of evidence and interpretations. The inquirer wishes to incorporate historical data into generalizations about the nature of all individuals and groups, in the widest possible frame of reference. And of course, such an investigation does not take place in a vacuum. The interpreter is socially and historically embedded. In formulating a theory of interpretation for our time, we have to ask: what are the relevant and pressing features of our own culture which impinge on us, here and now?

> I believe that the overriding fact of our time is violence; therefore a theory that attempts to make sense out of violence is more likely to orient us to the points in the field that are salient for our time.... Therefore, there is a congruence between our times, our texts, and our tradition that makes for a powerful interpretive constellation. (Hamerton-Kelly, 1992: 5)

Conclusion

The simple logic unifying this vast range of research runs as follows. Our desires are imitative, and mimetic rivalry is omnipresent in human affairs. An ensuing conflict and even violence is, for Girard, almost inevitable, overwhelming the community like a contagion (taboos and avoidance of impurity are to be attributed precisely to the primitive community's fear of unchecked violence). From this, he is able to explore the efficacy of sacrificial substitution as a containment of violence, and, finally, the unique role of the Judaeo-Christian scriptures in unmasking and denouncing this mysterious and pervasive mechanism in favour of Jesus' way of peace.

Girard offers two anthropological insights, therefore: mimetic desire, the scapegoating phenomenon. He claims to have discovered these in Christianity. We have seen that sacred violence reverses the state of affairs, so that the sacrificed victim 'becomes an appeaser of the gods, rather than the actual state of affairs – of the victim/god being the *appeaser of the mob* (Fleming: 61–2). According to Hamerton-Kelly, the gospel works as a 'hermeneutic of suspicion' which reverses the direction back again:

> The double transference is an act of misinterpretation by which the victim is transformed into the god by being blamed for the violence of the group. The group does not take responsibility for its own violence but transfers it onto the victim, thereby making it sacred. The theory of sacred violence as a hermeneutical device will simply reverse the direction of the double transference, returning responsibility for violence to its proper place and thus desacralizing the victim. Guile will be met with double guile. (Hamerton-Kelly, 1992: 40)

The Mimetic Theory of René Girard

The phrase 'guile will be met with double guile' echoes Ricoeur, where it is applied to the 'masters of suspicion', Marx, Nietzsche and Freud.[5] The decipherment of declarations of meaning must be a match for their initial encipherment by the strategies of social being, the will to power, and the cunning of desire respectively – or indeed 'violence', Girard's summary term for these forces:

> In this way the theory becomes a deconstructive 'hermeneutic of suspicion' in the sense that by exposing the cogs and levers of the sacrificial machine it dispels the mystery and enables us to withdraw cooperation. By categorizing (= accusing) sacred violence, the theory exposes it to public scorn. Simply by pointing it out, drawing attention to it, making it the subject of research and hypothesizing, the theory deconstructs sacred violence. Thus it overcomes the effects of the mechanism without destroying it, subjects it to deconstruction as distinct from destruction. (40)

Such a theory can only be demonstrated pragmatically, by its successful illumination of texts. 'The texts attest the theory and the theory in turn interprets the texts' (41), though Hamerton-Kelly stresses that there is no hermeneutical circularity: 'the theory is not derived from the texts by induction. The texts are merely one kind of evidence among others – from psychology, ethology and ethnology – which warrant the positing of the theory'. What Girard is proposing is in the end quite modest – a theory and a method, though the theory is a text that has to be composed after the event, derived from the posited nonobservables of scientific realism (Hamerton-Kelly, 1992: 59). Girard points us to 'a possible restatement of biblical faith that places it at the center of the struggle for a culture beyond violence', so that, in our reading of the Bible, it in turn 'speaks a clear word of criticism and hope to our time of limited violence' (60). It is this application of the theory of sacred violence which Hamerton-Kelly describes as 'the hermeneutic of the Cross'.

We will then proceed to a more detailed investigation of the engagement between mimetic theory and theology, including a survey of the incorporation of Girardian insights into the Dramatic Theology research project associated with the University of Innsbruck and the late Raymund Schwager. Four clear themes present themselves: in Chapter 5 Girard's 'anatomy of desire' will be examined for its convergence with and divergence from Karl Rahner's 'theological anthropology' and other accounts of how the human stands before God. The subsequent chapters will explore the impact of Girardian thinking on theories of Sacrifice and Atonement, Biblical criticism, and Political and Liberation theologies.

Girard and Theology

It is possible that even this survey will not provide the wherewithal for an overall judgement on Girard's work. A number of cautious theorists have suggested that such a judgement, even 50 years since *Deceit, Desire and the Novel*, may be premature (Fleming, 2004: 164). What cannot be denied, and what will serve as a provisional judgement on what we have seen so far, is the extraordinary generative power of Girard's mimetic theory: its capacity to generate or provoke additional theoretical work of enormous range and calibre, which is relatively independent of Girard's own intellectual commitments. 'Girard has proffered not simply research . . . but a research *programme*' (153; original emphasis). Imre Lakatos, as we shall see in Chapter 4, holds the falsifiability of a research programme to be a medium or long-term procedure (Lakatos, 1970); if this is the case, then mimetic theory will be around for some time yet.

Chapter 4
The Innsbruck connection: Dramatic theology

Raymund Schwager: 1935–2004

Innsbruck, the delightful historic university city which is the capital of the Tyrol, is an especially resonant location for theology. The Jesuit dogmatic theologian Karl Rahner, widely accepted to be the most influential Catholic theologian of the twentieth century, spent most of his teaching career at the Faculty of Theology. Rahner is buried in the crypt of the Jesuit church, and the Faculty is home to the Karl Rahner archive. Innsbruck also hosts the René Girard documentation centre; its theologians have been involved over a number of years with mimetic theory and its theological implications. The institutional expressions of this are two research projects: the 'Dramatic Theology' project, and an interdisciplinary programme titled 'Religion-Violence-Communication-World Order'.

For many years the inspiration behind much of this activity was Professor Raymund Schwager SJ, who was Professor of Dogmatic and Ecumenical Theology until his unexpected death in 2004 (he too is buried in the Jesuit crypt). Girard has on a number of occasions referred to Schwager as his most important theological interpreter. The present chapter will offer an overview of the 'Innsbruck connection', as it is manifested in the work of Schwager and his colleagues, and especially in the two research projects, as a prelude to the more specific investigations into theological themes: theological anthropology (Chapter 5), sacrifice and atonement (Chapters 6 and 7), biblical studies (Chapter 8) and political theology (Chapter 9).

Raymund Schwager was a key theological interpreter of Girard, but the influence was mutual. Schwager had made extensive use of the mimetic theory, especially in his construction of a 'dramatic theology', while Girard's understanding of 'sacrifice' developed in important respects under Schwager's influence. In his three principle works the Swiss Jesuit has used a Girardian anthropological framework to explore the theme of (God's) violence in the Bible in *Brauchen wir einen Sündenbock* (1978 [*Must There be Scapegoats?*, 1987]); to lay the basis for a systematic soteriology, or doctrine

33

of salvation (the articles collected together in *Der wunderbare Tausch*, 1986); and to construct a dramatic interpretation of the ministry, death and resurrection of Jesus (*Jesus im Heilsdrama*, 1990). His earlier work, before his utilization of Girard's theory, prefigures many of their common concerns: his dissertation on the Ignatian Exercises stresses a distinction between divine revelation – Ignatius' genuine mystical experience – and human impulse (Ignatius' psychological inclinations), and subsequent writings on Christian discipleship.

Brauchen wir einen Sündenbock?, Schwager's first major text, examines the Old and New Testaments for their attitude towards violence, and in particular for their attribution of violent intention to God. His conclusion reinforces Girard's, that in the Bible, God is progressively revealed as loving, non-violent and on the side of innocent victims. All the violence which is attributed to God by the Old Testament writers is an illusion, a projection of human aggression. The Servant Songs of Deutero-Isaiah represent the Old Testament's clearest revelation of this non-violent God, even though the rejection of sacrifice and the violence it perpetuates remains inconclusive in these mysterious passages. In the New Testament the crucifixion of Jesus is the event (cumulative of his ministry as a whole) which uncovers the hidden will to lie and kill. This uncovering renders the scapegoat mechanism ineffective; it points to a more positive way of uniting human beings based on non-rivalrous striving towards God.

Here the distinction between imitation and discipleship acquires systematic significance: discipleship does not produce conflict. Where Schwager seems to differ from Girard is in the latter's description of the choice of scapegoat as the irrational and arbitrary result of blind passion: the hostility towards Jesus, on the contrary, is not at all fortuitous, but Christological, since the source of provocation is the self-consciousness of Jesus.

Both Girard and Schwager point out the 'quasi-osmotic' immediacy of mimetic fascination (see 'Imiter et Suivre': Schwager, 1987). The Holy Spirit reveals the true nature of 'the Adversary' as *'la forme la plus subtile de la mimésis'*, operating as a demonic *imago Dei*. This is the significance of the Genesis account of the Fall, and also of the parable of the Wicked Husbandmen in Mk 12.1–12, whose desire to replace God (as the master of the vineyard) and Christ (as the inheritor) reveals the same original mimesis: the desire to be equal to God which leads to violence. In its most subtle form, conflictive mimesis takes the form of an imitation of the good, so that for Schwager even the Girardian notion of a positive mimesis is ambiguous. This is the force of his distinction between *Nachahmung* – imitation and *Nachfolge* – discipleship (Schwager, 1987). Schwager cites the examples of the young novice in Bunuel's film *Viridiana*, and the early Ignatius of Loyola, to show how even explicit imitation of Jesus can have

The Innsbruck Connection: Dramatic Theology

disastrous and violent consequences. How can we be sure that 'exterior' mimesis truly surmounts rivalry, and is not, as in these examples, a more subtle form of violence? Bonhoeffer's reading of the evangelical call to 'hate' father, mother, wife and so on, is seen here as a call to overcome '*la relation immédiate avec la monde*'.

Hostility towards Jesus also has its mimetic elements, as we see in the Gospel of John, where we read of those who believed in secret but were afraid of the Pharisees: 'for they loved human glory more than the glory that comes from God' (Jn 12.43), where this '*gloire*' or '*considération*' corresponds to the notion of mimetic regard. In the same way, when the people are forced to choose between two conflicting authorities, they forsake the charismatic attraction of Jesus for the more recognized and established authority of the Pharisees. Finally, even the disciples succumb to this external pressure. As long as Jesus is at liberty, his presence is strong enough to neutralize the force of mimetic pressure in his disciples, but once he is under arrest, his exterior 'gloire' disappears, and his disciples fall under the power of the established authorities. When the shepherd is struck, the sheep are scattered. Only with the encounters of the Resurrection and the descent of the Holy Spirit can the genuine radiance of the way of Jesus be re-established.

Jesus' response of non-vengeance delivers men from the evil and hatred from which they cannot free themselves. Very much to the fore in Schwager's account is the need to reinterpret concepts such as the 'wrath of God' and 'sacrifice' so that they do not impute violence to God, a point on which, as we shall see, he takes issue with Hans Urs von Balthasar. Two other works take this theme further: Schwager's contribution to the *Semeia* edition dedicated to Girard (McKenna, 1985) confirms the anti-sacrificial critique developed in *Sündenbock*, which is in turn recapitulated in 'The Theology of the Wrath of God' (Dumouchel, 1988: 44–52). Schwager's conclusion to the latter is a summary of the overall thrust of his theology and a brief *apologia* for it:

> The traditional allegorical method and the language of the just, divine punishment are inadequate to solve the problem of divine wrath. Simply to reject the Christian texts, as has been continually attempted since the seventeenth century, also leads no further. A comprehensive method is necessary, which assesses both pagan and Judaeo-Christian narratives by the same criteria. It must also be possible thereby to go beyond the ideal of justice and uncover and assess the collective mechanisms of aggression and concealment. This is precisely what Girard's theory attempts. So it offers progress where the greatest problems of Christian theology and occidental history have remained unsolved. (Schwager in Dumouchel, 1988: 52)

Subsequent to this work are Schwager's readings of soteriological issues collected together in *Der wunderbare Tausch*. In these essays Schwager returns to ancient themes: the unity-in-difference of the Old and New Testaments; the unity of the New Testament itself, thus the unity of the biblical conception of God; the tension between Jesus' message of divine mercy and his threats of eternal damnation; the apparent conflict between the unconditional offer of salvation in Jesus' preaching of the kingdom with later soteriologies which attribute salvific value, even necessity to Jesus' death. For Schwager, the vehicle most suitable for presenting the doctrine of redemption is a *dramatic* structure, which allows the various phases and dimensions of the divine offer and human reception of salvation to come to the fore in their proper context.

Dramatic theology

Schwager acknowledges his debt to Hans Urs von Balthasar, whose 'Theo-Drama' is the essential backdrop for the emergent project of a dramatic theology. Over five weighty volumes (1994–1980) von Balthasar expounds this second part of his trilogy, framed by a 'Theological Aesthetics' and a 'Theo-logic'. This exploration of Christian revelation from the standpoint of the 'good' seeks to assert the value of the theatre as a *praxis*, a form of human activity which is open to the transcendent:

> The world of the theatre will only provide us with a set of resources which, after they have been thoroughly modified, can be used later in theology. All the same, the model of the theatre is a more promising point of departure for a study of *theo-drama* than man's secular, social activity. For in the theatre man attempts a kind of transcendence, endeavouring both to observe and to judge his own truth, in virtue of a transformation – through the dialectic of the concealing-revealing mask – by which he tries to gain clarity about himself. Man himself beckons, invites the approach of a revelation about himself. Thus, parabolically, a door can open to the truth of the real revelation (*Preface to Prolegomena*; von Balthasar, 1980: 12).

Von Balthasar goes on to note the proximity of key themes in modern theology, such as 'event', 'history', 'orthopraxy', 'dialogue', 'political theology', 'role'. Above all, there is a new urgency attached to the problem of creaturely freedom and the possibility of evil:

> The confrontation between divine and human freedom has reached a unique intensity; the contest between the two has

The Innsbruck Connection: Dramatic Theology

moved into the center – the really dramatic centre stage – of the problem of existence . . . all these modes of approach seem to lead concentrically from the most diverse regions of contemporary thought toward a theodramatic theory. (1980: 50)

In this interplay of infinite and finite freedom, the person of Jesus takes the decisive role. The true drama comprises God expelling his Son into the powers of destruction so as to taste the depths of sin in the mystery of Holy Saturday. For all the profundity of this approach, there are limitations in von Balthasar's version of it, however. Schwager raises questions about the absence of the political dimension of reality, including the problem of violence, and about his interpretation of the Descent into Hell. Schwager suggests that von Balthasar's account would be more balanced if it addressed the theme of mimesis (in its account of sin) and included Jesus' preaching of the kingdom, as well as the rejection of that message. As it stands, there is a danger that the violence and evil of the Crucifixion is attributed to God, rather than sinful human beings.[1] John Galvin summarizes:

> A theology which conceived of the cross as the result of the human rejection of Jesus' public offer of divine forgiveness and salvation would find Jesus the decisive agent in his own passion; through his free acceptance of suffering he converted evil into good, respecting human freedom yet transforming it from within through his non-retaliation in death. The theodrama is thus performed in two acts, and the danger of attributing violence and evil to God, in contradiction to Jesus' message, is averted. (Galvin, 1989: 689)

In fact, Raymund Schwager's version of the theo-drama unfolds over five acts not two, though the structure described by Galvin is maintained.[2] Act I opens with Jesus' preaching of the *basileia* or Kingdom. This is an offer of unconditional divine forgiveness and salvation to Israel, inviting conversion to the God of the kingdom which is present and operative in Jesus' word and deed: 'The time is fulfilled, and the Kingdom of God is at hand' (Mk 1.15a). The conclusion of this first act is left open, because we do not know what the response of Jesus' listeners will be. Act II includes both the public resistance to Jesus' summons to repentance, and Jesus' reaction to the general rejection of his message. The failure of Israel to repent is a bitter disappointment for Jesus, and elicits from him the threats of punishment, even of eternal damnation, which such a refusal must surely entail.

The key moment in this phase is the disturbing Parable of the Vineyard which appears in two gospels (Mk 12.1–12; Mt. 21.33–46). The tenants of a vineyard kill the servants and then the son of the owner in a cruel strategy to gain ownership of the property. Jesus asks the question: what will the owner of the vineyard do with these wicked tenants? In Matthew's version Jesus' listeners, the Pharisees, provide the answer, in Luke it is Jesus himself: 'he will kill the tenants and give the vineyard to others'. As with the opening act, Act II is inconclusive.

The central Act III is a presentation and interpretation of the Passion of Christ. Despite his warnings, Jesus' proclamation still remains without the desired corporate response. Jesus symbolically completes his mission to Israel through the cleansing of the Temple, but instead of preaching resentful vengeance he moves towards a loving self-offering as an act of atonement for the collective force of human sin. This is still the *basileia* message of the first act, but now in very different circumstances. Schwager recognizes the process of a mimetic 'snowballing' – the scapegoat mechanism – as Herod, Pontius Pilate, the religious leaders and the crowd, all unite against God's servant and have him viciously crucified.

The judgement passed upon Jesus is a human deed, not a direct divine act, but the real truth of Jesus' message remains an open question, which can only be answered by an act of God. Here is the relevance of the Parable of the Vineyard: if indeed an atrocity has come to pass and the people of Israel have killed God's son, then the only imaginable response from God is the destruction of the tenants. This is the implacable 'logic' of the story. On the other hand, if Jesus was nothing but a deluded fanatic then those who put him to death as a blasphemer were justified in their actions. Still Jesus preaches the God of the *basiliea*, though this time by his steadfast insistence on forgiving and praying for his enemies. Both Jesus and those who put him to death cry out to God for support and vindication. Both cannot be right. The dramatic hinge, then, is: which 'version' of God is the true one? Once again there is ambivalence, though the silence of the Father at Calvary and his apparent abandonment of Jesus seems to indicate that Caiaphas and Pilate had a more accurate view of God than the crazed prophet from Nazareth.

In Act IV, this ambivalence is definitively resolved. God acts, and reveals himself to be the God whom Jesus preached after all. The Resurrection is the conclusive judgement of the heavenly Father, a vindication of his Son. For Schwager the raising of Christ encompasses both divine judgement in favour of the crucified Jesus, and an advance to a new and unexpected stage of God's self-revelation. This goes well beyond even the mercy of the Parable of the Vineyard, where even the owner's extensive patience was finally exhausted. God forgives even the murder of his Son: 'a mercy greater than which none can be conceived'. The final Act V deals with the descent of the Holy Spirit and the new gathering of the Church. The Spirit is operative above all in the internal transformation of individuals and in

The Innsbruck Connection: Dramatic Theology

the new assembly; Jesus' initial efforts to gather Israel failed: the Holy Spirit is a second aspect of the Father's response, able to reach and transform the innermost core of the human heart, in the light of the anthropology of the Cross, through celebration of the Eucharist and deepening of understanding in faith.

Schwager's dramatic soteriology represents the most thorough application of Girard's concept of the scapegoat mechanism to Christological questions. It is a scheme which has been subjected to extensive critique on several occasions, perhaps the most important being the 'Symposium on Dramatic Soteriology' at Innsbruck in 1991.[3] The symposium opens with Schwager's proposal of five theses for a dramatic conception of salvation, with each thesis containing a number of subtheses (Niewiadomski and Palaver, 1992: 13–15). What these make clear is that the events of Holy Week constitute a *Heilsgeschichte*, a sacred history, with actors exchanging roles: for example, in Act III Jesus takes the place of those who were judged and 'condemned' in Act II. The reversals which take place: judgement, turning to self-judgement and then salvation, constitute a hermeneutical key: 'the stone which the builders rejected has become the corner stone'. The whole drama becomes intelligible, now that we see the Old Testament as comprising of texts that mingle revelation with human projections: what Schwager calls 'mixed texts'.

The words and actions of Jesus Christ announce his claim to be the self-revelation of God. This can only be sustained if it can be shown that he presents an unchanging and non-conflictual image of God, otherwise his claim would be open to the charge of inconsistency. At the same time Jesus introduces differences from within Israel's faith tradition. A 'dramatic exegesis' allows for a bridge between the exegesis of individual texts and systematic theology; it is also comprehensible in non-biblical terms, such as social action theories and socio-psychological analysis. It therefore opens up perhaps the best possibility we have of a conversation between theology and the human sciences.

The essays which follow examine these theses from a variety of biblical and systematic theological perspectives, with a number of critiques engaging specifically with Girard's theory. Schwager presents a *Rückblick*, concluding analysis of the symposium, where he responds at length to a number of criticisms, including methodological concerns (339–54) about how biblical (historical-critical) exegesis and systematic theology might be coordinated through 'dramatic exegesis'. This takes us to the heart of some of the most intractable problems facing contemporary theology and its relation to biblical research.

Schwager then addresses the many concerns pertaining to Girard's mimetic theory which were expressed by participants at the symposium

Girard and Theology

(354–84), asking: 'Is it necessary for a dramatic doctrine of redemption in the long run to have regard to the scapegoat theory?' He points out that over 30 years new divergent theological currents have come into play, all practising theology from the perspective of the victim: political theology, theology 'after Auschwitz', liberation, feminist and ecological theologies. This convergence should be seen as a 'kairos' for contemporary theology, yet none has offered 'a thoroughly elaborated (anthropological, cultural, social, religious-scientific and theological) theory' which would focus on the victim: 'theology needs a religious theory of the victim that covers all fields of human science' – such as offered by Girard (355).[4] Mimetic theory is required, therefore, to enable theology to systematize and enrich its current priorities and intuitions. Without this, there is the danger of victims being played off against one another, or of victimhood status being used as a weapon for political advantage. If we are to be genuinely partisan for the victim, then a self-critical understanding of the mechanisms of victimization is essential.

Schwager also corrects a misrepresentation of Girard's theory, that it is an 'ontologization' of violence, attributing a naturally violent instinct to human beings. In fact Girard is offering no such philosophical-theological judgement on human nature, merely empirical observations which he has culled from literary and ethnological texts. He certainly believes, along with the Judaeo-Christian tradition, that an escape from mimetic entanglement is not at all synonymous with a denial of human nature. This is not to deny, however, that there are occasional ambiguities in the way Girard formulates the problem of violence. A further perceived problem, voiced by G. Baudler, is the apparent disparagement, or at least neglect, which Girard seems to show towards non-Christian religions. Schwager's response points to the revelatory power which Girard detects in Greek drama, though on a weaker register than the biblical writings, and to Girard's account of 'History and the Paraclete' (a chapter in his book *The Scapegoat*), the Holy Spirit who stands by all victims and whose activity corrodes the foundations of victimizing cultures. Schwager also refers to the phenomenon of the so-called Time of the Axle; this is the ethicization of religion which took place independently in a number of cultures across the world, about six or five hundred years before the Common Era; he responds to Baudler that this noted transformation, far from being counter to Girard's thesis, may be more comprehensible because of it.

Other difficulties are voiced here, concerning the lack of evidence for Girard's reconstruction of the scapegoat mechanism in primitive societies. From the side of systematic theology, John Galvin puts questions from a Rahnerian perspective, which will be taken up in a later chapter. Suffice to say here that this 1991 Symposium marks an important critical 'sifting'

The Innsbruck Connection: Dramatic Theology

of dramatic soteriology, not least insofar as it is underpinned by Girard's controverted mimetic insights.

The discussion continues through several *Festschriften* for Raymund Schwager. 'On the Curse and Blessing of Scapegoats', the symposium for his 60th birthday,[5] contains an important testimony from Girard of the relationship between these two thinkers (Niewiadomski and Palaver, 1995: 15–29). Girard quotes from the *Sündenbock's* conclusion, and remarks upon his own reluctance to follow through on the logic of Schwager's conclusions – even though their respective works (*Sündenbock* and *Des Choses Cachées*) contained many parallels. He accounts for this reluctance in terms of an apologetic impatience to clarify his insights, and a fear that recourse to the language of sacrifice would lay open the way to a regressive assimilation of the Gospel by archaic religious thinking: Girard congratulates Schwager for his boldness in reclaiming the language and conceptuality of sacrifice at a point when he himself was hesitant, for apologetic reasons, to blur what he saw as the crucial difference between the Christian revelation and other religions.[6]

> I believed that the overriding significance of the mimetic theory had to be in directing all apologetic efforts against religious relativism. It was to expose its weaknesses. I wanted nothing other than to make even more precise the clarity of this position, which pressed upon me almost like a proof. A recourse to the concept of sacrifice, which already designated the rite of archaic religions, as a description of the Passion of Jesus, stood in the way of me and my programme. I was afraid that the traditional definition of the Passion in terms of the concept of sacrifice would supply so many additional arguments for assimilating Christianity to the category of archaic religion. For this reason I have for a long time considered this usage to be degenerate. (Niewiadomski and Palaver, 1995: 24)

We will return to the question of Girard and sacrifice in a later chapter. Meanwhile, it may be asked: what precisely does 'dramatic theology' offer that is so distinctive? This may be best answered by saying what it is not, and in the expositions and refinements of these symposia and *Festschriften* it becomes clear that 'dramatic theology' is intended to be distinguished first of all from dialectical theology, and secondly from narrative theology. In a paper titled 'Redemption through Sin? Dramatic as Opposed to Dialectic Interpretation', Schwager addresses the theme of messianic agency in the context of Jewish–Christian dialogue (Schwager, 1995). This agency is presented, once again, as a drama between several free actors. The wrathful action of God is in fact no such thing: rather it arises from the underlying collective activity of sinful persons. Schwager is arguing for the superiority of this dramatic approach rather than a 'dialectical' one, because dialectic can only lock us into a continuous cycle of guilt and atonement (1995: 11):

> Where there is dialectic, there mercy changes into wrath (retribution, atonement), and out of this arises again a mercy, which leads again to wrath. In dialectical movements there lives a worm which gnaws away at everything, as Nietzsche and Freud clearly perceived. But I am of the opinion, that Paul must be understood in another way, that is, not dialectically, but rather dramatically and, what is more, in terms of the dramatic destiny of Jesus, as it is depicted in the gospels.

In Act II of the dramatic scheme, Jesus' preaching of vengeance after the initial refusal of his message looks like a dialectical counterblow. It would be the resentful response of a disillusioned prophet. But in his ultimate refusal to retaliate, and in God's fidelity in raising him from the dead, 'there was no dialectic, but there was indeed a very intensive drama, namely an interaction between the actors'. The incessant search by Nietzsche for a way to place existence beyond the cycle of guilt and propitiation therefore is fulfilled, not in a naive form, but in the form of 'a love which did not allow itself to be seduced by any evil power to commit evil; a love which responds to every evil inflicted upon it by an intensification of its own self-donation'. (12)

A 'loose' interdisciplinary research group in Innsbruck has been working on the themes of 'Religion-Violence-Communication-World Order' since 1979. Scholars representing various theological disciplines, and inspired in varying degrees by mimetic theory, are concerned with questions about the contemporary relevance of religion, and with the recovery of biblical and ecclesial traditions. This ongoing project coheres with the dominant motifs in Schwager's theology: divine non-violence in the Bible, a systematic approach to soteriological questions, and a dramatic interpretation of the ministry, death and resurrection of Jesus. According to Josef Niewiadomski, it is the last of these that provides the key, not only to the other two themes, but to the whole of Schwager's work: ' "the violent drama of Jesus" has become a hermeneutical key or a "faith-summary" for our day' (Niewiadomski and Palaver, 1995: 31).

The 'research programme' undertaken by the Innsbruck scholars accords with the stipulation of Imre Lakatos (Lakatos, 1970), that theories can never be falsified in the short term; instead, there can be competing research programmes, among which one must choose in a way that may be considered

The Innsbruck Connection: Dramatic Theology

rational. Research programmes are hypothetical reconstructions, requiring a certain rational choice as to their progressivity. According to Lakatos, a research programme consists of a body of theories and a collection of data. The body of theories has a hard core (central hypothesis) and a larger number of auxiliary hypotheses, by which the data are related to the hard core. The Innsbruck Group have elaborated their programme in three steps with subdivisions: (1) very general hypotheses, forming a comprehensive framework (2) a hard core of hypotheses which specify the framework in terms of the Christian religion and concrete human experiences (3) a surrounding belt of auxiliary hypotheses.

The two 'hard core' hypotheses specify what seems to be an uncontroversial fact: the extraordinary difficulty of establishing 'deep, true and lasting peace' among people, which is not based on sacrificing third persons or polarization onto enemies (scapegoating 'within' and 'without', as it were). If such a peace is achieved, it is surely to be seen as a sign of the Holy Spirit at work among people, the outworking of the logic of the Incarnation. Our failure to achieve such peace can be positively reappraised through belief in Christ, who allowed evil to fall upon himself. Only our repeated incorporation into Christ (forgiveness and conversion) makes social life and even the transformation of nature possible.

The group offers a number of auxiliary hypotheses, of which the first has an especially privileged status:

[3–1] René Girard's theory offers a set of instruments in order to relate in a critical analysis of human and social sciences the various religious, political and emotional experiences of people in the course of history to the central hypotheses of [2–1] and [2–2].

[3–2] As a theologically turned anthropology and an anthropologically turned theology, the understanding of theology implied in this research program is in line with Karl Rahner's thinking. The individual hypotheses are to be understood in this context.

[3–3] The analysis of the results of natural sciences is also part of these hypotheses. Here the view of Teilhard de Chardin, which shows a final convergence of historical and natural processes (Point Omega as the unity of mankind in Christ and in the cosmos), serves as a possible guideline. The development of a new type of science (cybernetics, information theory, game theory, chaos theory and catastrophe theory) arouses the conjecture that the contrast between natural and human science may be overcome. The hope standing behind this development to comprehend the unity of reality as a unity of universal structures is an explicit challenge to the research program 'unity without polarization'.

Girard and Theology

We should note a few points concerning this belt of auxiliary hypotheses. First, the high priority accorded to Rahner's anthropological theology. Its role is unspecified here, but it seems that Rahner is providing the theological filter through which the research project is to be understood. We will investigate further in the next chapter, when we look more closely at mimetic theory as a form of 'theological anthropology'. Secondly, one might say that the expectation of an increased convergence between the natural and human sciences, modelled for many by the vision of another Jesuit, Teilhard de Chardin, is being fulfilled in the kind of areas opened up by *Evolution and Convergence*, where Girard and his interlocutors note the emergence of mimetic models in neuroscience and in genetics (Girard, 2008).

Thirdly, the privileged status accorded to Girard's mimetic theory indicates its potential for relating a wide range of human and cultural phenomena to the central core of the research programme. This and the other auxiliary hypotheses are intentionally formulated so as to be independent of the 'hard core' hypotheses. Nevertheless, the auxiliary hypotheses contribute to the progressivity of the research programme – for the time being (Lakatos). It is possible that further data and the distinctions required to incorporate them may make the mimetic theory so ponderous as to impede this progressivity. The mimetic insight must continue to prove its usefulness, therefore. Its privileged position in the belt of auxiliary hypotheses is both its stamp of quality and its stumbling block.

Chapter 5
A theological 'anthropophany'

Naming humanity before God

The theme of 'Christian anthropology' has traditionally been developed around three interconnected areas: first, the doctrine of Creation as contained in the early chapters of Genesis; secondly, New Testament readings, which include primarily Paul's doctrine of the 'two Adams' and the Logos Christology of the Fourth Gospel; thirdly, the language and conceptuality of the doctrine of grace, as this was formulated in Christian tradition and most especially during the Reformation disputes around justification. All of these are aspects of the human attempt to give an account of how we stand 'before God'; such an attempt will normally include some account of human origins (hence the importance of the Creation narrative) which entails a description of human destiny. The technical phrase here is 'protology implies eschatology', or as T. S. Eliot puts it: 'in my beginning is my end'. To give an example: Kevin Vanhoozer (1997) sketches the contours of a theological anthropology, which unites origin and destiny according to three indicative themes from the book of Genesis. These themes are: being in the image of God; being finite and creaturely; being socio-sexual. From these descriptions he derives the imperatives which guide us towards the goals of human striving: righteousness (further explicated as the image of the Son); the creation-cultural mandate to work; and the sociality of worship and wedding – rest and feast. Vanhoozer reminds us that the eschatological and trinitarian implications of the human story are also significant: '[B]oth the beginning and the ending of the human story, both the origin and destiny of human being, are ultimately to be understood in the light of the triune God's creating, redeeming and sanctifying activity.' (163)

René Girard also presents a 'theological anthropology', but in a different key from a direct appeal to scripture and tradition as implied by the above (we have to remind ourselves once again that Girard is not a theologian as such). I would even suggest that the difference is so significant that it is worth proposing a new term: 'anthropophany', but if this word is just too clumsy then we can do without. The word is coined by analogy with 'theophany', which means an appearance or manifestation of the divine.

Girard and Theology

This is to be distinguished from 'theology', the logos or discourse about God. What a word like 'anthropophany' is meant to convey is the notion that Girard's two weighty assertions about the nature and origins of human beings – desire is mimetic; the scapegoating mechanism – are not so much a theory or discourse about mankind, but a startling discovery or revelation which is inseparable from a disturbing encounter with the divine.

Why this is important will become evident as the chapter proceeds, and in particular as we look at one extensive work of James Alison, *The Joy of Being Wrong* (Alison, 1998). Alison works closely with Girard's narrative of 'hominization', which takes up a substantial section of *Things Hidden since the Foundation of the World*. It is not, strictly speaking, a theological account, nor does it imply anything at all about human destiny. On the other hand, Alison would insist that it is indeed 'theological', because the light which has enabled us to see these things is the light of the Christian gospel. The difficulty with a term like 'Christian' or 'theological' *anthropology* is that it can draw too much attention to the *logos*, implying a neutral or rational account of 'how human beings stand before God'. A word like *anthropophany*, awkward as it is, might better convey the sense of dramatic surprise and discovery, 'the joy of being wrong', which is at the core of Girard's description of what it is to be human.

In *Things Hidden* Girard challenges the lack of ambition of the human and biological sciences when it comes to thinking about the origins of religion, suggesting that if Darwin has been similarly discouraged in the nineteenth century he would have never formulated the theory of evolution. The book opens with some very paradoxical statements from Girard, however, about the conditions under which this quest is being carried out. He is discussing the global disappearance of religion, a phenomenon which paradoxically will enable us to study religion further and come to a more accurate appreciation of its nature:

> There is no enigma, however complex, that cannot finally be solved. For centuries religion has been declining in the West and its disappearance is now a global phenomenon. As religion recedes and allows us to consider it in perspective, what was once an insoluble mystery, guarded by formal taboos, begins to look more and more like a problem to be solved. (Girard, 1987a [1978]: 3)

The passage seems to presuppose a secularist thesis about the decline and disappearance of religion which has been increasingly hard to sustain since *Things Hidden* appeared in 1978. Girard's overall project does not depend on such a theory, however, which is just as well. In a later work he suggests instead that we have been calling 'secularity' may be better understood as a

A Theological 'Anthropophany'

hiatus or interval between two phases of religion. In any case, the question as he posed it in 1978 does have a peculiarly 'modern' tone. What is the 'natural' human being like, stripped of religious or transcendental presuppositions and descriptions? For most generations who have lived on this earth, such a question would not make sense. It is only with modernity that, for the first time in history, we are able to pose it in these terms.

As a way of setting the scene for a true appreciation of Girard's 'anthropophany', let us consider two scenarios, addressing from different sides the same 'modern' question about God and religion (not, of course, the same thing). The first comes from Jean Jacques Rousseau, whose controversial educational treatise *Emile*, written in 1762, narrates the education of a young boy by his Tutor. The Tutor is in fact the boy's only companion, from just after his birth until the age of 15. Isolated from all other human influences, and under the benign manipulation of the Tutor, Emile learns to make 'independent' judgements based solely on his experience of and interaction with his natural environment. He grows up without even the slightest conception of God (or 'man' or 'world' for that matter), since such ideas have no practical value for him. The Tutor realizes, however, that when Emile enters the world of society he will come up against the notion of 'God' in conversations, and he will need to be prepared for this – even though in his natural, solitary state Emile manages perfectly well without any thought of the divine. This is the occasion for the Tutor telling the story, in chapter 5 of *Emile*, of the 'Savoyard Vicar', a benign pastor whose profession of Deist sentiment (as opposed to Christian faith) would get Rousseau into enormous trouble.

Two hundred years later, the Jesuit theologian Karl Rahner (1900–1984) invites us to a thought experiment in his 'Meditation on the Word "God"' (Rahner, 1978: 44–51). The argument is an interesting one. Rahner points out that believer and atheist can at least agree on one thing, that 'the word exists among us' – indeed its existence is prolonged as long as the atheist disputes its relevance! But what if we imagine that the word and all it stands for could disappear, 'without a trace and without an echo': what would this mean?

> Then man would no longer be brought face to face with the single whole of reality, nor with the single whole of his own existence. For this is exactly what the word 'God' does and it alone, however it might be defined phonetically or in its genesis. (Rahner, 1978: 47)

'Man would forget all about himself', overwhelmed by the details of the world and his existence. He would have forgotten the totality and 'forgotten that he had forgotten', regressing to the level of a 'clever animal'.

In fact, although the human race might survive biologically and technologically, it would have died a collective death: '[T]he absolute death of the word "God," including even the eradication of its past, would be the signal, no longer heard by anyone, that man himself had died'.

> It is not the case that each of us as an individual thinks 'God' in an active process and that in this way the word 'God' enters into the realm of our existence for the first time. Rather we hear and receive the word 'God'. It comes to us in the history of language in which we are caught whether we want to be or not, which poses questions to us as individuals without itself being at our disposal. . . . We should not think that, because the phonetic sound of the word 'God' is always dependent on us, therefore the word 'God' is also our creation. Rather it creates us because it makes us men. (50)

The turn to the subject

In the two scenarios, it should be noted that what is at stake is not the evidence for and against the existence of God, but the very comprehensibility of discourse about humanity without a religious or transcendental dimension. These scenarios address modernity's veering away from the early Christian conviction that the key to understanding humanity is to be found in the biblical doctrine of God. With the 'turn to the subject' initiated by René Descartes and Immanuel Kant (Kant, in particular, was greatly influenced by Rousseau's ideal of religious sentiment in *Emile*) we have become conscious that all our knowledge is mediated through the human condition. Human subjectivity has become foundational for comprehending both ourselves and the divine: '[m]odern theology reverses the polarity between God and human being; anthropology has thus become an "omnipresent element" correlated with each of the major theological topics' (Vanhoozer, 1997: 159).

The last century produced distinctive trends of theological reflection, from thinkers who accept and work with this change of emphasis — whose theological style is therefore 'anthropocentric' rather than 'theocentric' — and others who explicitly resist it. Karl Rahner is the best known of the first style, while the Reformed theologian Karl Barth is a 'resistance fighter' who from early on in his career condemned the mainstream liberal theology of his day for being disastrously incapable of moving beyond the human point of view.

Rahner's strategy was to accept Kant's assertion that the knowing subject has access only to sense phenomena, and not to things as they are

A Theological 'Anthropophany'

'in themselves'. We cannot know the world, much less God, independently of the conditions of our experiencing and reasoning: it is much preferable to concentrate our attention on these, rather than on what is strictly inaccessible (among other things, this puts paid to the traditional 'proofs' of the existence of God). For Rahner this is not a disaster. By scrutinizing human beings and noting how they are constituted – as creatures radically open to transcendence, 'hearers of the word' whose intellectual and affective response to what we hear is unlimited – we can still discern something of the God who has made us possible. Looking at a keyhole tells us something of the shape of the key. Rahner describes man as 'the event of God's free self-communication': this is why 'theology is anthropology', 'less the science of God than the study of humanity as it stands before God', with Christ as the culmination and ultimate realization of human openness to and capacity for the divine.

Karl Barth takes the opposite tack. To concede Kant's starting-point, as did Rahner, is a big mistake, because it means that theology never goes beyond anthropological parameters and is therefore doomed to fall short of satisfactory speech about either God or humanity. Theology is first and foremost God's word, which becomes imprisoned in what Barth describes as the 'Babylonian captivity' of enlightened modernity. The controlling factor for theology has to be the person of Jesus Christ: he alone is the place of God's self-revelation (therefore the revelation of humanity), not the consciousness of the human subject as such. 'Jesus is not simply an intense expression of the common, human experience of "God-consciousness"; nor is christology simply anthropology writ large' (Vanhoozer, 1997: 172). A similar concern is voiced by Hans Urs von Balthasar, who proposes a version of theology as aesthetics: similarly to Barth, he sees God's glorious action in history as interpreting itself to humanity in a way which cannot be surmised or extrapolated from human existence. In his most bitter criticism of Rahner, von Balthasar attacks what he sees as a theology which accommodates itself to the world of sinful humanity, and which therefore bypasses the Cross.

Not only is there no room for the Cross, says von Balthasar, a transcendental approach such as Rahner's also bypasses the unique significance of Christ. The difficulty is evident if we note that section six of Karl Rahner's *Foundations of Christian Faith* (1978) is titled 'Jesus Christ': after sections (and 175 pages!) dealing with 'Man as Hearer of the Message', 'Man as the Event of God's Free and Forgiving Self-Communication', etc. To introduce Christ in mid-story, as it were, is quite contrary to Barth's impulsion towards a rigorous biblical narration, one which has no space for alternative accounts of the human story. A Rahnerian approach stresses the convergence between God's self-communication and humanity's reciprocal reaching out in love and intellect; Barth, on the other hand, insists that God's first word to humanity is a firm 'No!' to all human projects, particularly our attempts to assert a likeness to or analogy with God.

Girard and anthropology

It is striking how dominant these two paradigms – Rahner and Barth – have been and continue to be in contemporary theology. It is important not to overschematize the differences, however, and in fact, as Vanhoozer suggests, it may be better to regard both options as theological anthropology, with one working 'from below' (Rahner), while the other is 'from above' (Barth). From the perspective of Girardian mimetic theory there are problems with each approach, and this section will concentrate on an attempt at a 'third way', drawing largely on James Alison's extensive study of the doctrine of original sin, *The Joy of Being Wrong*. He sets the scene much as we are doing here: chapter 2 is titled 'The Search for a Theological Anthropology' (Alison, 1998: 22–63), while chapter 3 is 'The Search for a Soteriology' (64–114). What Alison proposes is a 'wisdom anthropology', or an anthropology of conversion, meaning the arduous journey of discovery, Girard's 'Resurrection from the Underground' of mimetic entrapment. The term 'wisdom' deliberately evokes the Gospel of John, since for Girard and Alison the presence within the gospel texts of a certain rationality or awareness about mimetic relations must have come 'from above': 'At the text's origin there must have been someone outside the group, a higher intelligence that controlled the disciples and inspired their writings.' It is this 'wisdom' that I am suggesting we christen 'anthropophany'. Paradoxically, the fact that this rationality reaches us in garbled form, indicating that the evangelists and disciples did not themselves fully understand what they were transmitting, can be seen as an argument for its authenticity – what biblical exegetes call the *lectio dificilior*: the 'more difficult' puzzling or startling reading is very often the more likely to be the correct one.

What follows is Alison's recasting of the opening section of *Things Hidden since the Foundation of the World*, in which Girard, along with Oughourlian and Lefort, identify mimesis as the constitutive factor of the 'Self', 'the absolute condition for the existence of humanity' (28). The account of mimetic desire which follows from this is distinguished from the Freudian account of identification, leaving behind the problems of the Oedipus complex, but still with an understanding of the human self as 'an unstable structure, one that is changeable, malleable, and other-dependent, whether it likes it or not'. Alison cites the two main theses of

A Theological 'Anthropophany'

Oughourlian, to the effect that desire engenders the self and brings it into existence, and that desire is mimetic: it moves in imitation of the desire of another. We come into the world already programmed with the desires and patterns of behaviour of those who precede us. And of course if those desires or behaviours are wounded or distorted, we will also inherit these distortions, even before there is a 'me' to inherit! Each of us is, in short, a 'radically needy little anthropos', who from the start will shore up identity over against those whose desires conflict with ours.

This personal history, which is the history of every person, is also the long history of humankind, in the process of hominization. The mimetic capacity of human beings is a function of increased brain size, giving us a link between evolutionary development and mimetic interaction. Alison points out the importance of this kind of explanation: 'it inscribes the genesis of human culture in nature and relates it to a natural mechanism without depriving culture of what is specifically or exclusively human' (34). In this account it is the fascination of the object of death, specifically the victim who has been destroyed by the group and whose death appears to have brought peace out of violence. This awakening of attention is the first stirring of human consciousness, though we are positing a process that takes place over an extremely long time. The cadaver also becomes a sign, and so we have the origins of meaning and language: 'every possible signifying element has its starting point in the victim'. Hence the importance of anthropological evidence, such as myths, which refers us to but also conceals the founding murder. From here it is a question of linking the two narratives: the genesis of the self and the genesis of the species are similar processes.

> From the theological point of view it is of no small interest that we have here an anthropology that suggests that awareness of the other and awareness of the self come about simultaneously, and as part of the same process of (controlledly) violent desire. That is to say that both awarenesses and the attitudes that flow from them are simultaneously distorted. Not only that, but the only way of access into the formation of the distorted 'self' is via the distorted other, and thus the only access to any sort of transformation of the malleable construct which the 'self' has been shown to be passes through a change in the structure of the relationality with the other. (37)

There is no change in 'me' without change in my relation to the other; nor is there any change in 'me' unless it is initiated by the other. Quite simply, says Alison, we have here the foundations for an anthropology of grace, meaning here an account of what is required for human beings to change for the better. It allows such an anthropology to be constructed without all the false dichotomies which hamper clear thinking, such as individual versus collective, subjective versus objective (Alison, 1998: 37–9). This has considerable implications for how we conceive the social and political dimensions of the gospel message, as we shall see.

There is no space here to elaborate on what is required of a sound doctrine of grace: a pithy definition declares that '[t]he theological concept of grace tries to sum up God's relations with the human race with special attention to the fact that these relations are loving, generous, free and totally unexpected and undeserved' (Quessnell, 1990: 437). At the core of Alison's discussion is the sad and puzzled recognition that such a straightforward notion – the gratuity of God's action and loving – seems almost impossible to grasp. For whatever reason, it is astoundingly difficult to hang onto the notion of gratuitous love, without constructing some 'hydraulic' system of weights and pulleys, as it were; over time, the term 'grace' becomes the cornerstone of a complicated and highly technical theological discourse. The shift would seem to occur with Augustine, and his dispute with Pelagius in the fifth century; with Pelagius addressing the paradox at the heart of this divine gratuity: if it is really the case that we are incapable of saving ourselves without God's generous intervention, then there is no way that we can be held responsible or culpable for our sinful actions. Where Augustine emphasized our helplessness, Pelagius argued that we must, after all, be capable of keeping God's law and attaining salvation. Subsequent attempts to determine the exact point at which God's favour 'kicks in' led to an increasingly specialized vocabulary concerning grace, its causes, properties and operation. And holy scripture is drawn into the argument, specifically the account of the Fall in Genesis, chapters 1 and 2, and Paul's account of salvation in Romans 5.

With this controversy over the interaction of divine and human capabilities, the future battle-lines of Western Christianity are sketched out, though in the Eastern churches a clearer emphasis on the root meaning of 'gratitude' led in a different direction: the transformation of human nature through the action of Christ and the Spirit, called *theosis* or divinization. It would be wrong to suggest that this last dimension is entirely absent from the West, however, as is clear if we take up Thomas Aquinas' explication of human destiny as the eternal possession of God in a face-to-face beatifying vision. The concept of 'justification' in its richest sense brings together the different dimensions:

> Justification, God's act of turning the sinner into a just person, is God's greatest work, greater even than the original creation. It is

A Theological 'Anthropophany'

simultaneously conversion, forgiveness of sin and the infusion of grace. Grace in the sense of God's favour, benevolence and love is God's own self, eternal and unchangeable. (440)

Such an understanding of grace entails a habitual orientation of the entire person towards God, a 'new nature' which comes

> appropriately provided with new powers, new principles of operation, which heal and elevate and make the person able to be sweetly and promptly moved by God toward eternal shared divine life.

Unfortunately, the onset of nominalism sees a debasement of language and concepts and a falling away from the language of grateful attention to God's intimate self-gift. 'Grace' comes to be 'a mere name for the completely extrinsic reality of God's arbitrary will and absolute power' (441). The protest of the sixteenth-century Reformers and the considered response of the Council of Trent are attempts to recover a lost balance, which really only bear fruit in the decades before and after the Second Vatican Council (1962–1965). Historical and dogmatic researches allow much of the dead wood of misreadings and misappropriations of Aquinas to be cleared away, enabling a new appreciation that the word 'grace' can never refer to a third entity between human beings and the divine: God's action is identical with God, as implied in the 'conversion' experience of Rom. 5.5: 'For the love of God is poured forth in our hearts by the Holy Spirit who is given to us'.

It is this reality which Karl Rahner seeks to express in his description of the human being as 'the event of the absolute, free and forgiving self-communication of God'. This formula conveys the truth of humanity's openness to the transcendence in our intellectual and affective strivings towards the infinite, so that God has already communicated God's self as an inner constitutive element of every human being (God is the maker of the keyhole). Rahner's technical term for this is 'supernatural existential', meaning that we always already exist in the context of our intimate relationship to God. There never has been a state of pure nature, a 'neutral' zone.

While Rahner's account is a brilliant corrective of earlier distortion, it is not without its problems for Alison. He notes, quoting John Milbank, that a transcendental anthropology

> sees as a matter of philosophical truth, the human being as imbued with a somehow experienced orientation toward grace and glory

and therefore the concrete, contingent historical acts of salvation (the prophets, the coming of Christ, the existence of the Church, the sacraments) a merely making explicit the universal availability of grace. In such a view, 'the historical events, the human acts and images which can alone be the site of supernatural difference, are here reduced to mere signs of a perfect inward self-transcendence, always humanly available.'[1]

This is not to deny the universal availability of grace. The difficulty is that we have a *logos,* a truth which is announced in detachment from the process or journey of discovery of that truth ('anthropophany'). And it is precisely that discovery in hope, in specific social and historical situations, which is the core of the matter. We are left with a universal philosophical principle which 'shortcuts the way in which discovery of the universality of the call to *theosis* is, for each of its participants, a radical conversion and part of the revelation of salvation' (43). To anticipate Walter Brueggemann's distinction which we will encounter when looking at approaches to biblical theology in Chapter 8, Rahner's account is 'above the fray', rather than 'within the fray'.

There is a more serious problem however, with the simple affirmation that the human desire for transcendence is a natural desire for God. A mimetic point of view has to acknowledge that this desire, good in itself, may be misdirected or distorted. If our desire focuses on an object other than God, and if we desire in a grasping acquisitive manner, rather than reciprocating God's gratuitous love, then that desire is being 'lived as idolatry, a complete missing of the point'; it is the difference between the grasping appetite of a tourist and the calm possession of a resident. Here Alison agrees with those liberation theologians who see the antithesis of faith in the God of life as idolatry, rather than atheism. By contrast, a Rahnerian transcendental anthropology 'effectively pre-pardons idolatry without transforming the idolator, without giving him or her the chance of a real restructuring of heart' (47). Once again, this is the outcome of constructing an anthropology which is a neutral intellectual feat rather than the narrative of a struggle and a discovery.

A mimetic anthropology

Alison's strictures on transcendental anthropology need to be borne in mind, though in reply it might fairly be said that often the problem lies, not with Rahner necessarily, but with some of his adherents who fall into a sloganizing theology ('all is grace') without the careful safeguards and

A Theological 'Anthropophany'

nuances that Rahner himself puts in place. As we have seen, some proponents of mimetic theory, specifically the Innsbruck research group, favour a broadly Rahnerian approach alongside Girard's anthropology. John P. Galvin (1992) warns us against a too easy alignment of Rahner, Schwager and Girard, however. He does so by reminding us of von Balthasar's distinction between two fundamental approaches in contemporary soteriology: 'solidarity' (exemplified by Catholic theologians such as Hans Kung, Edward Schillebeeckx and Karl Rahner), and 'substitution' (as articulated by an evangelical tradition which includes Luther, Calvin, Barth, Pannenberg and Moltmann). Intriguingly, von Balthasar and Galvin place Girard and Schwager among this second group rather than the first. Rahner's theology of grace and salvation develops as an elevation of human nature into participation in the divine life. Grace is above all *gratia elevans*, presupposing a contrast between grace and nature; in this scheme the overcoming of sin receives little attention, and the challenge for Rahner is how to make room for the mediation of Jesus and the significance of his death (Galvin, 1992: 157). Raymund Schwager, on the other hand, begins with the reality of sin and violence; salvation is seen above all as God's answer to the violent injustice of human beings. This is *gratia sanans*, operating with the contrast between grace and sin, or with non-violence and violence (though this is not the same distinction). Galvin judges a synthesis of these two approaches – from Rahner and Schwager – to be impossible, though each offers worthwhile insights.

The construction of a 'theological anthropology' is a contribution to, and not the entirety of, a doctrine of salvation, a 'soteriology'. Having attempted a theological description of humanity, we can better articulate what is to be understood by God 'saving' or 'redeeming' human beings. We will look in the next chapters at the construction of a theoretical framework, and then at some of the traditional models and images of soteriology, through the lens of mimetic theory. Obviously, the discourses of 'theological anthropology' and 'soteriology' are closely related. We have seen that there are two broad paradigms or approaches, symbolized by the towering figures of Karl Rahner and Karl Barth. Though it is Rahner who more explicitly speaks of a 'theological anthropology', we have noted Vanhoozer's suggestion that these options be regarded as theological anthropology 'from below' and 'from above' respectively. Here once again René Girard's work falls intriguingly between polarities, as it seems to contain aspects of compatibility with each of these approaches.

As Alison argues, however, there is a strong case for construing mimetic theory as something of a 'third way'. We have seen how he regards the affirmation of universal grace as misleading, if it serves to characterize human desire for the transcendent as simply a desire for God, without acknowledging the possibility (or even likelihood) that such desire may be distorted or misdirected. Such an approach 'effectively pre-pardons idolatry, without transforming the idolator, without giving him or her the chance of a real restructuring of heart' (47).

The mistake here, of thinking that atheism rather than idolatry is the antithesis of faith in the true God, is in fact a costly one, if we read with Girardian eyes the two parables with which we began this chapter.

Rousseau's idyllic description of Emile as an untainted innocent who grows up in paradisal ignorance of the divine is of course the Romantic Lie writ large: Girard would reject as pure fantasy the picture presented here, of the isolated, non-mimetic, spontaneously good individual. Just as fantastical, however, is the version of man which we have from Rahner's parable about the disappearance of the word 'God'. Rahner suggests that in such a case, while there might be survival in a biological and technological sense, the human race would have died a collective death: '[T]he absolute death of the word "God," including even the eradication of its past, would be the signal, no longer heard by anyone, that man himself had died'. Human beings would continue to be 'clever and resourceful animals' who are nonetheless no longer confronted with the great question to themselves – the word 'God' – which makes them human.

What is missing from each of these scenarios, and what makes each of them deficient as accounts of the human, is mimetic (therefore potentially conflictual) desire. Rousseau's optimism is of course well known; but in Rahner's case also, the idea that the human appetite for transcendence will simply wither away, rather than attach itself to an idol, is a delusion. In *Jerusalem* William Blake declared that '[m]an must & will have some religion; if he has not the Religion of Jesus, he will have the Religion of Satan'; deprived of God, humans do not simply diminish or shrink into robotic existence, or an animal spontaneity. They turn instead towards false messiahs and false transcendencies, in search of the numinosity which will transform the emptiness within – with catastrophic results. When seeking to articulate this reality, we will find ourselves turning not so much to Karl Rahner as to his younger German contemporaries: Hannah Arendt (Adolf Eichmann and the 'banality of evil'), and the political theologians Johann Baptist Metz and Jürgen Moltmann; all seeking explicitly to make sense of how man stands, not just before God, but also 'before Auschwitz'.

Chapter 6
The drama of salvation

Having attempted to articulate the theological 'anthropophany' at the heart of mimetic theory, the next two chapters will explore the implications for soteriology, the doctrine of salvation. The first task is to establish an appropriate conceptual framework for such an exploration, which as we shall see has become a complicated business. The next chapter will take up a second task, an investigation of some of the key 'classic' metaphors of salvation, as they resonate in the work of Girard and Schwager.

For this chapter however, the challenge is to construct an adequate framework or scaffolding for a doctrine of salvation. One such structure which draws on mimetic theory is the 'dramatic salvation' doctrine (*dramatische Erlösungslehre*), elaborated by the late Raymund Schwager, which we have encountered in our survey of the Innsbruck theological appropriation of mimetic theory in Chapter 5, and adverted to once again on the last chapter. Schwager's contribution comprises two key works, first, *Der wunderbare Tausch*, or 'The Marvellous Exchange', an integrated study of selected controversies, all illuminated in important ways by the mimetic theory, and secondly in *Jesus and the Drama of Salvation* (*Jesus in Heilsdrama*).

Each of the ten controversies or problems addressed by Schwager in the essays in *Der wunderbare Tausch* is susceptible to a mimetic analysis, either because of some aspect of mimesis, or because issues of violence or scapegoating underlie the apparent problem.[1] This dramatic approach allows us to align Girard with important historical and contemporary contributors to the question of salvation, such as Irenaeus, Anselm of Canterbury, Karl Barth, and Hans Urs von Balthasar. To mention very briefly the first of these studies, in which Schwager examines the controversy between Irenaeus of Lyon and Marcion (Schwager, 1986: 7–31) Marcion's perception of diversity and conflict in the Bible led him to reject the Old Testament as inferior revelation to the God of Love revealed in Jesus. Schwager improves on the theological stance of Irenaeus by means of Girard's theory, which can better grasp the complex interrelationship between the testaments. Marcion's contribution is acknowledged for addressing head-on the issue of divine violence, the theme which Schwager has considered at length in his previous book, *Sündenbock*. For Schwager, the central problem of soteriology is precisely Marcion's dilemma: how to reconcile what the Bible tells us of God's wrath and God's love.

There is another dichotomy which has to be recognized, and which is beautifully conveyed in two imaginative 'versions' of the Incarnation of Christ from sixteenth-century Spanish mystics. In his *Spiritual Exercises*, St Ignatius sets the scene for a contemplation on the Incarnation and Nativity. First, he asks us to bring to mind the history of the subject to be contemplated, in this case 'how the Three Divine Persons look down upon the whole expanse or circuit of all the earth, filled with human beings'. With the Trinity, we observe from Heaven a vast diversity of people, how they swear and blaspheme, 'wound, kill and go down to hell':

> Since They see that all going down to hell, They decree in Their eternity that the Second Person should become man to save the human race. So when the fullness of time had come They sent the Angel Gabriel to Our Lady.

Then the camera zooms in, as it were, from the great globe of the earth to the little house in Nazareth where Mary encounters the angel, and after this we see her and Joseph journeying to Bethlehem for the birth of Jesus. We may set this 'narrative' alongside that of St John of the Cross, from his *Romance* 1, 'On the Gospel "In the Beginning was the Word"', in which the poet 'listens into' the tender words of love between Father and Son. John sees the Creation as the Father's gift to his Beloved:

> Son, I wish to give you
> A bride's tender love.
> A bride who is worthy
> For you to approve;
> And she shall dwell with us
> In company sweet,
> And eat at our table
> The bread which I eat.

The Son replies with gratitude:

> I will give all my brightness
> To your gift of a bride,
> So that she may value
> My Father's great worth
> And how my very being
> From your being had birth.

The Drama of Salvation

> In perpetual delight
> In my arms I will hold her,
> To praise your great goodness
> And in your love enfold her.

Here, the Incarnation takes place so that the Son may be united with his radiant bride. These readings ask us to think very differently about the Christmas story. In the account given by Ignatius, the emphasis is on the way Creation has turned out disastrously, and on the need for someone (the Second Person) to come down and fix things. W. H. Auden refers to Christ in one of his poems as the 'mild engineer'! The poem from John of the Cross has none of this: the Incarnation happens as the fulfilment of God's plan, the joyful coupling of the Son with His bride 'in perpetual delight'. The first approach reads the Incarnation in terms of our sin and our alienation from God, the second in terms of God's overwhelming love for us. They illustrate nicely the two approaches which were mentioned in the previous chapter, concerning *gratia sanas* ('healing grace'), which von Balthasar and Galvin associate with the evangelical theological tradition, but also with Girard and Schwager on the problematic of violence; and a *gratia elevans* approach ('elevating grace'), such as Karl Rahner's transcendental anthropology.

Christ, then salvation

With this framework in mind, we shall go on to consider the classic metaphorical clusters which have been used in discourse about salvation, specifically the images of *victory*, *justice* and *sacrifice*. Before we begin, however, we need to highlight an important point made by Walter Lowe in an essay called 'Christ and Salvation'.[2] The wording of the title draws attention to the 'classical' approach of theology, which treats first of the person of Christ and then his work. In contemporary theology, however, it is often the other way round: increasingly, we are given a prefatory notion of salvation – some account of why humans need or lack what Christianity has to offer – before looking at the person of Christ. This account usually includes four elements: a general *description*, a specific *diagnosis*, a general *recommendation* and a specific *remedy* (235). Addressing a sceptical or unbelieving world, we have to work 'towards' Christ rather than start from him. There are, however, two big problems with this approach:

> For by the very act of prefacing one's Christology with an
> explanatory sequence, one establishes a framework or context

to which the Christology must at all points conform. If at any point it does not so conform, the vital link between general recommendation and specific Christian remedy – the bridge across 'the scandal of particularity,' across Lessing's 'ugly ditch' – is lost and the project founders. (Lowe, 2003: 236)

The second difficulty with this sequence is that by beginning with an exposition of need or lack, the Good News is only presented in the context of the negative. There is a danger that this 'pact with the negative' may overshadow, or even defer altogether, the radical good of the Gospel (236). In fact, closer investigation reveals this to be a problem of both classical and contemporary soteriologies. James Alison tells the story as: 'God creates a good world, human beings mess it up, Christ comes to put things right again'. This is seriously inadequate, says Alison, because it is a story about our deficiency rather than God's initiative: 'The controlling factor in the story of salvation is the sin, and what Christ did fits in with that' (Alison, 1998: 7).

It can be said that from the outset that (despite Alison's argument) a Girardian-inspired soteriology seems to be caught in the same pattern, and therefore faces the same objections. What greater 'pact with the negative' could there be than Girard's dismal account of the debilitations of mimetic desire and the scapegoat mechanism? And there is the first difficulty: the risky strategy of making the Christological link, between 'general recommendation' and 'specific remedy'; Lowe draws a parallel with recommending an analgesic and advocating a specific brand. Even if we acknowledge the need to be 'resurrected from the underground' of violent mimesis, is it evident that Christ is the sole remedy – or even the best one, given institutional Christianity's atrocious track record?[3]

If the link between work and Christ is not established – if we fall into the ugly ditch – then the project is lost. To look at this from the other end, as Lowe invites us to do: does Girardian soteriology lack a robust and convincing Christology?

Lowe problematizes this further when he draws out the implications of the 'negative moment'. Salvation theories will usually include an 'economy', by which he means that 'a negative or deficit at one point must be offset by some positive valence at another point: the metaphorics of economy are quasi-hydraulic' (237). Just as Freud alerted us to compensatory or reciprocal psychological mechanisms, so the doctrine of salvation operates within an economic, 'quid pro quo' setting. The idea of humanity being 'bought back' from Satan was repugnant to Anselm: and yet even Anselm's *Cur Deus Homo* derives its power from an economy of exchange – though at least here Satan is taken out of the picture. It is probably unrealistic to think we can do without economic models altogether (a theme we will take up again when we look at sacrifice in the next chapter); the real question, once again, is whether any particular notion of 'deficit' is too dominant in our description, in a way that eclipses or distorts what we might want to say about Christ.

For Lowe, therefore, soteriological discourses, both classical and contemporary, confront problems of sequence, economy and negativity. They place 'a kind of soteriological preface – an account of the need for salvation which implicitly circumscribes what salvation, and the bringer of salvation, can be – before Christology'. This relies on an economy, the logic of which requires a negative element, the story of 'some form of need, offense or deficit' (Lowe, 242).

Girard and Anselm

Does mimetic theory rise above these limitations? Here, a close comparison of Girard with Anselm of Canterbury may be instructive. Anselm's doctrine of 'satisfaction' has proved to be enormously influential, but also controversial, as it seems to have prepared the way for the penal substitution theory put forward by later theologians. Here we may identify three characteristics of this doctrine which serve as a point of comparison with Girard. First, Anselm begins by declaring his dissatisfaction with a key understanding of salvation, the model or metaphor of 'ransom', which conveyed the idea that our redemption consists in God paying a ransom, his Son, in order to liberate us from the enslaving power of Satan. Anselm rejects not just this model, but in effect the family of metaphors which in one way or another give Satan a leading role in our salvation.

Secondly, and more positively, Anselm is one of the earliest theologians to attempt to systematize our thinking on salvation, to bring some order into the proceedings. It is now generally acknowledged that before Anselm's *Cur Deus Homo* the discourse of soteriology had been relatively unstructured. Instead of the precise and careful formulae of the great Christological councils of Nicaea and Chalcedon, what we are faced with in soteriology is a rich and considerable range of pictures and metaphors, each expressing some aspect of the reality of salvation in Christ. A dozen or more metaphors, mostly biblical, and largely untainted by the complicated philosophy which was enlisted for formal Christological debate, support and enrich one another. Some are incompatible, however, and sometimes the logic which unites them is at best implicit. This may not be much of a problem for a believer, but when it comes to giving an account of Christian faith to a non-believer, a more systematic and convincing approach is needed, rather than what looks like 'painting on a cloud':

> All these are beautiful notions, and are to be viewed like pictures. But if there is nothing solid underlying them, they do not seem to unbelievers to provide sufficient grounds why we should believe that God wished to suffer the things of which we are speaking. For someone who wishes to paint a picture chooses something solid on which to paint, so that his painting may have permanence. For nobody paints on water or on air, because on these no traces of painting last. Therefore, when we offer to unbelievers these notions which you say are 'appropriate', like pictorial representations of an actual past event, they think we are, as it were, painting on cloud. (Anselm, [1998]: 269)

Non-believers will not be convinced by mere pictures, however striking they may be. Anselm is thinking primarily of a Jewish dialogue partner, as represented by the character of Boso in the conversations of *Cur Deus Homo?* For people such as this, pictures are not enough to explain 'why the God-Man?'

Thirdly, Anselm offers his own account of the logic or necessity behind God's becoming man in the Incarnation, and he does so by referring to the specific reality of his own culture and society. The feudal background to Anselm's notion of satisfaction is well known, and is generally regarded a limitation upon this doctrine, which of course it is for anyone who does not inhabit a feudal society. The strength of the image, however, is its stress on our relationality to God, and to each other, with the implied rights and duties that such connectedness brings with it. However problematic it may seem, it serves precisely the purpose of taking the devil off the stage, as it were. Obligations or rights are no longer owed to Satan, as the narrative of ransom has it, but rather the question of salvation is now a matter solely between God and human beings. This is a significant advance, for which Anselm needs to be appreciated and applauded.

Three moments, therefore – the rejection of a model or metaphor which is seen to be problematic or no longer useful, the desire to establish an underlying logic or narrative which will bring some order and clarity to the profusion of different models, and an identification of the key aspect of his culture and society on which a more up-to-date understanding of salvation can be constructed. Raymund Schwager summarizes thus in *Jesus and the Drama of Salvation*:

> In order to reconcile God's goodness and justice with each other, Anselm's point of departure for his doctrine of redemption were

The Drama of Salvation

the very human concepts of offense, honor, punishment and satisfaction. These images were on the one hand immediately comprehensible, and on the other hand he was able through them to draw biblical utterances indirectly into the purifying process of his Christian thinking. These utterances, at first glance, speak of God in all too human terms. To reproduce the same procedure today would make no sense, as the immediate representations of his time are not the same as ours, and today's world is afflicted with tensions which differ in part from those of his age. But if the dominant representations and concerns of a given time are not drawn into the purifying process of a reflecting faith, then this latter easily becomes rootless, and it will offer solutions for problems which have not been accurately diagnosed, while those questions which actually concern people receive no further clarification. Anselm's method shows that a Christian theology which is to reach the furthest depths and heights must start from the dominant notions or representations of the age, and even from everyday images. (1999: 14)

It may be argued that René Girard's contribution to soteriology can be expressed in a threefold correspondence to Anselm's doctrine. Girard begins by expressing a radical dissatisfaction with one of the key images of salvation, namely the notion that Christ's saving action can be understood as a sacrifice. There are plenty of reasons why this notion is out of favour, given its abuse in the name of patriarchy and nationalistic militarism. There are many people who would be happy to leave behind the notion of sacrifice as inappropriate in Christian discourse, just as 'ransom' from the devil was judged to be unacceptable by Anselm. For Girard, who of course links ritual sacrifice with the scapegoat mechanism, the imperative to move beyond sacrificial thinking is overwhelming.

Secondly, Girard's theory provides a framework which allows the different picture and images to be placed in a meaningful pattern. There is need for a narrative or drama which demonstrates the underlying logical connection between the 'beautiful notions'. It is the solid surface which gives them permanence. Thirdly, just as Anselm chose for his starting-point the network of feudal rights and obligations to speak about how men stood before God, so Girard has focused almost obsessively on one of the most evident and widely acknowledged social phenomena of our day, namely the victimization of men and women in the name of religious or quasi-religious institutions and ideologies. The status of the religious victim is our key to the truth of Christianity. We have already heard from Robert Hamerton-Kelly: 'I believe that the overriding fact of our time is violence; therefore a theory that attempts to make sense out of violence is more likely to orient us to the points in the field that are salient for our time.'

In his essay on Anselm in *Der wunderbare Tausch* (Schwager, 1986: 161–91) Raymund Schwager draws attention to 'surprising parallels' as well as differences between Anselm and Girard (179). Neither wants to prove the faith in a rationalistic way; both are convinced that revelation opens up a perspective for the whole of reality, which in turn enables a deeper and richer awareness of revelation. Anselm proposes the outside limit of reason in the inability to conceive of something greater. By contrast Girard proceeds inductively, but is likewise concerned with the ground of thinking and indeed of reality: 'of things hidden since the foundation of the world'. Anselm takes the structure of the human soul (as image of God and mirror of the Trinity) as his point of departure; in this way the express formulation of doctrine is bracketed and the human self invited to proceed, step by step, to the faith realities, by a process of overcoming contradictions (Schwager, 1986: 180).

With Girard there is no such bracketing: he sees the biblical writings first and foremost as witnesses within the wider cultural and religious history of humankind. The distinctiveness of the biblical documents is made clear, and key texts within the scriptural canon are used to decipher all the other cultural and religious documents. Anselm's is an intensive journey of negation, asking about the significance of sin so as to move from a reflection on sin to an appreciation of God's mercy. Girard similarly begins with what Lowe calls a 'pact with the negative', insofar as he analyses the underlying mechanisms of lies, violence and pride. This is in order to move towards the true positive, the God of Jesus Christ, whose loving transcendence is quite different from the transcendence of violent idols.

The human situation is paradoxical, in that humankind must make satisfaction, but cannot. This, for Anselm, is the necessary reason for salvation in Christ. By analogy, Girard shows that all men are caught in a mechanism of lies and violence from which they cannot free themselves. Jesus' overcoming of this mechanism in his life and fate indicates for Girard that the prophet of Nazareth is both true God and true man. Anselm understands himself to be correcting a distorted tradition which precedes him; Girard is to some extent doing the same with respect to Anselm, or at least with versions of satisfaction theory which project elements of violence onto our picture of God. To this extent, their projects share a concern for free human action. A further complication, however: Anselm's approach, of purifying our notions of God in the light of our being in God's image and likeness (*imago et similitudo*) can too easily tend towards mirror imaging. For Girard, of course, a pure mirror image is a precursor to mimesis and rivalry.

The Drama of Salvation

The challenge of moving within and beyond Anselm is summed up in the formula 'neither punishment nor satisfaction' – the two alternatives which are presented to us within an Anselmian economy. A further possible parallel between Anselm and Girard suggests itself, with regard to the apologetic nature of Anselm's task, which is basically to answer the question 'Why the God-Man?' as it is posed by a non-Christian, a Jewish interlocutor, for example. Such a questioner will not be impressed by the 'beautiful notions' of Christianity, but will want to know what is the logic: why was it *necessary* for God to become man, and die on the Cross, as Christians claim, in order to bring about our salvation? There is a striking parallel with our own time, if we compare a document titled *Christian Answers to Muslim Questions*.[4] Chapter 3 of this very useful resource is on 'Cross, Sin and Redemption', and gives us some of the background as to why Muslims finds the Christian approach difficult. Specifically:

- How can the eternal God suffer and die on a cross? . . . How can the Father sacrifice his Son on the cross? This is all simply blasphemy.
- The death of an innocent and righteous person can neither wipe away the sins of another person nor can it redeem another person from his or her sins. For an innocent person to die in the place of a guilty person is an outrageous injustice.
- For God to forgive sins there is absolutely no need for the 'sacrifice' of which Christianity speaks. God is almighty and forgives all people from their sins provided they repent . . . God is kind; he is not an unmerciful judge. . . .
- Human nature is not radically evil. Why is Christianity so pessimistic?

We may point out, of course, that Muslims are not alone in putting these questions to Christianity. The challenge of an adequate response is exactly that which faced Anselm in the twelfth century; there can be no avoiding the 'ugly ditch'.

Does mimetic theory offer a plausible response? What characteristics should we be looking for? David Ford in *Self and Salvation* proposes six criteria for an adequate soteriology (Ford, 2006). Such a doctrine must go to the heart of Christian identity (i.e. it must be faithful to the specificity of the gospel setting and also have universal implications); secondly, it must be widely accessible, related to imaginative, emotional and pastoral concerns; thirdly, it needs to be capable of being focused through one or a few symbols, images or metaphors which have 'intensity and gripping power'; fourthly, it must have a conceptual richness, heuristically inspiring a diversity of investigations and discussions; fifthly, the theory needs to have practical promise of fruitfulness in the various dynamics of Christian living, such as worship, life in community, speech, action and suffering for justice; sixthly, it needs to be defensible against diverse attacks and be able to anticipate the criticisms of alternative theories.

We will return to this 'check list' in the next chapter, when we look at how Girard's theory makes sense of some of the key metaphors. Such a list still does not resolve some of the questions of basic orientation, where choices have to be made. We began with two imaginative accounts of the Incarnation, from St John of the Cross and St Ignatius, as illustrations of *gratia elevans* and *gratia sanans*, elevating and healing, respectively: it is suggested by Galvin in his presentation at the 1992 Symposium on Dramatic Salvation, that Rahner and Girard/Schwager are on either side of this divide, and therefore not compatible.

Here is a good place to summarize some specific areas of critique, the 'Rahnerian' questions which Galvin puts to Schwager's 'Theo-Drama'. First, the dramatic model is too one-sided in its presentation of the Holy Spirit (who only appears at Pentecost in the final fifth act); secondly, Galvin is concerned about the separation of the death and the resurrection of Jesus into separate acts (III and IV). In Rahner these are more tightly bound together; from a soteriological point of view 'salvation' does not proceed from one or the other; they are different aspects of the same event.

The third query concerns the salvific significance of the Cross and the necessity of Jesus' death. According to Schwager, this death becomes necessary (Act III) when the opponents of Jesus reject his message (Act II) and he decides to offer himself on their behalf. For Rahner, the death of Jesus is the definitive human acceptance of God's self-communication, an acceptance which only death makes possible; here, only here is the completion of the individual story of human freedom made categorically irreversible. The death of Jesus is the real symbol of the victorious grace of God; the implicit question to Schwager here is whether the significance of Jesus' death is only to be found in his rejection. Does this death have a meaning on the level of nature, or only in its particular circumstance? If Jesus' message had been accepted, would his death have no salvific significance? This is to ask (as Rahner has done) about the theological meaning of death as such, and not just this particular violent death. The unity of salvation and revelation is the core of Galvin's fourth concern; these are too sharply distinguished in Schwager by comparison with Rahner (see Rahner, 1978: 138–77). Fifthly, Galvin expresses concerns about Schwager's exegetical method in *Jesus im Heisdrama*, which places a needlessly high premium on the historicity of key passages. By contrast, Rahner's strategy in the *Foundations of Christian Faith* is to steer clear of the exegetical minefield, and work with a minimal dependence on assertions about the historical Jesus. Galvin's sixth point takes up the reproach of von Balthasar, that Karl

Rahner's soteriology avoids the 'decisive dramatic moments', specifically concerning the wrath of God. It is unclear to Galvin why the dramatic model should always be preferred over other literary forms, such as narrative theology, for example.

Conclusion: Beyond salvation

Galvin is just one of the many contributors to the 1992 *Symposium* who finds value in the dramatic theology model. If these connections hold good then we are looking at an extraordinarily elegant contribution to the debate about atonement. The truth is that the cure to our ills looks very similar to the ills themselves: the Greek term *pharmakon* refers to a poison which is also an antidote, just as a small dose of a virus is administered as a protection against more serious infection. This is why 'religious' solutions usually look as bad as, or worse than, the problems they are meant to address.

A number of contemporary theologians reinforce this paradox, arguing that the implications of Girard's mimetic anthropology go much further than breathing fresh life into jaded theological metaphors. Simon Taylor asserts that 'the paradox that Girard presents us with is that "salvation" is something from which we must be saved' (Taylor, S. J., 2006: 21), where the word 'salvation' is of course another term for the victimage mechanism. The same paradox, of our salvation from sacrifice is explored by S. Mark Heim, in a book titled *Saved from Sacrifice: A Theology of the Cross* (Heim, 2006). We need to take seriously that scapegoating is indeed 'saving' violence, because it saves us from the consequences of unchecked mimetic contagion. Religion performs an essential service for the community. But this religion is of course based on a lie, namely the supposed guilt of the victim; in any case, the 'salvation' which is achieved here is precarious, always requiring further victims in order to sustain its effects.

This is in effect a fresh version of the Anselmian dilemma, in other words: how can we think beyond both punishment and satisfaction: beyond the total violence of outright condemnation, and the controlled violence of substitutionary or 'hydraulic' solutions. Escaping from this mechanism is impossible on our own because it conceals its own foundations: 'we need literally to be saved from the salvation offered by scapegoating' (Taylor, S. J., 2006: 23). It is the revelation of this mechanism, made available to us in the Christian gospel, which makes possible an escape from it. Once its workings are revealed, it becomes impotent. What Taylor is at pains to emphasize once again is that Satan does offer stability and order, although of a strictly limited kind. He is not simply a force for destruction, otherwise he would destroy his own kingdom; rather, he offers a minimum and tenuous kind of stability. Taylor names manifestations of 'satanic forms of salvation in their various guises': nuclear deterrence during the Cold War; ecclesiastical homophobia; the 'war on terror'; and the offer of 'salvation' held out to the poorest nations of the world, namely the structural adjustment programmes imposed by the World Bank and the IMF. 'In our world there are numerous offers of salvation', and Girard's work is an invaluable critical tool for assessing these bogus soteriological strategies (Taylor, S. J., 2006: 28).

As we have seen, James Alison has argued that a mimetically inspired account of salvation is constructed in a radically different way from other soteriologies. Contrary to appearances, mimetic theory renounces any kind of 'pact with the negative' which makes the sinfulness and need of the human beings the controlling factor in the narrative. The reality is the other way round: we only have a sense of the mess because Christ has been raised from the dead. It is the event of the Resurrection which allows us to look at human origins and tell a narrative about them, one which happens to involve original sin. Our story begins, in other words, not with Adam and Eve in the garden, but with God's revealing action in the Risen Christ. This simple insight about our starting-point, about the 'order of discovery', runs through Alison's reformulation of the doctrine of the atonement in *The Joy of Being Wrong* and *Faith beyond Resentment*.

The task in this chapter has been to erect a theoretical scaffolding or framework for soteriology. From here we will turn our attention to the content of soteriology, specifically the metaphors or images which have been used to describe God's action *pro nobis*: 'for our salvation'. Paul Fiddes (1989) and Colin Gunton (1988) are agreed on the importance of three or four essential or abiding metaphors: *victory* (over the devil, over the powers of hell, over death, etc.) in a battle or contest; *forensic justification*; *sacrifice*. It may be said that in Western Christianity at least these three are predominant (in the East there is greater emphasis on the notion of atonement as *participation*, in such doctrines as *theopoiesis* or 'divinization'). The victory motif is certainly one of the earliest proclamations of Christianity, as it is present in the Letter to the Colossians, Irenaeus, Ignatius of Antioch, and in the ancient motif of the Harrowing of Hell, and is a staple of many well-known Easter hymns.[5]

The second theme, justice in a law court, is similarly to be found in Paul's epistles, and obviously speaks to the experience of the early Christians during the era of persecutions. In general, however, both Old and New Testaments have little interest in the theme of law in the abstract: the development of sin as legal transgression is to be explained partly with reference to the legal background of a number of the early Latin Fathers, such as Tertullian and Cyprian. Further development of the legal imagery occurs with the satisfaction theory of Anselm, the Reformation doctrine of justification as articulated by Martin Luther and the neo-orthodox theology of Karl Barth. Finally, the notion of sanctification through sacrifice comes to be central in the Catholic understanding of the sacraments, and especially of the Eucharist as the continued representation of Christ's sacrificial self-giving on Calvary, as well as the channel of sanctifying grace.

Chapter 7

'Painting pictures on clouds': The metaphors of atonement

How do we assess the adequacy of any theology of salvation? David Ford in *Self and Salvation* proposes six questions or criteria which may be borne in mind here (Ford, 2006). Such a doctrine must go to the heart of Christian identity (i.e. it must be faithful to the specificity of the gospel setting and also have universal implications); secondly, it must be widely accessible, related to imaginative, emotional and pastoral concerns; thirdly, it needs to be capable of being focused through one or a few symbols, images or metaphors which have 'intensity and gripping power'; fourthly, it must have a conceptual richness, heuristically inspiring a diversity of investigations and discussions; fifthly, the theory needs to have practical promise of fruitfulness in the various dynamics of Christian living, such as worship, life in community, speech, action and suffering for justice; sixthly, it needs to be defensible against diverse attacks and be able to anticipate the criticisms of alternative theories.

Can René Girard's mimetic theory give an account of these key metaphors and their interrelation which will satisfy the six criteria advanced by Ford for a decent soteriology? What do Girard and Raymund Schwager have to tell us about Christ's conquest of the devil, about God's justice, and about sacrifice?

First model: Christ's victory over the devil

The image of Christ's victory over demonic powers has been given classic expression by Gustaf Aulen, in *Christus Victor: An Historical Study of the Three Main Types of the Idea of Atonement* (Aulen 1970 [1931]). According to Aulen, traditional accounts of the atonement stressed a change in God's attitude towards us ('objective', Anselmian) or human beings towards God ('subjective', Abelard), whereas in fact the more basic model is that of a divine conflict and victory, Christ's triumph over the demonic powers.

That this model is referred to by Aulen as 'dramatic' should interest us, of course; how we are to make sense of the language of Christ's victory

The Metaphors of Atonement

over the devil has been a concern for mimetic theory. Girard has written at length on the meaning of Satan as *skandalon*, the 'stumbling block', and we will consider this in combination with Raymund Schwager's analysis of this theme. A chapter in *The Scapegoat* titled 'Satan Divided against Himself' (Girard, 1986: 184–97) follows on a masterful exposition of the incident of the Gaderene swine and precedes the final chapter of the book, 'History and the Paraclete'. The contrast between Satan and the Holy Spirit is immensely significant for Girard; where Satan is the 'accuser' before God, the Paraclete is the witness for the defence who declares our innocence (this is taken up in the second metaphorical cluster, that of juridical imagery).

More fundamental however is Satan's role in the economy of mimetic desire. Chapter 3 of Girard's book *I Saw Satan Fall like Lightning* (2001a) (French original 1999), is devoted to making the link between the figure of the devil and the biblical notion of scandal. As well as accuser, denouncer, the 'Father of Lies', Satan is associated with the promotion and the prohibition of desires: he is both model and obstacle. Jesus' rebuke to Peter is read in this way: because Peter seeks to instil his desire into Jesus (i.e. for a worldly Messiahship which avoids the path of suffering), he is chillingly reprimanded: 'Get behind me Satan, for you are a scandal to me'. Another important saying of Jesus concerns the casting out of Satan by Satan (Mk 3.23–6), which makes sense according to Girard if we pay attention to Satan's ambiguous role as the preserver of social order and the instigator of disorder. 'The devil, or Satan, signifies rivalistic contagion, up to and including the single victim mechanism' and may therefore be located either in the entire process or in one of its stages (Girard, 2001a: 43).

> The mimetic concept of Satan enables the New Testament to give evil its due without granting it any reality or ontological substance in its own right that would make of Satan a kind of god of evil. Satan does not 'create' by his own means. Rather he sustains himself as a parasite on what God creates by imitating God in a manner that is jealous, grotesque, perverse, and as contrary as possible to the upright and obedient imitation of Jesus. To repeat, Satan is an imitator in the rivalistic sense of the word. His kingdom is a caricature of the kingdom of God. Satan is the ape of God. (2001a: 44–5)

A later chapter in the same book, titled 'The Triumph of the Cross', takes up the metaphor which we are considering, commenting on Col. 2.14–15: the triumphal procession in which the disarmed principalities and powers are paraded in full public view. Girard comments: 'These metaphors are not at all fantastic and badly improvised; they are so precise it takes your breath away . . . What Christianity conquers is the pagan way of organizing the world' (139). For Girard this paradoxical description applies not to the history of the events of the crucifixion, which were brutal and hopeless, but to the *representation* of those events. This is the difference between mythical concealment and Christian revelation. The gospels 're-present' the murder, but they originate not in violence but in the self-giving love of Jesus. The defeat of Satan, that is the 'duping' of mimetic desire into revealing itself, has interesting echoes for Girard of images from Origen and other Eastern fathers, of the Cross as the baiting hook, or a divine trap to catch Satan. More precisely, Satan turns his own mechanism into a trap, and falls into it headlong. Such images have always seemed ridiculous or magical, but from the point of view of mimetic theory they contain an important insight about the self-ensnarement of mimetic desire (149–53).

Raymund Schwager writes in the second of the essays collected in *Der wunderbare Tausch*, on 'Christ's Victory over the Devil', where he considers patristic reflections upon the descent into hell, the deception of the devil through concealment of Christ's divinity, and the idea of the divine payment of a just ransom to the devil through the death of Christ (Schwager, 1986: 32–53). He concurs with Girard that the ultimate form of satanic deception may be our classification of Satan as a separate being. We should look instead for 'his' instantiation as the collective conspiratorial force, hidden too deeply to be recognized by the individual, but operative as a surreptitious human effort to usurp God. It is this satanic undertaking which is exposed by the crucifixion and resurrection of Christ. In this way Schwager is able to rescue most of the patristic soteriological themes – only the highly questionable motif of a 'just ransom' needs to be rejected outright.

So for both René Girard and for Raymund Schwager there is every possibility of retrieving the metaphor of Christ's victory over the devil, even in some of its more apparently outlandish expressions. They are following through on what Gunton writes about the effectiveness of a metaphor depending on a shocking inversion of its everyday, 'literal' sense – to the extent that the new inverted usage redescribes the literal reality. In the light of the cross, 'true' victory is achieved through apparent failure:

> To describe the cross as a victory is to use the metaphor in a bold way. It is what Ricoeur calls a 'category mistake that clears the way to a new vision'. It means that the cross is really but metaphorically but really a victory, and a victory whose significance is to be expressed in several ways. First, it 'clears the way to a new vision'

because it is revelatory of the nature of human life on earth. To be
victorious does not mean butchering your opponent with weapons
but refusing to exercise power demonically in order to overcome
evil with good. (Gunton, 1988: 77)

In Girardian terms, because the demonic makes us slaves to the lie, Jesus'
victory is a witness to and a revelation of the truth. According to Colin
Gunton 'the metaphor of victory enables us to bring God to speech':

If the victory of Jesus is the victory of God, then the language in
which the story is told is one of the ways in which we are enabled
to speak of God. We learn, that is, that God is the kind of being
who makes his presence felt in our world in the way in which
the life and death of Jesus takes shape. The metaphor of victory is
therefore one of the means by which God is enabled to come to
human speech as a saving God. (Gunton, 1988: 80)

Second model: The justice of God

The figure of Satan provides the link with the second of the key metaphors, that of language or imagery taken from the world of law,[1] with
Satan's 'debut' in the book of Job, as God's 'left hand', the adversary or
counsel for the prosecution.

He had therefore a legal function, representing the rule of law,
order and punishment. His defeat, therefore – whatever the
significance of his fall to earth in Luke and Revelation – signifies
that the will of God is not to be identified with abstract legal
justice. God is revealed by the cross as one who bears the power
of the demonic rather than punishes those who have fallen into its
power. (Gunton, 1988: 84)

Even in the book of Job this appearance is ambiguous: after the Prologue
Satan plays no further part in Job's drama, which focuses instead on the
arguments between Job and his comforters, and upon Job's encounter with
God. Girard makes it clear that what is important in this drama is the
human dynamic – the scapegoating mechanism which is the true cause of
Job's sufferings. The community has united against him and seeks to convict him of his guilt; on this reading Girard feels justified in bracketing the
entire Prologue, in which we are told that Satan, with God's permission, is
the originator of all his misfortunes. This is all a red herring; the juridical

situation is in fact irrelevant to the rest of the book, which consists of the dialogues between Job and his 'comforters'.

Schwager further explores the theology of justice in essays on Anselm, Luther and Barth. Regarding Anselm's doctrine of satisfaction, the challenge is to square the circle of Christ's efficacious self-offering with human free-will. Regarding Barth's theme of 'the judge who is judged' Schwager offers correctives to what he sees as distortions in Barth's doctrine of a double predestination, and takes up von Balthasar's suggestion of a similarity between the early Barth and René Girard (von Balthasar, 1980: 309; Schwager, 1986: 232–72).

Once again, with this idea of the direction of judgement being reversed, we have an overturning of the 'normal' usage which reminds us of Paul Ricoeur's 'category mistake clearing the way to a new vision'. For Ricoeur, the truth of metaphorical reference is built on the ruins of the literal. Here we have an understanding of judgement which amounts to a refusal to judge in the usual sense of the word. This last point is very similar to what Raymund Schwager tries to convey in his notion of a 'dramatic theology'. In *Jesus and the Drama of Salvation* Schwager describes the phases of Jesus' life, ministry, death and resurrection as successive acts in a drama. The second of these acts is Jesus' preaching of divine vengeance as the expected response to Israel's refusal to repent. The parable of the Wicked Husbandmen (Mk 12.1–12; Mt. 21.33–46) asks, what will the owner of the vineyard do with these wicked tenants? In Mark, Jesus himself replies, in Matthew his listeners, but in each case, the expected *just* response of the owner to the murder of his servants and his son is violent retribution. However, the fourth act of Schwager's dramatic scheme brings not apocalyptic violence but the resurrection, a vindication of Jesus which is also an action of quite unexpected mercy to those who are 'judged'. This reference may serve as a reminder that the ability of metaphor to shock and jolt us into new understanding must be accounted for in terms of a dramatic or narrative framework.

We are reminded of course of Paul's extended discourses on the uselessness of the Law to bring salvation, and how the Christian dispensation rests as it were upon the ruins of the Law. As the death of Christ makes clear, the Law has not obviated the need for sacrifice. To mark the transition from the second metaphor, the juridical, to the third – sacrifice – I quote a highly suggestive passage from the novelist Roberto Calasso's *The Ruin of Kasch*, in a chapter titled 'Law and Order':

> It is significant that we say 'law and order' – that it is not enough to say only 'law' or only 'order.' In fact the word 'order' does not repeat, does not echo, the meaning of 'law.' Order is what law, on its own, cannot achieve. Order is law plus sacrifice, the perpetual

supplement, the perpetual extra that must be destroyed so that order may exist. The world cannot live by law alone, because it needs an order that law alone is unable to provide. The world needs to destroy something to make order; and it must destroy it outside the law, with pleasure, with hatred, with indifference. (Calasso, 1994: 148; original emphasis)

Here the issues are greatly more contentious than with our previous two metaphors, as we register the emotional pressure behind the recent history of misuse of the term sacrifice (as an exhortation to nationalistic militarism, for example) which has caused it to fall into (irreparable?) disrepute in the modern age. And yet Calasso's highly disturbing assertions point us in the direction of the necessity of sacrifice, as enabling 'an order that law alone is unable to provide'.

Third model: Sacrifice

René Girard has paid a great deal of attention to the problematic of sacrifice, and his discovery of the scapegoat mechanism has had enormous effect as a theory about the nature and origin of sacrifice. Here it may be helpful to follow the French theologian Louis-Marie Chauvet in discerning three broad theological camps on the question of sacrifice: first, theories which insist that what is valuable or authentic in Christianity is incompatible with sacrifice, and that the contrast between the Christian and non-Christian dispensation in this respect is so vast as to make any notion of a Christian understanding of 'sacrifice' illegitimate. This would describe the position of many liberation and feminist theologians, and accords with Girard's position at the time of writing *Des Choses Cachées*. These 'non-sacrificial' approaches contrast directly with a second perspective, typified by Margaret Barker and Bruce Chilton, who assert that Jesus' identity as High Priest is crucial to early Christian self-understanding, and not peripheral, as the anti-cult protesters would maintain (Barker, 2003; Chilton, 1992).

The third, and arguably mainstream position, is to allow for a Christian usage of sacrifice, but with severe qualification, namely with a recognition that the notion has undergone a process of radical 'spiritualization' or interiorization. Since theories of this third type often agree that Christianity brings about the 'end' of sacrifice, meaning both its fulfilment and termination, there can sometimes be little difference between an espousal of a transformed notion of sacrifice and the first, non-sacrificial position. Chauvet designates this third approach as 'anti-sacrificial'. The terminology is potentially confusing, but what it seeks to convey is the recognition that

Christian sacrifice can only be understood in tensile contrast with another category: 'sacrifice in the "history-of-religions" sense of the word' (Robert Daly). So the term intends to convey a process of development, with elements of continuity as well as rupture. It is this third position which best describes Girard's considered view on the subject of sacrifice.

Girard's acceptance, as a result of conversations with Raymund Schwager, of a more nuanced understanding of 'sacrifice' than that contained in his earlier work, is one of the crucial developments in his thinking, one that has not always been noted by his critics. We have seen in Chapter 5 that Girard remarks upon a timid reluctance to follow Schwager's bolder soteriological logic, fearing a regression if the language of sacrifice were to be accepted in a Christian context (Niewiadomski and Palaver, 1995: 24). His concerns are similar, then, to those of Robert Daly, who wanted to distance Christianity from 'sacrifice' in this archaic sense. Between Christ's sacrifice and that of archaic religion exists a huge difference: Christ's self-offering is a refusal to 'play the sacrificial game', with the intention of bringing the game to an end. Girard refers to an important text for him, the dispute before Solomon of the two women concerning the rightful ownership of the baby. Here is to be found Girard's discomfiture with 'sacrifice', since the word is unable to distinguish between the 'blood' sacrifice proposed by Solomon (and which the false, mimetically obsessed mother is only too ready to accept) and the genuine sacrifice, through love, on the part of the baby's true mother.

In an interview in *Religion and Literature* (Adams, 1993) Girard admits to 'scapegoating' the Letter to the Hebrews and the word 'sacrifice', assuming it should have a constant meaning; in fact, the changes in its meaning constitute the religious history of mankind. He declares here that there is no serious problem over the issue of sacrifice, though at the time of writing *Des Choses Cachées* he was unduly influenced by his reading of primitive religion and by the psychoanalytic phobia concerning the notion of self-sacrifice; here he stresses once again the Judgement of Solomon as the text which liberated him from this reverse moralism.[2] So Girard's original 'non-sacrificial' approach has been explicitly modified in his subsequent work. His position now is that the term can only be understood in its transformative history, a view which corresponds to the third position designated by Chauvet as 'anti-sacrifice', but which may more helpfully be thought of as an 'exodus from sacrifice' (Keenan).

The exodus from sacrifice

There would appear to be a strong scholarly consensus that the Christian usage of sacrifice comprises a long process of 'spiritualization', both in the

The Metaphors of Atonement

Jewish scriptures and in the surrounding Hellenistic culture. Under pressure of the conditions of exile, and also of the prophetic critique of cult, 'sacrifice' evolved from the notion of a material immolation (destruction) ritual, towards a more spiritual prayer form, for which no immolation was necessary. Robert Daly distinguishes between 'normative' and 'descriptive' meanings of Christianity and sacrifice; he argues that 'sacrifice' has undergone a process of what he calls 'spiritualization'. This denotes an interiorization of the movement of 'offering' demanded in earlier ritual sacrificial acts: Christian sacrifice was not a cultic but rather an ethical idea, one which found its focus in the everyday practical life of Christian virtue. Synonyms would include: dematerializing, sublimating, humanizing, deepening, ethicizing, rationalizing, interiorizing, symbolizing, 'all those movements within Judaism and Christianity which attempted to emphasize the true meaning of sacrifice' (1978: 7).

A philosopher, Dennis King Keenan, concurs. 'The progressive interiorization and spiritualization of sacrifice did not, however, represent a repudiation of sacrifice, rather the necessity of the proper interior disposition accompanying the outward act' (Keenan, 2003: 189). While the contemporary crisis of sacrifice is acknowledged (systematic distortions of the concept due to economics, sexism and Christocentric evolutionism), Keenan argues against the conclusion that we should simply abandon the concept. Such an abandonment would be

> a sacrifice of sacrifice, which, if performed naively (i.e., without dwelling with the question of sacrifice), would unwittingly preserve some form of sacrifice. One would be duped into believing that one could be done with sacrifice, which could then return (relatively unchanged) in far more subtle and pernicious forms . . . one is called to remain attentive to the irreducible ambiguity of the sacrifice of sacrifice. (Keenan, 2005: 14)

Louis-Marie Chauvet agrees with Daly and Keenan. He declares that the interpretation of Jesus' life and death as a sacrifice is neither the earliest, nor the most important, in the New Testament. The Letter to the Hebrews represents a transmutation or subversion of the Old Testament cult. Jesus' priestly mediation is a feature of his whole life, and not just his death: his priesthood and sacrifice were exercised 'existentially and not ritually' (Chauvet, 1995: 299). Jesus' self-renunciation is an acquiescence to 'de-mastery', a sacrificial 'letting-be' which Chauvet prefers to call an 'anti-sacrifice'. He asserts that the language of sacrifice, whatever authority it may acquire in the New Testament, is not necessary to describe the meaning of Jesus' life and death, and remains only one symbolism among others. It should certainly have its place, but not a privileged status.

Chauvet has serious reservations about Girard's account of sacrifice as a scapegoating mechanism, and of Jesus' unmasking and denunciation of this mechanism (303–6), but he builds on Girard's insights so far as to propose a third term, 'anti-sacrifice', between the Girardian dichotomy of sacrifice and non-sacrifice (as we have seen above, this 'anti-sacrificial' position in fact coincides with Girard's considered view on the matter). Such a position insists upon the never-ending task of conversion: '[T]he anti-sacrificial regimen to which the gospel calls us *rests upon* the sacrificial, but it does so to turn it around and thereby to redirect ritual practice'; it is in ethical practice where the ritual practice is verified (307). For Chauvet, the evidence points to 'an undeniable anti-sacrificial and anti-priestly subversion . . . From now on . . . the sacred work the cult, the sacrifice that is pleasing to God, is the confession of faith lived in the agape of sharing in service to the poorest, of reconciliation and of mercy' (Chauvet, 1995: 260).

What he asserts as the 'basic principle' is drawn from Augustine: 'Christ, who was offered (sacrificed) once for all, is offered "everyday in sacrament" (*quotidie in sacramento*)' – a formula distinct from 'everyday in *the* sacrament' (St. Augustine, *The City of God*, Book X: 6; my emphasis). Augustine understands Christ's passion as a perfect sacrifice, a complete surrender to God: this is rooted in an ecclesial sense of our unity with Christ, whereby the gifts of bread and wine, which represent the sufferings of the faithful, are joined to the Christ-victim. At the altar we are exhorted to 'be what you see, and receive what you are'.

Girard's startling assertion in 1972 that 'violence is the heart and secret soul of the sacred' rendered problematic the notion of 'sacrifice' in a Christian context, and caused a widespread re-examination of this doctrine. Now it appears his settled opinion is much closer to a general scholarly consensus, which has been characterized as an 'exodus from sacrifice'. The validity of this Christian understanding lies precisely in recognizing the journey that has taken place, and in resisting what Keenan describes as a 'sacrifice of sacrifice, which . . . could then return (relatively unchanged) in far more subtle and pernicious forms'. A conversion, therefore, but not one which turns its back in denial of the sacrificial past. This consensus which acknowledges the 'irreducible ambiguity of the sacrifice of sacrifice' is surely one which René Girard himself has helped to create. It is in this light that we need to register the most recent published words of Girard on the subject of sacrifice, given in an interview in 2007. Having once again repented his too stark treatment of 'sacrifice' in *Things Hidden* Girard states:

> One has to make a distinction between the sacrifice of others and self-sacrifice. Christ says to the Father: 'you wanted neither holocaust nor sacrifice; then I said: "Here I am."' I prefer to sacrifice myself rather than sacrifice the other. But this still has to be called sacrifice. When we say 'sacrifice' in our modern languages it has only the Christian sense. Therefore the passion is entirely justified. God says: If nobody else is good enough to sacrifice himself rather than his brother, I will do it. Therefore I fulfil God's requirement for man. I prefer to die than to kill. But all other men prefer to kill than to die. (Girard, 2007b: 30)

The phrase 'God's requirement for man' certainly sends a chill down the spine for those who are still thinking of punitive substitution and other forms of retribution, but if this requirement is simply that in the midst of our conviviality each of us should be readier to die than to kill the other, then the argument makes perfect sense. As a matter of historical fact, most men have fallen short of this ideal, and it is here that we find the 'necessity' of Christ's incarnation, death and resurrection, as the only way of turning this around. Once again the judgement of Solomon is cited, and the distinction which Girard makes between two ways of 'channelling' homicidal violence – by enduring it, by venting it on another – is used to begin to make sense of the different notions of 'martyrdom' which we find in Christianity and Islam.

Conclusion

It remains to be asked whether this extraordinary cluster of insights satisfies the criteria which David Ford set out at the beginning of *Self and Salvation*, and which we listed above. I would wish to claim, not surprisingly, that the theory fares well. It attempts to go to the heart of Christian identity, in being both scripturally based and universally applicable; it is widely accessible, centred as it is on a few key metaphors which have 'gripping power'; it yields conceptual richness and heuristic fruitfulness, and can be integrated into the multiple dynamics of Christian living, such as worship, community and prophetic witness. David Ford's final criterion is that a theory of salvation should be able to anticipate and withstand criticisms from alternative theories, and we shall be looking at critics of mimetic theory in a later chapter.

As Anselm argued, it is not enough to just paint beautiful pictures; they need to be painted onto a solid surface if they are to endure. So an articulation both of the metaphors themselves and of their underlying logic and interconnection is required. We have examined three models which have demonstrated a fair amount of resilience over two millennia, at least in Western Christianity: special attention continues to be given to the metaphorical clusters of victory over the devil, justice and sacrifice. In each case the power and effectiveness of the metaphor (as with all metaphors) depends on a reversal or overturning of the literal sense. A fundamental redescription occurs, as a result of which 'victory' as used of the triumph of Christ means the exact opposite of what we normally understand by victory, namely forceful domination; just as the concepts of 'judgement' and 'sacrifice' come to denote very different realities from their ordinary usage.

A mimetic analysis would acknowledge the importance of these three metaphors and arrange them in a very compelling narrative (perhaps a drama, to be more accurate). The fascinating (fascist) power of mimetic desire and its cycles of resentment and violence are what we need to be 'saved from': our helplessness has been intuited, at various times in scripture and in tradition, through images of demonic enslavement, of our vulnerability before the law, and of the uselessness of our religious observances. Christ's death and resurrection have transformed and redescribed the world upon the ruins of these inadequate understandings – or rather, they too benefit from a 'resurrection'.[3]

The 'catch' is that we need always to be on our guard, because the possibility of regression to the earlier 'ruined' state is always possible. We are always liable to entangle ourselves once more in the false transcendence, the 'nonentity' of satanic mimeticism and its resentful will to power; just as we are quite capable of bypassing God's astounding 'judgement' – which is a proclamation of infinite, gratuitous mercy – for the more familiar securities of a judgemental or legalistic religion. Finally, as we have explored at slightly greater length, there is a constant temptation to forget that the Christian ideal of sacrifice (meaning a freely willed imitation of Christ's self-offering) is in fact an 'anti-sacrifice', an 'exodus' from the hellish practice of pious victimization.

Chapter 8
Girard and the Bible

From myth to gospel

With the publication of *Des Choses Cachées* in 1978, and especially its middle Book II titled 'The Judaeo-Christian Scriptures' (141–276), Girard ventures explicitly into the territory of biblical theology for the first time. It is not surprising, therefore, that the mimetic hypothesis comes to be subjected to a fair degree of scrutiny by biblical scholars in the years immediately following. A number of studies in the mid-1980s may be cited: Robert North's lecture to the Catholic Biblical Association in 1985 begins with a recognition of Girard's currency in non-English academic circles, while a special number of a journal of biblical studies, *Semeia*, was given over to 'René Girard and Biblical Studies' in the same year (McKenna, 1985); Mark Wallace writes on 'Postmodern Biblicism: The Challenge of René Girard for Contemporary Theology' (Wallace, 1989), while James Williams' study of violence in the Bible is heavily indebted to Girardian insights (Williams, J., 1991). Other applications include the work of Robert Hamerton-Kelly, using mimetic theory as a hermeneutic for reading the Gospel of Mark (1994). Sandor Goodhart (1996) has contributed a Jewish perspective, not least in the Jewish-Christian discussions with Raymund Schwager, while Gil Bailie's work (1995) attempts a cultural reading of contemporary America in the light of the mimetic theory's biblical insights. In Europe, Norbert Lohfink SJ has shown interest in the theory and collaborated with Raymund Schwager in refining it (Schwager, 1978).

Girard's argument for the unique revelatory significance of the gospels – the keystone of his argument – has been challenged by Burton Mack among others. We will examine these critiques, after first setting out the argument of this central section of *Des Choses Cachées* and then outlining a biblical theological framework which will help us to understand what Girard is doing and to assess his work more accurately.

As we have seen, Girard declares that '[w]e simply cannot confine our hypothesis to the area of hominization and primitive religion' (1978: 141) – even at the risk of being accused of scholarly ambitions worthy of 'Renaissance Man'. He then offers a comparative discussion of patterns of rivalry and exclusionary violence, in world mythology and in the scriptural narratives: the similarities between them are acknowledged, but as a prelude to exploring the 'absolute distinctiveness' of the Bible's treatment of myth. The divide is evident in the respective attitudes towards two fratricidal killings: the murder of Remus by Romulus, and Abel's death at the hands of Cain. In the first case the innocence of the victim is secondary to its 'good consequence' – the founding of the city of Rome – while in the second case the seriousness of the crime takes precedence over what follows (Cain is likewise the founder of the first town). The biblical text refuses to allow the ethical dimension – 'where is your brother Abel?' – to be overshadowed. A comparison of the story of Oedipus with that of Joseph (Gen. 37) shows the same difference. Both are persecuted figures, but Oedipus is overwhelmed by the accusations of parricide and incest made against him; Joseph, on the other hand, overcomes the collective violence and false accusations and becomes, eventually, a focus of genuine social reconciliation. In each of the two biblical stories, says Girard, '[t]he authors of Genesis have recast a pre-existent mythology, adapting it in the spirit of their special concerns. This involves inverting the relationship between the victim and the persecuting community' (151).

The mythic forms have been subverted in *Genesis* and *Exodus*, but still retain many of the characteristics of myth, and by themselves would not convey a sense of radical singularity. The same subversive tendency can be found, however, if we look at the relationship between the legal codes of the Old Testament and the prophetic books which follow them; there is a move from obsessive complexity of laws concerning hygiene and purity (all comprehensible from an anthropological perspective), to the simplicity of prophetic formulae. The exhortations and threats of the great prophets are evidently responses to real social and political crises, rather than adaptations of mythical and legendary sources. Whereas in the first books of the Bible the sacrificial mechanism is glimpsed but never completely described, the prophetic writings offer astonishing explicit and connected portrayals, specifically, the four 'Songs of the Servant of Yahweh' which we find in Deutero-Isaiah (156). The overall effect is something like a refinement of focus, an optician adjusting the lens as he examines a patient:

> Throughout the Old Testament, a work of exegesis is in progress, operating in precisely the opposite direction to the usual dynamics of mythology and culture. And yet it is impossible to say that this work is completed. Even in the most advanced texts, such as the fourth 'Song of the Servant', there is still some ambiguity regarding the role of Yahweh. Even if the human community is, on several occasions, presented as being responsible for the death of the

Girard and the Bible

victim, God himself is presented as the principal instigator of the persecution. 'Yet it was the will of the Lord to bruise him'. (Girard, 1987a: 157)

This ambiguity of God's role corresponds to how God is presented in the rest of the Old Testament: while gradually divested of the violence of primitive deities (as this violence is seen to be the product of mimetic social interaction, and therefore 'man-made'), yet the Old Testament never arrives at a conception of the deity that is entirely free of violence: 'Only the texts of the Gospels manage to achieve what the Old Testament leaves incomplete'; as Christianity has traditionally maintained, the New Testament completes an enterprise which had not been taken far enough by the Jewish scriptures.

What is it about the Gospels which refine the lens further? Girard begins with the 'curses against the scribes and Pharisees' which we find in the Gospels of Luke and Matthew; Jesus' ferocious attack on Israel's religious leaders is really an assault on a religious system which preserves its authority and integrity at the expense of sacrificial victims. Insofar as they perpetuate this system, the scribes and Pharisees are responsible for 'all the righteous blood shed on earth, from the blood of innocent Abel to the blood of Zechariah the son of Barachiah, whom you murdered between the sanctuary and the altar' (Mt. 23, 35). These are the 'first' and 'last' victims recorded in scripture, the A to Z of a very long list.

Girard connects this with the motif of the *tomb*, which we find in these same curses: 'For you build the tombs of the prophets whom your fathers killed . . . they killed them, and you build their tombs' (Lk. 11.47–8). Similarly, the scribes and Pharisees are 'whitewashed tombs', immaculate on the outside, but full of death and corruption within. Luke takes this one stage further: the Pharisees are underground, therefore invisible tombs, over which people walk without even being aware of the victims under their feet – a double concealment, therefore (Lk. 11.44; Girard, 1987a: 165)

The message, for Girard, is clear: the religious system of Jesus' day served as a retardation or concealment of the gradual process of discovery and enlightenment which was working its way through the Old Testament traditions. The killing of the prophets who were the vehicles of that revelation, and the 'cover-up' of those killings by means of construction of beautiful memorials or by hiding the tombs altogether, all signify a regression to the earlier way of thinking, the mythical sacralization of a founding murder. From here Girard's logic is straightforward, as yet another prophetic challenger, Jesus shares the fate of his predecessors, and is put to death by the unanimous group of persecutors – religious and political leaders as well as the crowd. The death of Stephen in the *Acts of the Apostles* follows the same pattern, of prophetic provocation followed by an angry scapegoating.

And yet the death of Jesus, followed as it is by the Resurrection, clearly breaks the pattern of previous lynchings. In short, the gospel text tells us that the story of Jesus' death is resistant to sacralization – at a minimum level, because there is no corpse around which the community can reorganize! The body of Jesus is simply not there to be decorously interred, while the reports of the Resurrection appearances make it clear that he cannot be simply forgotten. The action of the Father in raising Jesus from death is similarly a refusal to 'accept' or be placated by this death; it declares God's absolute non-complicity with the violence carried out by religious people in God's name. From this astonishing reversal, summed up in the quotation that 'the very stone which the builders rejected has become the head of the corner' (Lk. 20.17), Girard looks again at the teachings of Jesus, for example, the Sermon on the Mount. Jesus' entire mission and proclamation, we now see, are directed against the mimetic desires and processes which, when religiously blessed, are nothing less than the stark road to Golgotha.

To summarize thus far: Girard distinguishes between three phases of scriptural interpretation: first, the creative reworking of myths and legendary material which we find in the books of Genesis and Exodus, and which coexists with more primitive mythical elements; secondly, the prescriptions and admonitions of the prophets, which respond to contemporary crises seen in ethical and cultural-religious terms rather than mythical ones, though they are not ambiguously free of mythical traces; thirdly, the Gospel and the other New Testament records of the teaching, life death and Resurrection of Christ confirm the 'de-sacralizing' tendency of the Old Testament writings. 'The stone which the builders rejected' means that the fate of the scapegoated victim has become the great hermeneutical principle, enabling us to decode all such instances of persecution.

The logos of the victim

We will examine in later chapters the implications of this decoding, which Girard himself begins to draw out in *Des Choses Cachées*: the possibility of a non-sacrificial reading of Christianity (1987a: 180–223), and what such a reading implies for historical Christianity (224–62). For now, it is the final chapter of Book II of *Des Choses Cachées*, 'The Logos of Heraclitus and the Logos of John' (263–80), which concerns us. Girard is attempting to make explicit the hermeneutic with which he is working; to give it a 'logos', in other words. Following Heidegger, Girard discusses the term *logos*, as used by the pre-Socratic philosopher Heraclitus and by the author of the Prologue to the Fourth Gospel. In each case we are talking about 'the divine, rational and logical principle according to which the world is organized' (263), but in the Greek usage, as Heidegger recognized, there is present the idea of the attempted violent reconciliation of opposites: 'The Heraclitean Logos, in Heidegger's terms, is the Logos of all cultures to the extent that they are, and will always remain, founded on unanimous violence' (267) – meaning, of course, scapegoats.

The Johannine *logos* is similarly defined in terms of expulsionary violence, but here the *logos* is the victim: it shines in the darkness, but the darkness does not comprehend it; it comes into the world, but the world does not receive him, nor do his own people receive him (Jn 1.1–11):

> In the two thousand years since they were written, these words have attracted innumerable commentaries. Read them, and you will see that the essential point always escapes the commentators: the role of expulsion in the definition of the Johannine Logos. (271)

Girard maintains that this sustained misrecognition is not a puzzling accident, but an indication of something common to all cultures, namely, our blindness towards the singularity of the victim. It denotes therefore our refusal to admit that any other form of *logos* is by definition complicit with exclusionary violence, whether expressed in the guise of religion, or fragmented into the discourses of philosophy, psychology, aesthetics and so on. The connections between *logos* as 'the divine, rational and logical principle according to which the world is organized' and violent expulsion is further confirmed for Girard by considering the opening sentence of the Prologue: 'In the Beginning was the Word . . .', and its echo of Genesis, 'In the Beginning God created the heavens and the earth'. What we have is nothing less than 'the whole Bible being *recommenced* from the point of view of the Logos as victim', an enactment of the kind of deciphering which we are empowered to undertake with the Passion of Jesus as a hermeneutical key. Both the opening chapters of Genesis and John's Prologue establish the relationship between God and humanity in terms of expulsion: 'The only difference is that *in the story of Adam and Eve, God manipulates and expels mankind* to secure the foundations of culture, whilst *in the Prologue to John it is mankind who expels God*' (275; original emphasis).

With this simple reversal of direction, says Girard, the relation of the gospel to the Old Testament and the basis of his anthropology are both made clear. The opening sentence of the Prologue is the repetition and translation of another sentence, 'with one crucial difference – the replacement of the God that inflicts violence with the God that only suffers violence'.

Genesis bears witness to an ambivalence, an 'internal travail on the subject of victimization'; the Johannine text does not.

An exegetical response

I have referred to Robert North's address, 'Violence and the Bible: The Girard Connection', which coincidentally appeared in the same volume of the *Catholic Biblical Quarterly* as Brueggemann's review of Childs and Gottwald, which we consider below. North begins with a sympathetic summary of Girard's thesis, and then a critique. As an exegete he is concerned by the 'casualness and generalisation with which OT allusions are pressed into service', as well as the scant treatment given to some important passages. North in short sees the Old Testament evidence cited by Girard to be on the thin side: 'His use of the passages, rather than a true exegetical analysis (which it would be unfair to expect of him), is a sort of "gut-hunch" combining common-sense with anthropological exotica' (North, 1985: 14).

On the other hand, North recognizes the complementarity between Girard and Raymund Schwager, and is able to commend Schwager's 'excellent' book (*Must There be Scapegoats?*): 'By contrast with Girard, Schwager has done his own exegetical homework', in scrutinizing the six hundred examples of violence which are condemned, but also no fewer than one thousand cases of Yahweh's own violence which need to be deconstructed. North does suggest that there is a divergence, however, as 'Schwager finds underpinning for Girard along totally different and more imposing exegetical lines' (16). Regarding the New Testament passages invoked by Girard, once again North finds a thinness of exegesis, a 'sort of common-sense outlook made subtle by anthropology' (17). As North observes, the lines of critical resistance to Girard are understandable when we note that he accuses all exegetes before himself of misreading the biblical evidence. There is also opposition to Girard's dismissal of the conceptuality of sacrifice and especially the book of Hebrews – a judgement which Girard was later to reverse, as we have seen.

North's is a level-headed analysis, sympathetic but by no means uncritical. He specifies seven 'points of unfinished business', among which he notes that the transition from private hostilities to unanimous scapegoating is too casual; similarly the equation of 'sacrifice' with simple violence, and an exaggerated claim for the universality of mimetic desire. He is concerned about the way Girard has set up the debate as 'all or nothing', since to question any part of his theory is merely to confirm one's own mimetic blindness (the problem one has arguing with Freudians also!).

But North also stresses eight positive features of Girard's work which he hopes will enrich exegesis, suggesting his general intuitive agreement with Girard's argument, rather than a satisfaction that it has been sufficiently demonstrated.

Figura and ambivalence

Such, therefore, is the considered judgement of one prominent biblical exegete, who interestingly suggests that Raymund Schwager's exegetical approach is more reliable than Girard's. I wish to complement this with an exposition of two other approaches to the reading of Old Testament texts. While recognizing Girard's vulnerability in the presence of biblical exegetes, it is important to stress that he follows in a hallowed tradition of interpretation which predates the concerns of modern biblical criticism:

> Throughout the Middle Ages, traditional interpretation, taking its cue from particular passages in the Gospels and the Epistles of Paul, tried to read the Old Testament in the light of the New. The results became less and less interesting, and this type of interpretation was finally abandoned as being irrational and mystical. Medieval exegesis was not capable of gauging how right it was to see the great figures of the Old Testament as prefiguring and announcing Christ. Because the intuition could not be justified, subsequently it was rejected as groundless by modern rationalist research, whereas in reality – in spite of its limitations – it goes far beyond all that contemporary criticism has ever told us. (Girard, 1987a: 274)

The exceptions, among modern authors, are Paul Claudel, Henri de Lubac and the 'outstanding essay' by Erich Auerbach.[1] The figural approach is more explicitly set out by Girard in *Evolution and Conversion,* where he links Auerbach's figural interpretation to his own discovery of 'novelistic truth' as contained in *Deceit, Desire and the Novel* (Girard, 2007a: 181). The use of *figura* here means 'a technique of reading that related two historically distant facts in a unique form' (180), reading backwards and forwards, as it were, which sees the facts related as prefigurement and fulfilment. He praises Auerbach's insight, especially his reading of Peter's denial, even though this does not go beyond the level of literary analysis, whereas for Girard mimesis is about content as well as description:

> It is impossible to represent the mimeticism of our relationships without writing what critics would call a 'realistic text'. Because

that is just the way human relations are! That is also why I am interested in 'Figura'. I never wrote about it, but I remember reading and rereading it because of its relevance to the Christian notion of prophecy. Auerbach sees something essential about the mimetic structure of these relational configurations. It is this mechanism that provides a sense of totality within which myths can be reread in the light of Christianity (Girard, 2007a: 181–2).

We find a very early example in the Acts of the Apostles, where we hear of an Ethiopian eunuch, on pilgrimage in Jerusalem, who is trying to make sense of the Suffering Servant passage from Isa. 52.13–53.12:

> Look, my servant will prosper, will grow great, will rise to great heights.
> As many people were aghast at him – he was so inhumanly disfigured
> That he no longer looked like a man – so many nations will be astonished,
> and kings will stay tight-lipped before him, seeing what had never been told them,
> learning what they had not heard before.

Far from being punished by God, the Servant is in fact bearing the sins of the people, 'and we have been healed by his bruises'. Clearly baffled, the eunuch asks Philip to explain the passage to him: 'does the writer speak of himself or of someone else?' The tone is one of bewildered astonishment, as the bystanders recognize in this despised, disfigured man 'a revelation of Yahweh's arm'. Since the isolation by Duhm of four 'Servant Songs' in chapters 42–53 of Isaiah, the literature as to the identity of the Servant has burgeoned. Interpretation within Judaism has oscillated between a collective and an individual assignation, although the Christian tradition, starting with Philip, identifies the figure with Christ.[2] Here we have a distinctive complex of theological ideas: the highest expression in the Old Testament of the transfer of many violent actions onto one innocent individual, and the most sublime articulations of monotheism and critique of idolatry.

And yet this important transitional text (from the point of view of mimetic theory) had a paradoxically lowly status; the statements in the fourth Song about universal and vicarious suffering were, in the words of Koch, left for centuries 'lying there misunderstood, like an eccentric addition'; not a single biblical author refers to them explicitly. As with the other writings in the Old Testament concerning violence and the sacred, the Songs await the reinterpretation which comes about in the light of the fate of Jesus.[3]

Girard and the Bible

So much for figural interpretation. A second approach is opened up by Walter Brueggemann, whose template for organizing Old Testament theology has considerable implications for Girard's approach.[4] Brueggemann highlights two programmatic books, from B. S. Childs and N. K. Gottwald, which go in nearly opposite directions but which need to be read together:[5]

> Childs seeks to elaborate a notion of the OT as a normative canon which moves beyond critical dissection and historical developments. The completed form of the text offers a base line for normative theology. The implication of Childs's work, it seems to me, is to put the faith claims of Scripture beyond the interplay of historical and literary analysis.
>
> Conversely, Gottwald rigorously moves in the other direction. He sees the text not only as a result of societal conflict, but as a *literary legitimation* of a social movement. In his view, the canonical literature is primarily a settled ideology of a certain partisan experience of reality. In its finished form it claims to be normative, but the really important fact is that it has reached that form through partisan social interaction. Thus, the canon as canon is the outcome of social conflict, insisting on a certain settlement of the conflict. (Brueggemann, 1985a: 29–30; original emphasis)

We need to take both these authors seriously, says Brueggemann, even if holding them together is difficult, though it becomes apparent that it is Gottwald's socio-literary reconstruction of Israel's revolutionary origins which has caught Brueggemann's imagination. Gottwald's materialist reading of the Old Testament stresses that the texts are shaped by and 'in the fray', while with Childs the text as we have it is 'above the fray' of historical interaction and historico-critical analysis. 'Whereas Gottwald is sociologically relentless, Childs is theologically reassuring. . . . The Bible is both fully engaged in the struggle for faithfulness, yet also out of reach of that struggle' (30). To ignore either perspective would be an impoverishment.

On the basis of these two contrasting but supplementary approaches, Brueggemann advances a proposal for Old Testament, and by implication biblical, theology: his version of a bipolar construct is that Old Testament faith serves both to *legitimate structure* and to *embrace pain*. Insofar as it partakes of the 'common theology' (the structure of belief found across the Near East) Old Testament theology is structure-legitimating; but as part of the struggle to be free from this theology, it is open to the embrace of pain experienced 'from underneath'. By entering the fray of Israel's experiences, Israel's theologians experience ambiguity concerning structure and the pain caused by structure (this is Gottwald's argument in *The Tribes of Yahweh*); at the same time they seek a normative standpoint, different from that of the 'common theology', but above the fray of contestation (Childs' position).

> A careful understanding of the literature shows that we are not free to resolve the tension. The OT both partakes of the 'common theology' and struggles to be free from it. The OT both enters the fray of ambiguity and seeks distance from the fray to find something certain and sure. (31)

It should also be noted that, in putting forward a theological proposal, Brueggemann is less concerned with the process and character of the texts, but rather 'with *the process and character of the God* met in the text' (30; original emphasis). On this account,

> [T]he God of Israel is presented variously as the God above the fray who appears like other Near Eastern gods and as a God exposed in the fray, who appears unlike the gods of 'common theology', a God peculiarly available in Israel's historical experiences. (31)

Steeped as it is in a providential sense of a life and cosmos ordered around the sovereignty of a creator God, the 'common theology' tends to serve the ruling class. The Old Testament shares many of its elements, but recognizes also a crisis in common theology because it does not square with Israel's experience of life and her discernment of God. 'Israel's strange linkage with Yahweh' involves two moves, an intensification of Yahweh's anger and impatience, while at the same time there is in the heart of God

> an enormous patience, a holding to promises, even in the face of disobedience, resistance to the theological categories which conventionally give God self-definition. . . . The God of Israel wills to be other than 'the enforcer.' And so there emerges an unbearable incongruity. The incongruity concerns a God committed to a structure of sanctions, and yet with a yearning for a relationship with this disobedient partner. (1985b: 397)

The dilemma which faces this God, and which is usually recast as the problem of 'theodicy', is 'how much he is committed to the "common theology," how much he must implement its claims, and how much he can resist' (398). It is in the book of Job where the two aspects – the question of structure legitimation and the embrace of pain – are brought into dramatic tension. By 'embrace of pain' Brueggemann understands a posture of both

Girard and the Bible

Yahweh and Israel, 'the full acknowledgement of and experience of pain, and the capacity and willingness to make that pain a substantive part of Israel's faith-conversation with God'. Brueggemann goes on to explore the theological aspects of this embrace, recognizing that a sociological analysis, such as Gottwald's, will not be enough. So the category of the 'restlessness of lament' is found in Israel's counter-tradition, which includes Moses, the Psalms, Jeremiah and Job. But Yahweh shows hints of the same restlessness and unease: the troubled heart of God in the episodes of the flood (Genesis 6) and of Sodom and Gomorrah (Genesis 18), take us 'into the interiority of God, where things are troubled and far from clear'. Where one would expect straightforward stories about floodwater, fire and brimstone, we have, for example, the astonishing negotiation over the minimum number of righteous people to save the city: 'Abraham and Yahweh had gone as far as they could with this bold and dangerous characterisation of God and a new practice of righteousness' (410).

These are stories of God's genuine probing of an unknown future, and just as Israel had to decide whether or not to be 'like the nations' or to be a 'holy people', so its God, Yahweh, is portrayed as having to decide between being 'like the other gods' or being a holy God, 'the Holy One in our midst', learning new dimensions of mercy and righteousness from his conversations with Abraham (415). The question of God and the character of Israel are intimately linked:

> Israel as a social experiment could have little positive prospect unless it sojourned with a God who noted, responded to, and embodied the pain that Israel was also to embody. Yahweh's probe of godness away from the gods of the Egyptian empire is at least as important as Israel's probe of a sociology alternative to that of the empire. (415)

I have dwelt at length upon two approaches to reading scripture which are directly related to a Girardian mimetic analysis, and which arise out of traditions of biblical scholarship. The aim here is to show how René Girard's arguments for the specificity of the gospel revelation are not idiosyncratic, nor are they the unanchored speculations of a maverick thinker who is not, after all, a biblical scholar. Girard links himself tentatively, then firmly, with the practice of figural interpretation, which allows him to read back and forth between New and Old Testament passages, and between biblical and non-biblical texts, plotting patterns of prefiguring and fulfilment. The freedom to do this is vital to Girard's mimetic theory, and while it is a literary theorist, Erich Auerbach, who first alerts him to figural reading, the method itself is nothing new, and continues to inspire biblical theologians.[6] Whether or not one agrees with such an approach, it should at least be clear that some of the hard questions which biblical scholarship might want to put to Girard, concerning critical-historical issues, for example, are simply not appropriate.

Walter Breuggemann's outline of the shape of Old Testament Theology, at least as it stood in 1985, confirms the need to hold together the same tensions which appear in Girard's work. Brueggemann's use of Gottwald and Childs to articulate a framework both 'above the fray' and 'in the fray' is surely an exact description of the ambiguities and tensions in what Girard calls 'texts in travail', or 'mixed texts': or texts like the book of Genesis, which contain an 'internal travail on the subject of victimization'. Indeed, the Fourth Servant Song, which asserts that 'it pleased the Lord to crush him', can also be said to be such a mixed text, containing traces still of a persecutionary violence which has been projected onto God.

For Girard, these texts are a site of contestation: between the mythical perspective of sacralized persecution and the minority voice of the innocent victim. It is the same for Walter Brueggemann, though he articulates this as a struggle between 'structure legitimation' and the 'embrace of pain'. Most astonishing in Brueggemann's account, perhaps, is his picture of a God 'deciding' to what extent he should identify with the 'common theology', and when to pull away from it. Mimetic theory may not want to go this far; even so, we can say that the mutual adventure set out by Brueggemann (following Norman Gottwald), of Yahweh's 'probe of godness' and Israel's 'probe of an [alternative] sociology', contains plenty of parallels with the biblical drama described by Girard.

Chapter 9
Political theology

The violent return of religion

René Girard's mimetic theory holds out promise of helping to fill the vacuum vacated by crude and now discredited theories of secularization. Prophecies that religion would wither on the vine of increased global economic prosperity and development have not been fulfilled, and new paradigms of explanation are required, if the 'return of religion' in its many forms is to be comprehended.

In this respect mimetic theory is in competition with many other attempts at diagnosis of our post-9/11, 'post-secular' condition. Some of these are happy to incur the label of 'political theology', as a protest against closure and exclusion in political discourse – yet have only the most tenuous connection with traditional religious or faith traditions. Two recent collections of essays illustrate this trend.[1] Within the pages of these challenging volumes, contributors as diverse as Jürgen Habermas, Pope Benedict XVI, Judith Butler and Slavoj Zizek rub shoulders, recognizing with Hent de Vries that 'religions contain both an integrative and a potentially disintegrating or even violent aspect of modern societies', an ambivalence which leaves us in need of new concepts and new research practices: 'No unified theory is currently available to hold these trends together in a compelling explanatory account or historical narrative' (de Vries and Sullivan, 2006: 8). Rowan Williams suggests that there is a common conviction beneath this extraordinary variety, namely a rejection of the 'barbarism' of meaningful action understood as pure assertion, conjuring 'the spectre of the purest fascism'.

A further attempt at defining political theology is proffered by Scott and Cavanaugh (2004), in terms of an affinity between the two terms: 'both are constituted in the production of metaphysical images around which communities are organised'. What might these 'metaphysical images' be? For Girardian mimetic theory, of course, there can only be one answer. Attentiveness to the *paradox of violence* in social formation, insisted on by mimetic theory, will discern the traces of ambiguity in many classical accounts of political origins. Marcel Detienne's discussion of the foundation of early Greek cities shows how 'a number of aspects of action, decision, and the strategies of politics took shape and were analysed with reference to the divine powers' (2006: 91–101). As well as Apollo, the founder (*Archēgetēs*) and Hesta, 'the Aphrodite-Ares pair, which is of major importance and represents the relationship between the rituals of warfare, on the one hand, and harmony and concord, on the other, introduces a set of major tensions that must be taken into account in any analysis of the political field' (de Vries and Sullivan, 2006: 101).

For René Girard, for whom sacrificial violence is the foundation of all cultural differences, there is a thematic connection between all four deities listed by Detienne. The pairing of the god of war and the goddess of love hints at the problem of violence, but the activities associated with Apollo and Hesta (demarcation of space, preservation of a sacrificial flame) themselves carry echoes of foundational sacrifice. Similarly, the ambiguity of violence in social formation is evident in Greek drama, notably the tragedy by Aeschylus, *The Eumenides*. The central problem of the play is: how is civil strife to be overcome? The Chorus of the Eumenides (formerly the goddesses of wrath, but now mysteriously turned benevolent) promises an end to the civil war, as 'man with man and state with state / Shall vow the pledge of common hate / And common friendship' (*Eumenides*, 978–87). There is rejoicing over 'these alien Powers that thus are made Athenian evermore'.

In *Deceit, Desire and the Novel*, and then in *Violence and the Sacred*, Girard formulates his anthropological insights by reading texts: first, his treasured European novelists, then in the myths and legends of the history of religion as filtered through ancient drama. Burton Mack summarizes: 'Texts are in touch with the mechanisms and events that generate social structures and their history . . . By combining the two literatures (novels with mimetic plots and myths of killing), Girard produces the full dramatic sequence.' Literature and myth are complementary sources of insight: the myths are closer to the events of sacrificial scapegoating, but they need great literature to interpret them, and reveal what they attempt to conceal (Mack, 1987: 17).

The golden question, once again, is whether it is possible and legitimate to move from fictional to actual violence. Is it conceivable that assertions about violence within symbolic and literary constructs can be extrapolated to the 'real world'? 'Texts are in touch with the mechanisms and events that generate social structures and their history', claims Girard. Is this true?

Violence and the sacred in the modern world

A 1992 collection of essays records an attempt to test Girard's hypothesis in actual situations of conflict,[2] with participants asked to consider how the mimetic hypothesis shed light on conflicts across the world. Two questions emerged, which Juergensmeyer sets out in the Introduction: why are images of violence, destruction and death so central to religion, and 'what is the relationship between symbolic violence and the real acts of religious violence that occur throughout the world today?' (Juergensmeyer, 1992: 1). These questions are addressed directly by Girard's mimetic theory, but this colloquium was one of the rare occasions where Girard has found himself face to face with social scientific investigators of religious violence. Juergensmeyer expounds the mimetic hypothesis, though differs from Girard in the importance of Christian revelation: 'Like other aspects of Girard's theory, however, one can accept or reject this aspect of it without disturbing the rest of his theoretical design' (4).

Most of the contributors to *Violence and the Sacred in the Modern World* seem to be in agreement as to the usefulness of at least some aspects of Girard's work: that symbolic and actual violence are not so far removed from each other. It is interesting to note that the contributors are drawn to different bits: for some, it is mimetic desire which is most important, for others, the role of sacrifice as a containment of violence. Mimetic rivalry is to the fore in essays on the strident Israeli ideologue, Rabbi Meir Kahane, and on the curious affinity that exists between fundamentalist Muslims and fundamentalist Jews; the sacrificial motif is considered in an essay on the 'self-sacrifice' of suicide victims in the Lebanon. A number of other essays, including Juergensmeyer's own contribution, 'Sacrifice and Cosmic War' (case studies of India, Sri Lanka, Nicaragua and the Middle East), and a broader context from David Rapoport, scrutinize particular aspects of Girard's theory and call for modifications.

It is the response to these contributions, from René Girard and Mark Anspach, which concerns us here. The common thread, as far as they are concerned, is that anything which gets labelled 'fundamentalism' is a reaction to the fear of undifferentiation, the dissolution of differences which Girard refers to as the 'mimetic crisis'. Our contemporary culture is in the midst of a deepening mimetic and sacrificial crisis (a view which Girard repeats in his reaction to the 9/11 atrocity). They do not see a middle of the road position between 'fundamentalism' and 'post-enlightenment rationalism', though insist that an approach which does not take seriously the view of the fundamentalist, seeing it as a form of pathology, is inadequate.

They touch, perhaps all too briefly, on the question of the relationship between religion, nationalism and the state (146–7), noting that Rapoport remarks on 'the similarity of the origin of religion proposed by *Violence and the Sacred* to the origin of the state conceived by Hobbes and other political theorists'. Girard and Anspach respond by noting the differences: for mimetic theory, the solution is a war of all against one – the victim – while in *Leviathan* we have a war of one against all (the sovereign's retention of the unlimited right to force). There is a big difference between them insofar as mimetic theory posits a spontaneous mechanism, while classical social contract theory makes an unlikely assumption of rationality. 'It is, after all, much easier to choose a victim than a sovereign': Girard here repeats his view that monarchy is more likely to have evolved gradually, from a divine victim awaiting sacrifice, to a 'ruler' who, over time, acquires real power.

There is one further point of difference, which may in fact be seen as a broadening out of mimetic theory, rather than a refutation of it. Mark Juergensmeyer is not wholly convinced of the central planks of the theory: he questions whether the concept of mimetic desire is necessary, and doubts that the notion of sacrifice is the fundamental religious image. The quest for order, which involves a struggle between order and disorder, is in his view more basic. This struggle is often exemplified in the grand metaphor of cosmic or sacred warfare, 'a dominant motif in the rhetoric of modern-day religious activists' (7). Girard expresses interest in this perspective: 'order contains disorder, but it also emerges spontaneously from it – and refers to a symposium which sought precisely to locate mimetic theory in this broader theoretical perspective.[3]

The doctrine of the katēchon

There is a potent tradition in political thought which sees this process – of containment and re-channelling of violence – as the fundamental meaning and purpose of politics: or at the very least, as an important aspect or criterion of 'the political'. The theological component of this is the New Testament notion of the *katēchon*. The Greek word *katēcho* means 'to hold back, hold fast, to bind, restrain', and is used by St Paul to refer to the restraining hand of God before the chaos of the end times is unleashed (2 Thess. 2.1–12). Mark 13 and Luke 21 similarly refer to a delay or deferral of the apocalypse. It is in the book of Revelation, 20.7–8, however, where we find the most graphic portrayal, in Michael's struggle to contain Satan.

The *katēchon* refers, therefore, to the political force whose function is the restraint of chaos and disorder. We will find aspects of *katēchon* theology in a number of theologians, notably Augustine in the *City of God*, and in his *Retractions*, and Martin Luther, who draws a contrast between the high gospel standards by which Christians live, and a less demanding ethic, based on fear and coercion. Luther is under no illusion about the dangers of getting these confused:

> If anyone attempted to rule the world by the gospel and to abolish all temporal law and sword on the plea that all are baptised and

Political Theology

Christians, and that, according to the gospel, there shall be among them no law or sword – or need for either – pray tell, friend, what would he be doing? What do you imagine the effect will be? He would be loosing the ropes and chains of the savage wild beasts and letting them bite and mangle everyone, meanwhile insisting that they were harmless, tame, and gentle creatures; but I would have the proof in my wounds. Just so would the wicked under the name of Christian abuse evangelical freedom, carry on their rascality, and insist that they were Christians subject neither to law nor sword, as some are already raving and ranting.[4]

Thomas Hobbes in *Leviathan* (1651) attempts a secularized solution of the same problem which confronted Augustine and Luther. Hobbes announces his conviction of the equality of all human beings, though the sociological and political implications of this theological affirmation are extremely fraught. The natural equality of humans engenders equality of hope, which in turn breeds envy (*Leviathan*, ch. 13), therefore, universal competition and strife. The famous 'war of all against all' is a condition 'of continuall feare, and danger of violent death; And the life of man, solitary, poore, nasty, brutish and short'. Christianity's pernicious doctrine of human equality is a recipe for conflict; yet the religious category of the *katēchon*, once secularized, provides a way out of the difficulty. In this state of nature, only an absolute power can prevent the outbreak of civil war. The people agree on a social contract, and cede absolute power to this sovereign. He would then be a mortal 'God', with authority over both politics and religion. The State which evolves functions as a *katēchon*, with no positive goal other than the restraining of the apocalyptic state of war and the alleviation of fear:

> The war of all against all is the natural condition of humankind. It is cold fear and the need for security, the foundation of both religion and the social contract, that drives humans from their nasty and brutish circumstances and into the arms of Leviathan. This soteriology of the State as peacemaker demands that its sovereign authority be absolutely alone and without rival. In Hobbes it is not so much that the Church has been subordinated to the civil power; Leviathan has rather swallowed the Church into its yawning maw. (Cavanaugh, 1995: 406)

Carl Schmitt has been described as the 'German Hobbes'. Many commentators would agree that the analogy holds, insofar as Schmitt attempts a similar appropriation of the language and concepts of Christianity (more precisely, in Schmitt's case Roman Catholicism), for what is in fact a purely immanent political project. Schmitt's classic text *Political Theology* sets out the roots of sovereignty as a secularized theological concept, while *The Concept of the Political* defines politics in terms of the *Freund-Feind* ('friend-enemy') distinction. This differentiation is an extension of Hobbes' concept of the State: according to Schmitt, the world is divided into states which are aligned with or against one another. Political stability arises from the balance between them; a state needs alliances, but it also needs the unifying power which comes from having enemies.[5]

Schmitt regards any attempt to unite where God has instituted separation and strife is a grave mistake. This 'denial of difference' upsets the balance between states, and therefore has the opposite effect of what was intended. There is a theological enmity between Christianity and liberalism, and Schmitt refuses to allow the apparent harmonizing neutrality of the modern liberal state to mask the brutal reality of the modern revolt against God. The liberal Enlightenment dream of 'perpetual peace' is a chimera: a world free of aggression is not possible, since such a state could itself only be achieved by aggressive means. Substituting war with economic competition merely disguises the coercion; it does not remove it. Like the Eumenides, Schmitt proclaims the intensity of two sentiments: love for fellow citizens and hatred of one's enemies.

Carl Schmitt's second major concept is the relationship between *nomos* (law) and space or territory (summarized here from Palaver, 1996). *Nomos* means a 'total concept of law that contains a concrete order and a community', including therefore the religious dimension of *nomos*. The term connotes originally a 'sacred location': Apollo as 'founder' of a city was invoked as the one who measures out and marks off its dimensions, including those of the *agora*, the place of assembly (Detienne, 2006: 97). For Schmitt there are more sinister overtones to the *nomos* and territory link, since it helped him to justify Nazi annexation policies: 'The great primal acts of law . . . remain earthbound locations (orientations). These are land appropriations, the founding of cities and colonies.'

Wolfgang Palaver asserts that '[t]hroughout his life, Schmitt feared nothing more than a unified world' (Palaver, 1996: 111) because the pacific ideology of the League of Nations, peace movements and so on ignored the *Freund-Feind* distinction. They were also oblivious of this territorial dimension of *nomos*, namely, the arrangement of space as the foundation of international order. These two concepts, as used by Carl Schmitt, are of course highly problematic. The dualism of the *Freund-Feind* distinction is unacceptable, and its Hobbesian reduction of the state to a mere question of power leave us well short of the refusal of barbaric fascism articulated by Rowan Williams: '[T]he fundamental requirement of a politics worth the name is that we have an account of human action that decisively marks its distance from assumptions about action as the successful assertion of will.' What is required is a theological critique which will respond to the genuine concern which is expressed in Schmitt's arguments – namely, the fear of undifferentiation which is at the origin of both religion and politics, and which always threatens to engulf and appropriate an authentic evangelical political vision. Political theologians such as Wolfgang Palaver believe that René Girard and mimetic theory contribute to such a theological framework.

Such a framework needs to enable us to do the work set out by Rowan Williams, who as we have seen valiantly attempts to draw together the wildly incompatible strands of contemporary 'political theology'. This he does under the banner of resistance to the 'barbarism' of meaningful action, understood as pure successful assertion of will (Davis et al., 2005: 1). Whatever else may be said on this topic, it is at least clear that Girard distances himself from any such conception of action. Like Freud and Marx, he sees social interactions unfolding as a result of the misunderstanding (*méconnaisance*) of the agents concerned. A community, newly reconciled to itself by the expulsion of a victim, disguises its violence from itself by means of myths, prohibitions and rituals. Even as he is done to death 'at the hands of political and religious meaning makers', Jesus cries out: 'Father, forgive them, they know not what they do'. In place of this 'barbarism', Rowan Williams appeals to an understanding of action as *testimony*, and to theology as 'the discipline that follows what is claimed as the supreme act of testimony, and thus the supremely generative and revisionary act of all human history: the Cross for Christians, the gift of Torah and communal identity for Judaism' (3).

The 'apocalyptic feeling'

Girard himself has expressly considered it the duty of an intellectual to be 'above the fray' when it comes to right or left wing labels in politics. He has also responded to the accusation that he is a cultural pessimist by insisting that in the long run neither optimism nor pessimism is justified by the much more complex movements of history. At the same time, it is not the case that history is carrying along at the same pace and rhythm as before; Girard has become increasingly explicit about specific aspects of the contemporary situation which make it unique. The phenomenon he is trying to describe, namely the decomposition of the sacred mechanism since the Second World War, is in fact a highly ambiguous one, summed up in *Things Hidden* by the injunction from the book of Deuteronomy to 'choose life or death'. How we react to the collapse of sacrificial safeguards will be determinative of whether or not we have a future at all, as Girard repeats in *Evolution and Conversion* 20 years later:

> [T]he Gospel does not provide a happy ending to our history. It simply shows us two options (which is exactly what ideologies never provide, freedom of choice): either we imitate Christ, giving up our mimetic violence, or we run the risk of self-destruction. The apocalyptic feeling is based on that risk. (2007a: 237)

In other words, precisely the uncomfortable ambiguity of our situation, which could go either way, at least shows we are not dealing with an ideology, such as the 'end of history', or the inevitable triumph of the proletariat, which leaves us no choice in the matter. Instead, what lies ahead will consist of 'dialectical turns so astonishing that they are going to take everybody by surprise' (261). There is, it seems, paradox at every turn, just as Christ comes to bring not peace but a sword: 'Satan is still with us, but only as a source of disorder. Indirectly, therefore, because of our inability to live without scapegoats, Christianity is a source of disruption in our world' (262). What chance is there, we might ask, of figuring out what is happening, when both Satan and Christianity are disruptive influences?

This has been the situation over the past 50 years or so. Girard speculates that because of the ferocity of the cruelty towards the Jews during the Holocaust, the modern care for the victim is a kind of 'return of the repressed'; the postwar period has seen an acceleration of concern for the victim and the destruction of sacrificial bulwarks. While on one level this is good news, from another perspective it means we are left vulnerable without the protection those bulwarks afforded us. The situation has been further complicated by the sequence of events from 1989 to the crisis initiated by the 9/11 attacks. During the Cold War a precarious stability was achieved by the fact that enemy superpowers faced each other and were able to predict their actions. However terrible the logic of 'Mutually Assured Destruction' (MAD), there was at least a predictability to the situation, which enabled beneficial courses of action to be undertaken. For all its nastiness, Cold War communism operated within a humanist perspective, as did its Western opponent. The example Girard has cited a few times is the Cuban missile crisis of 1963, in which Khrushchev 'turned the other cheek' by recalling his missiles, and thereby avoiding catastrophe. This was when the Soviet Union showed that it was human after all (2007a: 28); we are dealing here with choices and free-will. What concerns Girard about the present threat to global security is its complete unpredictability.

Political Theology

The confrontation with militant Islam is to this extent far more serious than the Cold War stand-off.

We have no way of understanding this new enemy, of predicting their logic and intentions. It is this unknowability which is behind Girard's rather shocking declaration at the Colloquium on Violence and Religion, 2008, to the effect that we are beyond the point where politics can help us. The search for a political solution merely prolongs the illusion that we are in charge of things, that the world is predictable. The title of this Colloquium, *Catastrophe and Conversion*, reiterates the biblical imperative, of choosing between life and death. This biblical alternative is taken in deadly earnestness by Girard, and not at all as a hyperbolic figure of speech. While he explicitly disassociates himself from Derrida's sense of an 'apocalyptic tone in philosophy' (Girard, 2007a: 235) there is no doubt that the theme of apocalyptic or eschatology has played an increasingly large role in his thinking. It is a 'feeling' which he identifies very precisely with the conviction of the early Christians that 'the time is short' (1 Cor. 7.29).

> The apocalyptic feeling is the consciousness that the scapegoat business has run its course, that therefore nothing more can happen. What else could happen after the Christian revelation? And at the same time, what might happen to our world if the precarious order of false transcendence imposed by the scapegoat mechanism ceases to function? Any great Christian experience is apocalyptic because what one realizes is that after the decomposition of the sacrificial order there is nothing standing between ourselves and our possible destruction. How this will materialize, I don't really know. (235)

The question which this raises here is, is whether the renewed stress on this complex biblical reality enhances or undermines the effort to derive a 'political theology' from Girard's mimetic theory. Is apocalyptic awareness (which, as Girard describes it, is all about the problem of violence without sacrificial protection) a *corrective* to our politics or a *substitution* for it? A comparison with Hannah Arendt suggests itself, as an important thinker who was alert to the ambiguities of mimetic interaction and violence. In *The Human Condition* (1958) Arendt sets out an understanding of politics as entirely free of any kind of coercion. Political action, the public association of free human individuals, is distinguished from work and labour, which in different ways arise from human necessity. Politics begins where violence ends, in other words. She stands on the other side of the divide from Carl Schmitt, who, as we have seen, defines politics in terms of violence: the channelling violence of the *katēchon* and the 'Friend-Foe' distinction.

Girard and Theology

Arendt puts forward a high ideal of politics as 'action' and makes a strident case for Christianity's incompatibility with politics, not least because the Christian ideal of goodness is a secret rather than a public one, with the right and the left hand being ignorant of one another.

More to the point for our present discussion, Arendt draws attention to the way that the Christian's awareness of living out the end time distracts from the exigencies of the present world. Why worry about the social and political order when 'the time is short'? The fact of Christians tolerating such realities as slavery suggests an essentially conservative or indifferent perspective on the present world. A further argument from Arendt may be noted here. She insists that no politics is possible without some purchase on the future, through the two activities of promising and forgiveness. *Promising* is of course what politicians do all the time as they lead us into a bright new dawn: *forgiveness* is also required, however, because it is rarely possible that all our plans and predictions are fulfilled, and if we were to be rigidly held to them we would never dare express any intention towards the future. As it happens, Arendt sees the notion of public forgiveness as a specifically Christian contribution, deriving from Jesus himself: we do not find it in Roman political theory, as we do the notion of promising. Taken together, promising and forgiving allow us to have a purchase on the future, they enable political action to take place. If Girard's account of 'apocalyptic feeling' is correct, however, we no longer have that purchase, and politics is no longer possible.

There is no necessity to accept Arendt's critique, of course, and we have already implied that her understanding of politics as free from and antithetical to coercion and violence may itself be too optimistic. Mimetic theory would seem to have more in common with the kind of *katēchon* theology associated with Hobbes and Schmitt, although the differences between them are even more significant. Two recent writings of Girard take us further into this theme. First, a collection of essays in *SubStance*[6] on 'Cultural Theory after 9/11' contains an interview with Girard, as well as contributions from several Girardian scholars; secondly, there is Girard's contribution to a collection titled *Politics and Apocalypse*, edited by Robert Hamerton-Kelly. A third text, Girard's most recent work, and what he himself describes as a 'bizarre book', *Achever Clausewitz* (French original, 2007b), is a study of the famous military theorist Carl von Clausewitz (1780–1831), likewise composed (in part) according to an interview format.

The interview with Girard in *SubStance* treats of 'Apocalyptic thinking after 9/11' and takes up Girard's comments from 2001, just after the atrocities. Seven years on, he still sees 9/11 as a 'seminal event' and questions the wisdom of allowing its importance to be minimized. Rather than just being 'more of the same', a continuation of twentieth-century violence, in fact it represents a new global dimension to violence. An accommodation of 9/11 to our everyday perceptions is nothing less than a denial or evasion of its religious character. In order to comprehend this, religious categories are needed, specifically the apocalyptical dimension of Christianity. Clausewitz is cited and paraphrased: terrorism is a form of war, and war is politics by other means. Beyond this, for all its technological superiority, the West is baffled and helpless, 'powerless' before Islam; for example, the fighting between Shia and Sunni is incomprehensible to us. How the West responds to this experience of weakness will be crucial in the years to come (22).

Interestingly, Girard is now less convinced that it is simply resentment at work; another motivating force is needed to explain the readiness of terrorists for suicide attacks and so forth, and this Girard now thinks to be more directly religious. At the same time, Girard follows James Alison in being very cautious about 'sacralizing' the events of Ground Zero. Making this a holy event at a holy place can only ever have one effect: the mobilization of a unanimous grieving crowd for a holy war (24). The use of the Greek term *katharsis* (in its religious sense a 'purgation') casts the 9/11 disaster as a piece of theatre, which indeed it was for those watching the events live on television.

For Girard, the significance of 9/11 is as a kind of hermeneutical key to understand what is happening around us: 'This is the event which makes possible an understanding of the modern event, for it renders the archaic more intelligible' (25). The root of 'apocalypse' is of course 'unveiling', and we need to pay attention to what is being unveiled, namely the perishing of the powers. Such a destruction brings with it an unleashing of violence, bringing us to the end (Girard differs from fundamentalists only in that they believe this to be God's violence, not that of human beings). Once again, we are taken beyond categories of optimism and pessimism: there is more good and more bad in the world all the time (Maritain), and the world is both more Christian and less Christian. There will be 'spiritual and intellectual revolutions in the not to distant future'; and 9/11 will continue to be highly meaningful, however much we seek to evade its message.

Politics and Apocalypse (Hamerton-Kelly, 2007) brings these issues into focus, not least in its title. Hamerton-Kelly cites Peter Thiel to the effect that 'the brute facts of September 11 demand a re-examination of the foundations of modern politics', in recognition of the increasingly evident inadequacy of Western political philosophy. The essays are the outcome of an intensive conference in 2004, with just eight participants, gathered to scrutinize three themes – politics, mimesis and apocalypse; and three political theorists – Carl Schmitt, Leo Strauss and Eric Voegelin. Girard's essay,

Girard and Theology

'The Evangelical Subversion of Myth' (29–49) is an extended reflection upon Jesus' 'Curses of the Pharisees' in the gospels of Matthew and Luke. Hamerton-Kelly's commentary on this essay (after he has sifted through the many contemporary expressions of 'apocalyptic' writing, including the *Left Behind* literature) makes clear that

> mimetic theory is ironically apocalyptic because it is the opposite of what normally passes for that genre. It is non-violent, while the vulgar apocalypse is violent, it decodes while the vulgar encodes; nevertheless it is apocalyptic because it deals with universal history and human nature and assumes that historiography is possible and the human story is not 'a tale told by an idiot.' It is apocalyptic because it decodes the encryption of violence in the vulgar apocalypse, in symbols such as the divine judgement and the torture of the guilty. (15)

This may be as helpful a clarification as we can hope for on the question of apocalypse. It has clearly become a major theme for mimetic theory and we shall return to it briefly in the Epilogue. In the meantime, the question raised above, with the help of a brief overview of Hannah Arendt's critique of Christianity, remains: is the discourse of apocalypse a substitute or replacement for politics, or a corrective of it? In fact, as far as political theology goes, we have been here before. If we examine the work of postwar German political theologians like Johan Baptist Metz, Jürgen Moltmann and Dorothee Sölle, we find the same note of bewildered disbelief: first, that the horror of Auschwitz could have happened at all (Sölle asks of her parents' generation: 'Where were you when the transports were put together? Didn't you smell the gas?'); secondly, that the realization of what had taken place did not utterly transform our theology and politics, but in fact people continued to theologize 'after Auschwitz' as if it had not happened. For Metz and Moltmann, a recovery of the eschatological dimension of Christianity is needed so as to 'interrupt' the complacency and amnesia of the present. With Girard and his interlocutors, the situation seems to be similar: a 'normalization' of the 9/11 catastrophe, meaning a willingness to live with such violence in the world, is an act of complacency or denial, a blind trust that we will somehow muddle through.

But here is the difference also; for all his dissatisfaction with the bourgeois complacency of European Christianity, Johann Baptist Metz saw himself as keeping faith with the project of the Enlightenment. His 'eschatological' critique of the present in the name of a messianic future is a corrective of a forgetful modernity, not a despairing rejection of it. With the mimetic apocalypticists, such as Girard, Hamerton-Kelly and

Thiel, there is a sense that we have reached a 'tipping point' – comparable to the challenge posed by the Holocaust. Thiel speaks of the need for 'a re-examination of the foundations of modern politics', but his overall tone is bleak: in a commentary on Girard titled 'The End of the City of Man', he dismisses the liberal as one who knows nothing of the past, while the conservative knows nothing of the future:

> Indeed, one may wonder whether any sort of politics will remain possible for the exceptional generation that has learned the truth of human history for the first time. It is in this context that one must remember that the word apocalypse originally meant unveiling. For Girard, the unveiling of this terrible knowledge opens a catastrophic fault line below the city of man. (Hamerton-Kelly, 2007: 212)

Chapter 10
Views from the South

René Girard and mimetic theory have been, for the most part, a transatlantic phenomenon. Girard himself has lived and worked exclusively in First World academic environments in Europe and the United States; the *Colloquium on Violence and Religion* which was formed to explore his ideas has mirrored this geographical and cultural bias, and while the charge of Eurocentrism is a complex one in Girard's case, it seems to be an easy one to make. How should a Girardian theorist respond?

There are principally two contexts for replying to this. First, in terms of explicit engagement or utilization of Girard's theory with 'the South', we have the colloqium in 1990 with Latin American liberation theologians. Because this is still to date the only occasion on which Girard has been present in such a setting, this conference seems to possess an iconic status. Secondly, there is the utilization of mimetic theory for exploring the theme of witchcraft and conflict by a number of African authors, who have drawn attention to the social and political pressures which underlie witchcraft accusations and persecutions.

Before exploring these, however, I wish to draw attention to another 'French' thinker, an almost exact contemporary of Girard, whose influence in twentieth-century thought is considerable. Frantz Fanon (1925–1961), was a psychoanalyst and revolutionary, and a key inspiration for anti-colonial liberation movements for more than four decades. *Black Skin, White Masks* analyses the effect of colonial subjugation on the human psyche, while *The Wretched of the Earth* (*Les damnés de la terre*) appeared in 1963, about the same time as *Desire, Deceit and the Novel*; it is a classic 'handbook' for post-colonial liberation, powerfully introduced by a Preface from Jean-Paul Sartre. Among other things, Fanon later discusses in depth the effects on Algerians of torture by the French forces which he had come across as a practising analyst during the liberation wars. While there is a great deal in this revolutionary text that would not much appeal to Girard, there are nevertheless themes where Girard and Fanon converge.

The possible synergy is tantalizing. Like Girard, Franz Fanon's work is interdisciplinary, as his psychiatric concerns are enlarged to encompass politics, sociology, anthropology, linguistics and literature. He distances himself from the conceptuality of *Négritude* (which implicitly based consciousness in racial difference and tension), opting instead for a psychological analysis which attributes consciousness not to 'racial essence', but to political and social situations. Between Girard and Fanon hovers the figure of Hegel, whose Master–Slave dialectic is fruitful for both thinkers. We will recall that the Master–Slave dialectic (*Herrschaft und Knechtschaft*)[1] is a story or myth elaborated by Hegel in order to explain his idea of how self-consciousness dialectically sublates into what he variously refers to as Absolute Knowledge, Spirit and Science. For Hegel, Absolute Knowledge, or Spirit, cannot come to be without first *a self-consciousness recognizing another self-consciousness*. To illustrate this, Hegel tells the story of how two people meet. This account can be read on various levels: as self-consciousness coming to itself, or self-consciousness coming to be in beginning of human history (hominization), or the self-consciousness of a society or nation realizing its freedom.

Hegel's master–slave trope, and particularly the emphasis laid on *recognition*, has been of crucial influence on Frantz Fanon's description of the colonial relation in *Black Skin, White Masks*.[2] We have come full circle since our attempt to 'place' Girard in the opening chapter began with Kojève's famous lectures on Hegel, and the explication of 'desire according to the other'. Kojève declares that '[h]uman history is the history of desires that are desired', and of course Girard's life and career are spent in following up this insight. For Hegel, of course, the desire is for 'recognition': I desire that you should desire me; for Girard, the desiring subject desires what the model desires, not the model himself. With this background in place, we are able to tune in to the Conclusion to *The Wretched of the Earth*, which is worth quoting at some length:

> Let us waste no time in sterile litanies and nauseating mimicry. Leave this Europe where they are never done talking of Man, yet murder men everywhere they find them, at the corner of every one of their own streets, in all the corners of the globe. For centuries they have stifled almost the whole of humanity in the name of a so-called spiritual experience. Look at them today swaying between atomic and spiritual disintegration.

This call to leave Europe behind nevertheless coheres with a sense of admiration for European success:

> Europe undertook the leadership of the world with ardour, cynicism and violence. Look at how the shadow of her palaces stretches out ever farther! Every one of her movements has burst the

bounds of space and thought. Europe has declined all humility and all modesty; but she has also set her face against all solicitude and all tenderness. She has only shown herself parsimonious and niggardly where men are concerned; it is only men that she has killed and devoured.

It is time to recognize that 'we have better things to do than to follow that same Europe', whose triumphs of the mind have been accompanied by such immense suffering: '[t]he European game has finally ended; we must find something different'.

We today can do everything, so long as we do not imitate Europe, so long as we are not obsessed by the desire to catch up with Europe. Yet it is very true that we need a model, and that we want blueprints and examples. For many among us the European model is the most inspiring. We have therefore seen in the preceding pages to what mortifying set-backs such an imitation has led us. European achievements, European techniques and the European style ought no longer to tempt us and to throw us off our balance. . . . Let us decide not to imitate Europe; let us combine our muscles and our brains in a new direction. Let us try to create the whole man, whom Europe has been incapable of bringing to triumphant birth.

Fanon points out that a previous example of a former European colony intent on catching up with Europe was a disaster. The United States became 'a monster, in which the taints, the sickness and the inhumanity of Europe have grown to appalling dimensions'. The temptation to create a 'third Europe' must be resisted. Fanon calls on his readers to cease paying tribute to Europe by mimicking her states, institutions and societies; an obscene caricature. If it is about turning Africa into a new Europe, and America into a new Europe, then 'let us leave the destiny of our countries to Europeans' since they will do it better:

But if we want humanity to advance a step farther . . . we must seek the response elsewhere than in Europe. Moreover, if we wish to reply to the expectations of the people of Europe, it is no good sending them back a reflection, even an ideal reflection, of their society and their thought with which from time to time they feel immeasurably sickened. For Europe, for ourselves and for humanity, comrades, we must turn over a new leaf, we must work out new concepts, and try to set afoot a new man. (Fanon, 1963).

Views from the South

Girard and liberation theology

From these apposite comments from Fanon, we can move to an understanding of how Girardian theory maps onto liberative politics. As we have found in the previous chapter, a Girardian politics seems hard to envisage, especially as there seems to be a tension in his most recent work between 'politics' and 'apocalyptic'. Girard has set himself early on against the modality of 'liberation', in what is understandably, but unfairly, read to be a reactionary stance towards modernity. His analysis of desire, and in particular his insistence on the destructiveness of mimetic desire, leads him to assert that ideologies of liberation are self-defeating:

> The more people think they are realizing the Utopias dreamed up by their desire – in other words, the more they embrace ideologies of liberation – the more they will in fact be working to reinforce the competitive world that is stifling them. . . . All modern thought is falsified by a mystique of transgression, which it falls back into even when it is trying to escape. (1987a: 287)

In this respect, the colloquium between Girard and liberation theologians which took place in Brazil in 1990 – less than a year after the collapse of communism in Europe – is a fascinating encounter. There is, to begin with, a degree of mutual suspicion, before the participants begin to find common ground, to the point where Girard is commended by Leonardo Boff for his 'immense intellectual holiness'. The discussion pushes forward a general analogy, between the mechanism of sacrifice as Girard understands this process, and the liberationist critique of capitalism, understood as an idolatrous and deadly phenomenon.

A strong point of agreement, therefore, between René Girard and the theologians is their common rejection of 'Opferideologie', which can translate as the 'logic of sacrifice' or the 'logic of the victim'.[3] This means a repudiation of the deconstructionist tenet that 'everything is only language . . . there is nothing beyond or outside language'. The liberationists' contact with the poor, and Girard's discernment of the victim, respectively prevent them from subscribing to deconstructionist doctrine, and to the alienating jargon that too often goes with it. Once again, for Girard, literature is not self-contained but links us with the 'real world'; the conference is significant for Girard's own self-disclosure, concerning his conversion experience and those aspects of his life where he was enabled to take the perspective of the victim. There is some degree of mutual critique: Girard expresses concern about the liberationist stress upon social critique to the detriment of popular piety and religion, while the liberationists question whether Girard's anthropology is too negative. His account of social formation as scapegoating, it is alleged, does not do justice to the possibility of solidarity and collaboration among the poor.

Witchcraze

The question of witchcraft in Africa is, of course hugely complex; even within the African contexts there is a notable diversity of practice and terminology, and the range of (largely non-African) hermeneutical approaches has been considerable. Van Binsbergen lists the different phases which can be discerned in the academic study of witchcraft in Africa: as a manifestation of Africans' allegedly fundamentally different modes of thought; of a particular logic of social relations; of the African subject's confrontation with the problem of evil, meaning and competition in a context of rapid social change; as an African path to modernity in the context of globalization. This alone would discourage the kind of comparative study (e.g. with the European witchcraze of the sixteenth and seventeenth centuries) towards which Girard's mimetic theory would urge us. On the other hand, a more general interest in the phenomenon of witchcraft shows no sign of abating: 'The Past Which Will Not Go Away' is the title of the opening chapter of Rainer Decker's book, to accompany a recent TV documentary series on German television.[4]

For our purposes, we can identify two approaches to this phenomenon. First, sources make clear that a more general 'culture of violence' is the context for witchcraft activity, since witchcraft and witch-hunts are manifestations of larger patterns of violence and counter-violence. It is difficult to claim, for example, that the high incidence of witchcraft activity in South Africa in recent decades is unrelated to the wider political unrest surrounding the death throes of the apartheid regime. South Africa's *Commission of Inquiry into Witchcraft, Violence and Ritual Killings* (May 1996) reported more than three hundred deaths at the hands of vigilante groups in a 10-year period, with thousands of people evicted from their homes. Persecution has been particularly intense in the mid to late 1990s; ten farms had been set up in the Northern Province to harbour hundreds of refuges found guilty of witchcraft at kangaroo courts. Six hundred deaths between 1990–1999 are attributed to witch-hunting in this province alone; with hundreds of instances of crimes perpetrated against suspected witches, including murder, damage to property and assault. Victims of such accusation are typically women between 55 and 72 years of age; killings occur most commonly in the rainy season, when witches are accused of directing lightning at their alleged victims. Elsewhere in

Views from the South

Africa, the estimated figures are even more graphic, as a news report of 2001 makes clear:

> Suspected Witches Dead in Congo: 200 Believed Killed in Northeast: Ugandan Official[5]
>
> KAMPALA, Uganda, July 5, 2001 – Villagers have hacked to death about 200 suspected witches in rebel-held northeastern Congo since June 15, blaming them for diseases that have gone untreated since Congo's war broke out three years ago, a senior Ugandan army official said today. Ugandan troops, which had withdrawn this year from the district near the border, were sent back to the area to stop the killings and make arrests, Brig. Henry Tumukunde said.
>
> 'Villagers were saying that some people had bewitched others, and they started lynching them. By the time we discovered this, 60 people had already been killed by early last week. About 200 people lost their lives,' Tumukunde said. Tumukunde refused to say how many people had been injured or arrested. It wasn't clear whether the witches were mainly men or women.
>
> The killings began three weeks ago in Aru, 50 miles south of Sudan, but spread deep inside northeastern Congo, a country the size of Western Europe. The region of rolling savannas was once a rich agricultural area where wheat was grown and cattle raised, but a series of rebellions have left communities destroyed since the 1960s.
>
> The war that began three years ago has only made matters worse. 'The war forced people to move to other areas, and the internally displaced were the targets of local villagers, who accused them of witchcraft,' Tumukunde said.
>
> He said diseases endemic to the region were being blamed on witchcraft, noting that drugs to treat the diseases have not been available during the duration of the war. In much of the rebel-held 60 percent of the country, routes that would carry trade and aid back and forth are cut off. With no immunization programs or other health programs, measles and other diseases are killing people in large numbers. Plague has even made inroads. In the worst-hit areas, people are dying from a combination of disease and starvation.
>
> Some charities have estimated an indirect wartime death toll of about 2 million out of a population of 50 million in the former Belgian colony.

> In a report released jointly today by UNICEF and the World
> Health Organization, experts said after a recent 12-day visit to
> Congo that 'every facet of society – whether human rights or
> economy, education or water and sanitation, housing or
> social care – has collapsed.'

Such a nightmare scenario accords very closely with Girard's account of the dynamics of a society in mimetic meltdown, when the search for scapegoats begins. The discussion concerning witchcraft in Africa, however, has a second, less dramatic but more complex dimension. This concerns societies or groups which are not undergoing this kind of extreme meltdown, but which nevertheless find their identity or sense of coherence to be under threat from external pressure. Austen (1999: 1) speaks of 'the new discourse of witchcraft' in Africa, in which scholars have expanded their horizons from classical ethnography into what has been called 'modernization studies'. He cites Peter Geschiere, author of *The Modernity of Witchcraft* (1997), as representative of a new generation of scholars concerned with the pressures upon a post-colonial world: a world whose nationalist aspirations have not been realized, and which finds itself marginalized in a global economy and culture. Current beliefs and practices regarding witchcraft, therefore, are to be understood not as a logically closed system, which either thwarts modernization or is overcome by it, but rather a flexible and deeply ambivalent means of contemplating and reacting to traumatic and problematic confrontations (globalism with localism, culture with political economy).

Wim van Binsbergen conceives of witchcraft in modern Africa as the virtualized boundary conditions of the kinship order: 'virtuality' here is about 'discontinuity, broken reference, de-contextualisation, through which yet formal continuity shimmers through'. This approach is essential if we are to appreciate that we are dealing not so much with 'real' communities, as with the increasingly problematic *model* of the community village, and its nostalgic pull on urban groups:

> Virtuality equips us for the situation, which the global spread of
> consumerism and electronic technology has rendered increasingly
> common also in Africa, that meaning is encountered and
> manipulated in a context far removed, in time and space, from the
> concrete social context of production and reproduction where that
> meaning was originally worked out; where meaning is no longer
> local and systemic, but fragmented, ragged, absurd, maybe even
> absent. (van Binsbergen: 4)

Views from the South

Van Binsbergen goes on to define witchcraft as everything which falls outside the kinship order, is not regulated by that order, and which challenges rejects, or destroys it.

> As such, witchcraft is opposed to kinship, group solidarity, rules of kinship, incest prohibitions, avoidance rules concerning close kin . . . [O]utside of the kinship order is the realm of witchcraft; and it is here that we must situate kingship, trade, and the specialities of the bard, the diviner, the magician and the rain-maker.

Witchcraft in contemporary Africa, therefore, is to be regarded neither as a timeless atavistic continuation of an essentially unaltered cosmology right into modernity, nor as a predominantly new phenomenon marking Africa's road to modernity (as Geschiere maintains). Instead, says van Binsbergen, we are talking about the resolution of a tension: between witchcraft as the boundary conditions of the kinship order at the village level, and witchcraft as the idiom of power struggles in modern situations (the context of urban life, formal organizations, the state). Witchcraft is available for appropriation and virtualization by African middle classes and elites in their struggle to create meaning in modernity and postmodernity, precisely because it has traditionally played an important role in defining the moral productive order in many parts of the African continent (van Binsbergen: 19). In this way he is able to account both for its continuity, and for the transformed and virtualized modern context. 'Witchcraft has offered modern Africans an idiom to articulate what otherwise could not be articulated: contradictions between power and meaning, between morality and primitive accumulation, between community and death, between community and the state' (19).

Gerschiere and van Binsbergen agreed that it is the fundamental ambiguity of African witchcraft which allows it to insert itself into the heart of modernity. If it is a discourse of 'power', it is power in a specific context: 'the individualising self-assertion which while challenging the kinship order, constitutes that order at the same time'. This second type of witchcraft discourse – concerned with the articulation of contradictions of self and society in a modern, post-colonial context – offers a relatively benign account of the function and purpose of witchcraft; for the most part it appears to have little to do with the violent manifestations discussed earlier. Van Binsbergen does make some reference to the victimization process, though here it is viewed as the price of transgressive success rather than a question of survival as such:

> Extremely widespread in Africa is the belief that for any type of excessive, transgressive success – such as attaining and maintaining

the status of ruler, divine priest or monopolist trader – a close
kinsman has to be sacrificed or to be nominated as victim of occult,
anti-social forces. I have extensive reason to take such beliefs as
indicative of actual practices. . . . In view of the above discussion
of the kinship order and of witchcraft as its boundary condition,
these beliefs are eminently understandable as ritual evocations of
how these specialist statuses challenge the kinship order through
their individual assertiveness, violence and denial of reciprocity and
community. (van Binsbergen: 14)

Joseph Kufulu Mandunu (1992) has addressed directly the possible application of a Girardian hermeneutic to the question of African witchcraft, specifically the '*kindoki*', the term used in his native Kikongo. He describes how certain categories of illness such as psychosocial disorders, social misfortunes, etc. are attributed to the work of an evildoer ('*ndoki*'). Healing consists in the divination by religious healers of the cause of the disorder, and the subsequent elimination or neutralization of the person deemed responsible (usually a relative or member of the same community). Though the *nganga* or healer is expected to use his powers only for good, he is making use of the same dangerous powers as the *nkoki*.

Kufulu Mandunu outlines two Christian theological approaches to this phenomenon which have been inadequate: suppression (the old mission churches) and accommodation (independent African Churches). In the latter case, witch-finding is incorporated into the socio-therapeutical practices of the church, though it goes against the commandment of neighbourly love. A third approach is argued for, one which acknowledges the real effects of *kindoki* in the lives of Africans, while avoiding the practical implications. Girard's mimetic theory offers a tool for this translation of the gospel into the idiom of African beliefs. Simon Simonse, in a review of Mandunu in *Contagion*, 1995, summarizes as follows:

> The tool for translating the gospel into the idiom of African beliefs
> is Girardian theory. *Kindoki* is the African perception of the human
> reality of deadly mimetic rivalry. The *ndoki* and the drive of the
> community to eliminate the *ndoki* correspond to the scapegoat
> mechanism. The Christian message reveals that the selection of
> the *ndoki* is arbitrary, and that, in fact, in the drive for the victim,
> all are *ndoki*. A Christian practice of divination should therefore
> reverse the arrow of victimage and confront the scapegoaters with
> their *ndoki*-ness. (original emphasis)

Simonse acknowledges the importance of this approach, though expresses reservations as to whether witchcraft practices are identically structured throughout Africa and the rest of the world (as Kufulu Mandunu claims). Simonse also sees the use of Girard's mimetic theory as setting up an unnecessary polarization, since it is a messianic 'great refusal' which condemns (in order to 'redeem') all cultural practices which betray evidence of mimetic rivalry and scapegoating. He wishes to speak up more positively for the rich diversity of our cultural responses to violence. Theologians will recognize this 'Barthian' dimension to Girard's thought, and many will regard it as a fair comment.

> Cultural institutions are not one-dimensional emanations of mimetic dynamics and the scapegoat mechanism. They play a twofold role: they facilitate the operation and, simultaneously, keep their potential violence within certain bounds. Witchcraft as a socially accepted set of beliefs has a regulating function with regards to scapegoating. Divination often functions as a check on the arbitrary selection of witches, and on the outbreak of witch-hunts. The same twofold dynamic of allowing and constraining violence is operative in the institutionalized forms of warfare and economic competition (the latter strongly condemned by Mandunu, p. 224). This openness to the ambiguity of cultural institutions creates a space in which the different cultural experiences, including the African one, can be compared and evaluated.

This is an important nuance, though I would suggest that what Simonse is here presenting as a counter-argument to Girard's mimetic theory is in fact contained within its scope. The twofold role of cultural institutions, of facilitating but also restraining violence, is precisely Girard's description of the violent sacred, whose most dramatic expression is the scapegoat event, but which is also present in preventative or apotropaic form (in a lower dosage as it were) in sacrificial rituals, taboos and myths, as well as apparently non-religious cultural phenomena. Mimetic theory exhibits precisely that 'openness to the ambiguity of cultural institutions' which creates the important critical space Simonse is looking for.[6]

Conclusion

The resounding prophetic words of Franz Fanon which opened this chapter have indicated the way forward for a liberative politics, and how Girard's mimetic theory might help to construct such a politics. Fanon's use of

Girard and Theology

Hegel's 'Master–Slave' dialectic to describe the pathology of post-colonialism is entirely apt, and entirely consonant with Girard's own recognition of the mimetic factors at work in global conflict: for example, in his reading of the crisis engendered by the 9/11 atrocity, he sees the perpetrators as caught up in a simultaneous hatred of and fascination for the West, denoting a 'mimetic crisis on a planetary scale'.

Less dramatically, something similar can be asserted in the later waves of liberation theology, whose analysis, it is suggested, needs to be corrected in a number of ways which are compatible with mimetic theory. In retrospective, it may be said that the encounter in Brazil in 1990 may have been premature; the events of 1989 in Europe were still to be assimilated by all concerned. Certainly in the decade following this encounter, a number of key revisions to liberation theology have taken place which suggests a broader convergence with mimetic theory.

First, the revision of its economic reliance on dependency theory: liberation theologians have continued to identify the roots of global poverty in the systemic inequalities of an unjust capitalist system, but have also acknowledged that there are other factors at play. People are poor because of corruption and poor governance, civil war, environmental disasters, tribal and racial disputes, and a host of other reasons, and not just the systemic impoverishment by richer colonial nations. A refinement of this analysis – in Girardian terms, a readiness to move away from simply 'scapegoating' the West – has been an important element in the maturation of liberation theology. There is a similar refinement in the recent work of Jon Sobrino, a prominent liberation theologian, who has proposed that a discourse on 'the victims' is actually more helpful than the traditional liberationist category 'the poor'. This last category is fraught with difficulty, as people wrestle with socio-economic definitions: a description instead of Christ 'from the perspective of the victims' (Sobrino, 2001) takes us more surely to the heart of the gospel message. Finally Daniel Bell Jr's judgement of liberation theology 'after the end of history' (Bell, 1992) similarly calls for an expansion of the liberationist imagination. For Bell, using a Deleuzian framework, Christianity and capitalism are to be understood as alternative 'disciplines of desire'. Liberation theology's neglect of the theme of 'desire' has been detrimental to its credibility, as it has been seen too often as a negative critique of capitalism, without addressing directly the positive achievements and attractions of a market system on its own terms. As commentators have suggested, liberation theology needs to revise its blanket negative judgement on the market if it is to continue to be taken seriously by social theorists (see the essays on a 'paradigm shift' in liberation theology in de Schrijver, 1998).

Liberation theology can best be understood as one of the voices of theological modernity, expressing with prophetic clarity and gospel urgency the 'dialectic' of that modernity, that is, its shadow side, the brutality and exclusion which seem inevitably to accompany our strivings towards freedom and prosperity. Although the dialogue between Girard and liberationists has not for the most part been sustained, it is clear that there is a great deal of common ground between them. As liberation theology has refined and corrected itself, the commonality has become more evident. It is unlikely now that there will be a reprise of the 1990 colloquium between Girard and liberation theology, but such an event, taking on the 'paradigm shifts' indicated above, would have been an interesting encounter.

Regarding the African utilization of Girardian theory, specifically to understand the phenomenon of witchcraft, I have discerned two poles of discourse. One concerns the fate of the victims: real men, women and children, in their hundreds, who are sacrificed and continue to be sacrificed because of the turbulence and violent chaos of the communities to which they belong. Another theme, less dramatic, has to do with how (often middle class and urban) Africans use the idiom of witchcraft to articulate for themselves the contradictions of modernization. The first of these, humanly speaking, takes priority, and yet the second discussion, about the articulation and resolution of contradictions, offers important signposts and refinements. The first seems to match exactly the template which Girard offers for a society describing its social unrest in mythical terms: the coincidence of witchcraft with political turmoil in South Africa and Uganda, to name just the two examples we have considered, seems undeniable. At the same time, an analysis of less violent manifestations of witchcraft makes clear its function in negotiating the transition to modernity, in a way which also seems consonant with a Girardian perspective. Joseph Kufulu Mandunu sees Girardian theory as a tool for establishing a 'third way' in dealing with the problem of witchcraft. Simply anathematizing witchcraft is ineffective; simply accommodating witchcraft into Christian belief and practice is morally unacceptable. What is required is an approach that acknowledges the reality of witchcraft in people's lives, without their being committed to the practical manifestations of scapegoating.

This critical translation of the gospel into the idiom of African beliefs is reminiscent of the current debates about 'inculturation', in which it has been observed that Western Christianity has had the tendency to veer wildly between the extremes of cultural vandalism and cultural romanticism, with not always very much in between. René Girard's theory has the merit of avoiding these extremes: in insisting upon the ambiguity of all cultures (insofar as they are founded upon a violence, from which they nevertheless struggle to distance themselves) it is able to engage critically with them. The refusal to 'vandalize' the other culture, even when that culture has been as rapacious and exploitative as the European one,

Girard and Theology

brings us back to the post-colonial plea from Franz Fanon: 'We today can do everything, so long as we do not imitate Europe, so long as we are not obsessed by the desire to catch up with Europe. Yet it is very true that we need a model, and that we want blueprints and examples.' It is a plea to outdo Europe, to achieve where Europe has failed, and yet not to mirror Europe. This is to recognize once again that there is a 'dialectic' or ambiguity to European modernity, which must therefore be imitated only selectively and with care.

Commentators have occasionally referred to Girard's work as 'a kind of liberation theology', which is true if the term is carefully understood. In general, as we have seen, he believes liberation as an ideology to be self-defeating, and much of his work is directed in particular at the false claims to emancipation which are made in the name of Freud or Nietzsche. And yet mimetic theory insists on the liberative dimension of the gospel, which for us is manifest at the heart of modernity, and is only comprehensible in terms of its inception. Witchcraft discourses, which as we have seen are both archaic and within modernity, provide the key. In the context of the European witch-hunts, Girard has asserted that '[t]he invention of science is not the reason that there are no longer witch-hunts, but the fact that there are no longer witch-hunts is the reason that science has been invented'. The precise challenge from Girard comes in a highly suggestive passage from his 1986 book, *The Scapegoat*:

> The scientific spirit cannot come first. It presupposes the renunciation of a former preference for the magical causality of persecution so well defined by the ethnologists. Instead of natural, distant and inaccessible causes, humanity has always preferred causes that are significant from a social perspective and which permit of corrective intervention – victims. In order to lead men to the patient exploration of natural causes, men must first be turned away from their victims. This can only be done by showing them that from now on persecutors 'hate without a cause' and without any appreciable result. In order to achieve this miracle, not only among certain exceptional individuals as in Greece, but for entire populations, there is need of the extraordinary combination of intellectual, moral and religious factors found in the Gospel text. The invention of science is not the reason that there are no longer witch-hunts, but the fact that there are no longer witch-hunts is the reason that science has been invented. (Girard, 1986: 204–5)

The persistence of witchcraft beliefs and practices, alongside and within an admittedly problematic and ambiguous scientific modernity, means that this judgement from Girard may need to be re-examined if it is to hold true for the African experience. Nevertheless, Girard's valorization of the Jewish and Christian revelation as the truly 'scientific' demystifying power in European history remains a dominant and disturbing counter-intuition at the core of mimetic theory; the source, for Girard, of all true liberation.

Chapter 11
Girard and the religions

We have been looking at Girardian approaches to the Judaeo-Christian scriptural revelation, where it is argued that to some extent Girard's vulnerability in the fact of hostile or even sceptical scriptural exegetes may be offset by his claim that what he is doing with scripture is immune from their strictures. Girard is simply undertaking a recovery of the practice of figural interpretation, such that the figure of Christ, crucified and risen from the dead, is the *figura* or 'hermeneutical key' for interpreting all of human reality. This ancient practice predates contemporary biblical criticism and should not be molested by it. Put biblically: 'the stone which the builders rejected has become the corner stone'.

As we have seen, an early example of figural interpretation is found in the Acts of the Apostles, where the Ethiopian eunuch, on pilgrimage in Jerusalem, tries to make sense of the Suffering Servant passage from Isaiah, asking Philip: 'does the writer speak of himself or of someone else?'

In this encounter, and in this question, is the starting-point for a discussion of mimetic theory in relation to non-Christian religious traditions. Who is the suffering victim? Does the description in Isaiah point us exclusively and ultimately to Christ (who is in turn the key to all human suffering, the 'Lamb of God' who stands for all victims of whatever time and place)? In which case, there is a concern to be addressed about Christian exclusivism, since a rigorous assertion of this hermeneutical key would seem to devalue and depreciate what other religions may have to say about the overcoming of sacred violence.

The revelation of Holy Week

Confronting the issue of 'Girard and the religions' is a salutary exercise because it brings mimetic theory up against its own potential dogmatism and particularity; these must be addressed if its general claims are to be upheld. It has not proved an easy dialogue, as was appreciated at a Colloquium in Boston, 2000, which took as its ambitious theme 'Violence and Institution in Christianity, Judaism, Hinduism, Buddhism and Islam'.

Girard and the Religions

The exchanges from this conference will form the bulk of this chapter, as much for what they have to say about conversational method as for their content, but we will begin with an elaboration of the 'hermeneutical key' as Girardian theory understands the Judaeo-Christian revelation, so as better to assess concerns about Girard's Christocentrism.

Girard's conversion experience in 1959 coincided with the Christian holy season of Lent and Easter, as we have seen; the weeks of anxiety about his health, and the joyful news of an 'all-clear' from his doctor, mapped onto the transition from Lenten penance to the Easter commemoration of Jesus' death and Resurrection. Girard sees his own life in these terms: 'Never before had I experienced a feast to compare with this liberation. I saw myself as dead, and suddenly I was risen.'

As far as mimetic theory is concerned, this is far from being a biographical coincidence. The initial insights into the nature of desire (mimetic) and social formation (scapegoating) came to him from modern European literature, but they did not originate there. Girard's use of Resurrection language to describe his intellectual discoveries, as well as his own release from anxiety, is a recognition that both are ultimately rooted in the Paschal mystery, the suffering, death and Resurrection of Christ. We have seen how other authors have thought similarly: the literary theorist Erich Auerbach argues that unique Western modes of representing reality, or *mimesis*, are shaped by the figural mode of interpretation, centred on the suffering, dying and risen Christ. The systematic theologian Raymund Schwager, following von Balthasar, constructs revelation as a drama whose *dénouement* is very precisely structured around the events of Holy Week. To refer again to Schwager's five act scheme, it is in Act II that the opposition to Jesus' preaching of the Kingdom becomes apparent. The 'dramatic' tension between human and divine freedom is revealed – our resistance to the light – a resistance which catalyses the events of Acts III, IV and V.

It is worth staying with the liturgical dimension of Girardian mimetic theory for a moment. Certainly as far as the Roman Catholic celebrations of Holy Week are concerned, there is much that lends itself to a mimetic interpretation. In fact it is possible to see Holy Week, as interpreted ritualistically by the Church, as a kind of 'Girardian pedagogy'. Two examples will suffice. First, the 'role' of the crowd, played by the congregation gathered for Mass: in the traditional celebration for Palm Sunday, 1 week before Easter Sunday, the triumphant entry of Jesus into Jerusalem is re-enacted, with the congregation waving branches and singing *hosannas* in welcome of the Messiah. Then, immediately, the priest leads the congregation in a dramatized reading of the Passion, with the crowd calling out 'Crucify Him!' at the appropriate moments. For a Girardian, the 'logic' of this sudden transition is evident: 'see what we are like, see how swiftly our mood can swing and our allegiance be totally switched around, even within the space of a few days.' Holy Week begins with a very harsh 'anthropological' lesson, about the volatile nature of mob sentiment, especially when mobilized for nationalistic or religious ends.

The second example concerns the readings which are proclaimed during the celebration of the Passion proper, on Good Friday. One of these is the strange prophecy from the book of Isaiah, which we have already examined: the Song of the Suffering Servant which puzzled the Ethiopian eunuch until he asked Philip to explain it to him. For Girard this is culmination and climax of the Old Testament's insight into the innocence of the suffering victim. What is especially powerful is to read this text alongside the traditional Good Friday 'Reproaches' which within the Roman Catholic liturgy are said or sung as the congregation venerates the Cross on which Jesus was crucified. The refrain is an anguished cry from God:

> O my people, what have I done to you?
> How have I hurt you? Answer me!

The anthem is a haunting litany of the blessings which God has poured out on his people, and the torturers and insults which they have vented on His Son in return. The message is sharp and clear: all the violence of Good Friday comes from spiteful human beings, and is in no way to be attributed to God, whose bountiful goodness has been returned with cruelty. Once again, there is a very powerful pedagogy at work.

There are two reasons for this liturgical excursus. First, taking seriously the Holy Week setting of the 'Theo-Drama' should remind us that religious texts or scriptures do not stand alone, but are embodied in communal practices such as liturgy, and that we should look for analogous settings when we come to consider the sacred texts of other religions. Most importantly, however, is what comes to light if we compare the clear-sighted message of the 'Reproaches' with the confused bewilderment of the Suffering Servant song of Isaiah 52. Here is the crucial difference that Girard is trying to highlight: the Suffering Servant song, for all that it insists on a innocence of the victim, is still a 'mixed text', in that there are traces still of sacred violence: 'it was the will of the Lord to punish him'. God is still somehow complicit in the violence which has been vented onto this man – this is the source of the confusion of the bystanders, who really do not know what to make of it. With the 'Reproaches' there is no such confusion and no such ambiguity. The violence which destroys Jesus is clearly ascribed to its true source: the scandalized mob. In the very moment that Christians gather in veneration of Jesus, dead on the Cross, an ancient liturgical hymn forbids them from sanctifying its violence by placing it on God's shoulders.

The difference between the 'Reproaches' and the Song of the Servant is like an optician adjusting a lens; what was blurred and indistinct has now become crystal clear. The challenge of Girard and of mimetic theory to non-Christian faiths is simply stated: do these traditions contain texts (especially texts which are embedded in practices of liturgy and worship) which perform the same task, of clarifying the link between religious assertion and exclusionary violence, and which do it to the same degree as the Christian gospel? Girard does not claim that such a process is absent altogether, but that as a matter of empirical fact no religious culture or institution has done a demonstratively better job of 'deconstructing' sacred violence than Christianity, and those cultures which have been substantially exposed to the Christian revelation.

A stuttering conversation: Boston 2000

With this in mind, let us turn to the Boston Colloquium of 2000, which undertook a comparative study of 'violence and institution' across five different faith traditions. A distinction which Robert Daly introduced early on, between 'normative' and 'descriptive' accounts, has been used before, as we have seen when discussing whether Christianity was a 'sacrificial religion.' This distinction sought to get at what religions aspire to by way of non-violence or critique of violence (normative), and what in actual fact has occurred through history, by way of inquisitions, holy wars, crusades and exclusionary prejudice (descriptive).[1]

While there is a note of disappointment that the exchanges did not go as well as hoped, for various organizational reasons, there is much to be learnt from the various contributions if we see this as COV&R's first, 'stammering' venture into new territory. The successful reception of papers depended in part on the familiarity of the speakers with mimetic theory, and their willingness to engage with it. There is a rather lively exchange between Rabbi Reuven Kimmelman, and his respondent Sandor Goodhart: Kimmelman's 'legalistic' survey of Jewish traditions concerning warfare is stingingly castigated by Goodhart, for its twin neglect both of Girardian mimetic theory and of the tradition of prophetic, ethical Judaism to which Goodhart adheres. To this extent, he suggests, Kimmelman is waging a 'holy war' against interpretations other than his own.

Though Goodhart later softens his critique, he insists on calling attention to the interplay between text and history which he feels his interlocutor has missed out, and which is central to the claims of mimetic theory: '[i]t is never clear that the Rabbis were offering any commentary whatsoever on what actually happened – politically, historically, morally, or otherwise, except as what actually happened passed through scripture' (70). This is a matter of reading and praying, never of sacrifice; if we are dealing with texts, not history, says Goodhart, we are asking about scriptural context, and therefore about its prophetic significance.[2]

The paper from Qamar-ul Huda, on 'The Problems of Violence and Conflict in Islam' is an extended survey of how such problems derive from the Islamic conception of God as perfect and unitary Peace. The life of an individual Muslim is conceived as a struggle – *jihâd* – to achieve a connection with this peaceful divine consciousness. Huda goes on to consider Qur'ânic verses on violence, before outlining a 'new hermeneutics' for an Islamic liberation theology, one which not only reinterprets the concepts and vocabulary of Islam, but seeks to answer 'something very elementary: whether or not the acting, doing and thinking of surrendering are really freeing us' (96). Though this is argued for as a return to the original message of the Prophet, it will also entail the unshackling of many layers of dogmatic thinking and doing.

In other words, Huda is also trying to work within the dichotomy of descriptive and normative, to envisage a normative version of liberative Islam which is certainly compatible with mimetic theory. He underlines the point by using the word *islâm* in the lower case, meaning 'the personal piety of surrendering to the divine and the journey of making one's faith meaningful' (81), as distinct from a capitalized Islam which denotes the impersonal institutional, political and cultural dimensions. The response from the Christian theologian Robert Hamerton-Kelly prefers to stay with the latter however. As far as mimetic theory is concerned, all the great religions are more or less in reaction against the pagan sacred, against generative violence of the 'pagan sacred', and 'one of the marks of their greatness resides in the candor with which they address the problem of the residual sacred violence in themselves' (99).

He does not entirely find such candour in Huda's paper, having already found it lacking in Reuven Kimmelman's presentation on Judaism. It seems that in the so-called Abrahamic faiths a strong assertion of monotheism coincides with a recognition of the innocence of the victim; nevertheless, the residues of sacral violence need to be accounted for. With this, Hamerton-Kelly puts his finger on the 'neuralgic' points of Islamic tradition: the history of warfare; the attitude towards non-Muslims or towards Muslims who convert; the alleged priority of the Mecca and Medina *suras* of the Qur'ân; and finally the treatment of women, specifically the relation of Islam and clitoridectomy. Hudar acknowledges the validity of these concerns, but they are more to do with 'the capital "I" Islam, the institutional Islam, the cultural/social/political Islam' which he has chosen not to speak about. In the wide-ranging discussion which follows Huda's clarifications, at least one voice expresses the uncomfortable possibility that the COV&R group is instinctively 'scapegoating' Islam, though there appears to be at least the beginnings of a genuine dialogue.

The presentation on Hinduism is different from the preceding ones in that it is not given by an adherent of that faith. Francis X. Clooney, a Jesuit, emphasizes his reluctance to simplify the reality of Hinduism, let alone its understanding of violence and non-violence. Within these parameters, he examines a variety of strategies within Hinduism for resolving the problem of sacrificial violence: by internalization; substitutions; renunciation and non-violence. He also describes resources within Mimamsa ritual theory and Vedanta theology for limiting violence according to the intention of the actor, as well as the political aspects of state coercion. Clooney goes beyond the previous presenters, however, in arguing that a sociological perspective is needed to supplement the exegesis of scholarly texts, and he refers us to two instances of contemporary work: Beth Roy's analysis of riots between Hindu and Muslim villagers in Bangla Desh in the 1950s, and the writings of Mahasweta Devi, an activist who has written extensively about the victims of violence, especially tribal people. A properly theological analysis of the phenomenon of violence and non-violence in India requires attention to both classical textual materials and other literary and social resources.

Clooney's closing comments merit our attention. He recognizes that a Christian viewpoint may see the Hindu scheme deficient, given the lack of a valorization of suffering (such as we find in the notion of sacrifice), or of the sense of the victim. But this can be misleading if we are looking at local or isolated parts of the comparison:

> But comparative study also and more immediately tells us that such deficiencies are rarely as significant as they may seem to have been, before one knows enough about another tradition actually to begin to understand how it works. 'Deficiencies' are more often signs of larger differences in traditions. What is valuable in one tradition 'disappears' (or never appeared) in another tradition which is configured differently in its parts and as a whole. From a Hindu perspective, if indeed there is no real vocabulary of victims this is probably because (as just mentioned) there is a different sense of human experience and agency in the face of the possibility of violence. The question is then turned back upon the Christian observer: can the Christian tradition of reflection on violence and non-violence find room for reflection on violence and non-violence which is not based on the image and vocabulary of oppression, victims, and suffering for others? (137)

For 'Christian tradition' here, read 'mimetic theory'. And here is the rub. What is the reaction of Girardian theory when it encounters, not neglect or hostility, but simple incomprehension? A religious tradition which does not have the straightforward vocabulary and concepts of mimetic desire and victimization may seem, from the viewpoint of mimetic theory, highly deficient, as Clooney maintains. And yet here is a gaping temptation, to leap in and supply what is missing: to finish the sentence of the stammerer for him, instead of patiently allowing him to speak, however falteringly. The painstaking task of genuine interreligious dialogue does not mesh easily with the impatient zeal of mimetic theorists to share insights which are at once highly generative and very simple.[3]

The final exchange of the 2000 encounter, Christopher Ives on 'Dharma and Destruction: Buddhist Institutions and Violence' with Leo D. Lefebure responding, presses this issue further. According to Hamerton-Kelly, Ives is the most successful in speaking with 'candour' about the residual violence in his respective tradition, namely Buddhism, especially given the general perception of gentle monks in saffron, the Dalai Lama, and so on. In fact, says Ives, the Buddhist reputation as a religion of non-violence is betrayed by its historical record, and proceeds to list hair-raising examples, even in recent contexts such as Japan, Korea and the early decades of the Chinese Revolution. The various justifications of this violence are then discussed.

Ives finds a number of points are enlightened by a Girardian analysis, though he has reservations about mimetic theory's applicability to Buddhism (170–2), especially given its apparent lack of ritual sacrifice. He is unsure whether the catch-all term 'pagan' to describe non-Christian religions is helpful, similarly the assumption that all these religions are doing the same thing, that is, struggling to overcome the 'pagan sacred'. Nevertheless, there is a role for mimetic theory in that it can help Buddhists bring actual historical Buddhism into line with its core doctrine of non-violence – his own historical survey having indicated how extensive a gap there is between them.

What needs to be avoided is the kind of engagement which Leo D. Lefebure warns about in his response, where the 'application' of mimetic theory to all kinds of religious phenomena becomes another version of 'Orientalism', such that 'only Western concepts are capable of understanding Asia's experience' (176). A two-way conversation around the core themes of mimetic theory (the mimetic construction of desire as the core of human identity; the surrogate victimage mechanism; the uniqueness of the biblical revelation) is a provocative challenge to Buddhist perspectives, which can respond from its own resources – provided the exclusive claims of mimetic theory are not allowed to drive out non-biblical religious voices from the conversation.

Lefebure has explored this previously in another essay, on Socially Engaged Buddhism, interestingly subtitled an 'overture to a dialogue' (Lefebure, 1996). He notes the similarity between Buddhism and mimetic theory in their respective denials of an autonomous independent self, and in their concern for awakening from illusions of selfhood and desire. However, a dialogue will be impossible unless the Western stereotypical notions of Buddhism (deriving from Arthur Schopenhauer and Max Weber) are rejected. These hold Buddhism to be pessimistic and world negating, with the notion of *karma* interpreted in fatalistic terms. Girard himself is taken to task for holding to this stereotype: Lefebure quotes from a 1981 interview in which Girard declares himself 'profoundly Greco-biblical-occidental in contrast to this complete nirvanesque renunciation' (Lefebure, 1996: 122).

For Lefebure, this oppositional attitude is merely indicative of Girard's depreciation of all non-biblical religions, 'as chaneling violence but powerless to break the cycle of violence'. This exclusivist claim is 'almost Barthian', and sits ill at ease both with the biblical revelation itself (which recognized the value of wisdom cultures outside Israel) and Christian theological tradition, from Justin Martyr in the second century through to Karl Rahner in the twentieth. In the famous phrase from the Vatican II document *Nostrae Aetate*, the Church 'rejects nothing of what is true and holy' in other faith traditions.

Lefebure takes this as his cue for an extensive investigation of Girardian and Buddhist similarities, beginning with the resonances between Girard's intersubjective view of the self and the no-self of Buddhism. Lefebure asserts that the link between mimeticism and scapegoating is present in the teaching of the Buddha, though implicit in comparison to Girard's formulation.

What we do have in Buddhism are precise prescriptions for dealing with the problem, even if that problem is not as delineated as in mimetic theory. Concrete strategies such as meditation practice are the ways to take responsibility for one's feelings and desires and dealing with them appropriately. Such practice is 'not a struggle against desire but rather a heightening of awareness of desire' (133). It is this practice, rather than any theoretical correspondence, which resonates most strongly when he compares with Girard's account of conversion in *Deceit, Desire and the Novel*.

Regarding 'Girard and the Religions': the view of sympathetic interlocutors such as Leo D. Lefebure, and indeed of much of Christian tradition, is that René Girard's Christocentric claims should not be understood in rigorously exclusivist terms. In fact, Girard clarifies this, in the discussion at the 2000 Colloquium once again: mimetic theory does indeed put forward an 'exclusivist' claim, but it is not a question of who does and does not have the truth. As Daly's distinction between 'descriptive' and 'normative' implies, there is no religion that has fully lived up to its ideals of non-violence. The 'truth' of sacred violence and its overcoming is not the unique possession of any faith tradition, and there is no justification for supersessionism. 'Rather it's a question of language we all have to use. Ninety percent of the words we use to talk about this are exclusively Western (e.g. the idea of "humanity")'. The task is to present an alternative language, which may look as if it is antagonistic but is in fact really an expansion of and improvement on what was there before. The Enlightenment, which thought of itself as excluding institutional Christianity was in fact a broadening out of Christian perspectives; Girard thinks something similar is happening today (189).

It is also the case that recent writings by Girard have softened the accusation of an exclusivist Christocentricism. In *Evolution and Conversion*, he claims to find rich material in the Indian *Vedas* to illustrate the phenomena of mimetic rivalry and its relation to sacrifice (Girard, 2007a: 62). But there are also Indian traditions which go beyond simple description: 'the mimetic theory does not exclude the possibility that a given society or religious group could reach a form of radical awareness of the violence nature of human beings', the Jains being cited as an example (212–13). Nevertheless, his verdict on the 2000 COV&R conference repeats his customary answer to the question which we posed at the beginning of this chapter: are there texts in other religious traditions which present the truth with the same powerful lucidity as the Christian Gospel?

> What I gathered in that conference is that all these religions are fully aware, from a normative standpoint, of the injustice of violence and I fully acknowledge that the Eastern traditions have contributed in making those societies less violent. They know that the human being should withdraw from anger, resentment, envy, violence, but they are not fully aware of the scapegoat mechanism. They know what sacrifice is and they progressively try to forbid it. The difference that I see between them and Christianity is that the latter was able to formulate in the Gospels and unmask in a full light the anthropological mechanism of mimetic scapegoating and sacrifice. (214)

The 2000 Colloquium was a watershed for mimetic theory and the religions, though it seems to be as significant for its limitations and stuttering beginnings, as for the insights achieved and shared. Robert Daly sums up the key points in his Epilogue: amid the intensive conversation, a pull towards scapegoating and mimetic hostility on the part of participants was recognized and repented; there is also an acknowledgement that mimetic theory is a Western theory, which has something to offer non-Western cultures provided it is not applied in a Procrustean manner; at the same time there is a keener awareness of the limits of mimetic theory's exportability (Daly, 2002: 196). It is interesting to note that Daly refers to the Jesuit philosopher and theologian Bernard Lonergan, on conversion as an indispensable aspect of the move from violence to non-violence. Lonergan understands the term on several levels – intellectual and ethical as well as religious – and though his system largely failed to provide the methodological structure that Daly hoped for, this concept at least brings us back to the centre of Girardian thinking, as explored in the opening chapter. And it is encouraging that Leo D. Lefebure's account of Buddhist mediation practice may have something to offer Girardian theory: concrete strategies by which the goal of renouncing mimetic violence may be achieved. The conversation needs to be two-way.

We may wish to return here to the difficulty which Walter Lowe articulated in his essay 'Christ and Salvation', and which we explored in an earlier chapter. There is no place here to explore the theme of 'salvation' in other religious traditions, but such a discussion is central to what is at stake here. As Lowe puts it, the danger with contemporary approaches to soteriology is that a prefatory notion of salvation has to be offered before we can begin to speak of Christ. The narrative which needs to be constructed will contain a general *description*, a specific *diagnosis*, a general *recommendation* and a specific *remedy* (Lowe, 2003: 235). But how are we to bridge the gap between general recommendation and specific remedy? Or in the present case, from the problem of sacred violence, to Christ as its definitive resolution? As the discussion so far has indicated, it may be the case that a common, interreligious description of the problem has to be arrived at, and it is far from obvious that this will be possible.

In this respect, there is a tension between the clean, streamlined attractiveness of mimetic theory – which perhaps commends itself to a jaded post-Christian culture in need of refreshment – and the painstaking labour of authentic interreligious dialogue. Whatever the zealous impatience of mimetic theorists, there can be no short-cut to this kind of engagement. In cases where even the basic vocabulary of mimetic theory is lacking, such as 'victim', 'mimetic desire', and so on, what may be needed is a patient search for analogies, rather than a triumphant demonstration of straight correspondences. To use the phrase of Lefebure, such a conversation may as yet be only an 'overture to a dialogue'.

There remains a specific set of difficulties regarding the relationship of mimetic theory to Islam; here too we might want to speak of an 'overture to a dialogue'. The responses of Girard and other mimetic theoreticians to the attacks of 9/11 are treated in several places in this book, and it is perhaps inevitable that this event should colour perceptions. Girard's initial response was to see the atrocity as a massive outburst of mimetic rivalry which is now on a planetary scale, with Islam merely being one symptomatic expression. While never rejecting this view, he later qualifies it by stressing the specifically religious aspect. Islamist extremism is an example of a return of the archaic sacred, for which the West is quite unprepared, particularly when the respective attitudes towards death and martyrdom are considered. It is this which, for Girard, makes the present crisis of the 'war on terror' more frightening than the crises of the Cold War. Communism at least was operating out of a humanist paradigm, just like the West, so that systems of deterrence could operate with a degree of predictability. Khruschev's recalling of the missiles during the Cuban crisis of 1963 is a recognizable action, 'turning the other cheek'. With the readiness of Islamist bombers to 'sacrifice' themselves and others, to love death more than life, as we are told, we are plunged into a new and frighteningly unknown world.

As Hamerton-Kelly insisted at the Boston Colloquium 2000, according to mimetic theory the monotheistic religions, including Islam, are 'a powerful antidote to the pagan sacred'; the growth of monotheism goes hand in hand with an increasing awareness of the victim (as with the Servant Songs of Deutero-Isaiah). How can this potential for compassion be harnessed, therefore, in resistance to extremism? Among the many facets of this challenge is a hermeneutical one: interpretation of the Qu'ran, especially of key verses and concepts such as *jihad*.

Here we come across the question of *naskh*, or 'abrogation' (Wicker, 2006: 2–3). which refers to a way of adjudicating a potential difference of meaning between two Qur'anic verses. If a preference is made, then the earlier verse, according to some scholars, is held to be superseded or 'abrogated'. This has meant were militant readings of the later, so-called Medinan 'sword verse', being favoured over an earlier pacific one (see Afsaruddin, 2006: 15–31), as well as the more violent understandings of *jihad* and *shahid* (martyrdom) have come to hold sway. It is difficult to see how extremism can be overcome without addressing the use and abuse of the doctrine of *naskh*. And yet, Islam lacks a central doctrinal authority which takes on this decision.

Whatever is the way forward with this, I mention it here as a point of contact between Islamic hermeneutics and mimetic theory. The Christian gospel, as understood by mimetic theory, does indeed carry elements of both abrogation and supersessionism which properly understood should help rather than hinder interreligious understanding. For Girard, the primitive sacred is annulled and abrogated by the revelatory self-offering of Christ on the cross. The crucifixion reveals the innocence of all victims and the ineffectiveness of all attempts at social order which are founded on victimhood. This 'revealed' perspective of course supersedes, has priority over, the system it has exposed as worthless. At best such systems might imply or hint at the truth, just as in figural interpretation the figure points towards Christ.

What makes this acceptable is a change in meaning for the word 'supersessionism'; it is usually taken to mean the doctrine by which Christianity has 'superseded', rendered null or made redundant, the religious dispensation of the Jewish people – for most people, an unacceptable assertion of superiority. By contrast, what Girard describes and celebrates is the annulment of the 'violent sacred', the false transcendence which underpins and justifies the actions of the scapegoating mob. This is indeed 'supersessionist', but not in a way that privileges any group or faith community over others.

It may be that Islam has in its notion of *naskh*, or 'abrogation', a concept which can open up possibilities for mimetic awareness. As mentioned above, the struggle for pacific rather than militant versions of Islam would seem to require a modification of this doctrine, in such a way that violent interpretations are not given priority.

This looks to be the Girardian way of proceeding, not just for Islam but with the other faiths also. It means the assertion of a robust supersession, not of one group or faith tradition by another, but the 'abrogation' of the false and violent sacred – no matter in which faith tradition it raises its head – to be replaced by a transcendence which is truly merciful. It may be that contestation of terms such as *jihad* and *shahid*, can be seen as precisely analogous to the history and meaning of the words 'sacrifice' and 'martyr' in Christianity. If so, such terms carry within themselves the long history of humanity's religious adventure.

Chapter 12
Girard and the theologians

Girard's astounding hypothesis has elicited a wide range of responses over the past 35 years. While its broad outlines are clear enough, it is still too early to say how significant its impact will prove to be: Chris Fleming ventures the opinion that an overall judgement is premature. James Williams declares that 'there are those who believe that by the middle of the twenty-first century, if not before, Girard will be known as one of the intellectual pioneers of the twentieth century. I am one of those holding that opinion' (Williams, J., 1988: 320). Those who would concur with Williams as to the seminal importance of Girard's contribution have met since 1990 as an international Colloquium (COV&R) to explore his ideas, while a French research group is also in existence. An even more recent development is the establishment of Imitatio Inc. for the furtherance of mimetic theory, which we will examine below.

There have been several extended assessments of Girard's work, including special editions of journals such as *Diacritics* (1978), *Sciences Religieuses/Studies in Religion* (1981) and *Etudes* (1973). *Violence et Vérité: Autour de René Girard* (Dumouchel, 1985) summarizes a conference at Cerisy, and is partially translated in *Violence and Truth* (Dumouchel, 1988). *To Honor René Girard* (Juilland, 1986) is a *Festschrift* for Girard's 60th birthday. These collections show varying degrees of allegiance to the mimetic theory: all testify to its immense impact across a wide range of disciplines.

Regarding specifically theological engagement: Hans Urs von Balthasar offers a respectful critique of Girard and Raymund Schwager in his *Theodramatik* (1980), while the work of Robert Daly has been strongly marked by his reading of Girard, as we have seen in our discussion on sacrifice. William Schweiker (1990) has shown the importance of the mimetic theory for theological hermeneutics. James Alison's enthusiasm is evident throughout his writings, as he has applied it to the doctrines of the resurrection, to original sin, to eschatology and soteriology. Other British theologians who have given sympathetic appraisals include Rowan Williams (1985) and Fergus Kerr (1986: 81–2; 1992a; 1992b), though the latter has since expressed more reservations. John Milbank has acknowledged his indebtedness to Girard in *Theology and Social Theory* (1990), but his overall assessment is very guarded – despite, as has been remarked, the broad similarity of their respective projects. We have noted the 1992 symposium on Dramatic Theology in Innsbruck, which undertook an examination of Raymund Schwager's Girard-inspired *Theo-Drama*, and charts the construction of a research programme which continues still.

Regarding the more negative responses, we have to recognize a misunderstanding and downright carelessness of some of his commentators, Haydon White, and a number of feminist critiques being notable examples.[1] The number of such misreadings should give pause for thought, however. Among the fears most commonly expressed is that of totalization, the sense that Girard offers yet another 'grand narrative' of the oppressive kind associated with 'modernity'. Charles Davis has written an ultimately unfavourable review of Girard's work, in which he declares:

> The difficulty with a hermeneutic of suspicion, to use Ricoeur's phrase, or with the critique of systematically distorted communication, to adopt Habermas' analysis, or with the uncovering of a mechanism of structuration under the written text, to adopt Girard's account, is that there is no innocent starting point, no absolute beginning, no unquestionable *a priori*. Suspicion, critique, uncovering: all can be turned upon oneself. This should keep us humble and prevent us putting forward grandiose systems and universal visions . . . apart from the multiple questionableness of Girard's theory, there is this basic inconsistency: in the name of nonviolence, he is advocating the kind of exclusiveness that has been an endless source of violence in Christian history.[2]

Jean-Marie Domenach (1988: 159) expresses similar misgivings:

> If I voice an objection, is it to avoid succumbing to the seductiveness of an audacity that would return Christ on the cross to the centre of the world? It seems to me it is out of fear of meeting up again with some demons I thought I had exorcized: the claim to close off in a global explanation, the myth of a social transparency finally realized, the dream of a City that the Spirit would penetrate and dedicate to the Good. In short, a desire to know that does not know its limits and claims suddenly to illuminate all history, past, present and yet to come, like a pyrotechnics expert igniting a Catherine wheel. The tragic, in my view, will continue its dialogue with certitude. For there will subsist until the end a share of night that is not the reverse side of day, but the place for the propagation of light.

Girard and Theology

Here it is important to draw attention to the modesty of the Girardian scheme as well as its audacity. As James Alison suggests, we have here a *petite idée* of infinite applicability,[3] rather than yet another totalizing system – an idea, moreover, that Girard is more than happy to be 'turned against' him in the manner Davis suggests. Quite a few of Girard's critics differ with him on the question of sacrifice, but as we have dealt at length with his own change of perspective on this theme, I would suggest that the remaining theological themes or objections can be considered under three headings:

1. 'The slaughter bench of historical Christianity'
2. Girard's God
3. Girard's gnosticism

1. 'The slaughter bench of historical Christianity'
We should address what seems to be the most glaring objection to mimetic theory. The anthropological claims about mimetic desire and the scapegoating mechanism have at least an initial plausibility. But in the third phase Girard goes on to claim that the scapegoat mechanism is fully unmasked in the New Testament. Why, then, in the course of the Church's history, have so many events occurred which follow the same pattern of original collective persecutions? Specifically, how is it that, despite its most cherished texts standing in total opposition to persecutory myth, Christianity could bring itself to tolerate the coercion of heretics, Jews and witches? The single, most telling counter-example to Girard's theory, in other words, is the bloodstained history of the Christian church.

This objection has taken several forms. First of all, as has been noted there are Girardian thinkers who see the claims about Christian revelation as separable from the valuable anthropological insights of mimetic theory: for these commentators, this objection is irrelevant. A second approach is to confront the difficulty head-on and deny outright that there is any special demystifying power in the gospel texts. Burton Mack has gone so far as to claim the opposite, that the gospel stories themselves are, in their very structure, precisely the kind of persecution text which (according to Girard) are meant to unveil and deconstruct (McKenna, 1985: 135–65). Written as they are at a painful juncture in Jewish-Christian relations, namely the 'parting of the ways', their scapegoating of the Jewish people as the rejecters and killers of Christ is not incidental, it is crucial to their theological structure.

Mack's objection invites a response on the level of New Testament exegesis, such as Robert Hamerton-Kelly (1994) who is at pains to disallow the charge of anti-Semitism: the gospels make it clear that *everyone* was united against Jesus. The Jewish and Roman authorities joined the mob in complete harmony, and even the disciples, in fleeing and denying him,

Girard and the Theologians

succumbed to the universal mimeticism of the scapegoat. That later generations of Christians should corrupt these insights into an excuse for persecuting the Jews is not the fault of the evangelical text as such. But this still leaves us with the overall objection, that the demystifying potential of the gospels has simply never been sufficiently realized in the history of Christianity. It may be possible, therefore, to acknowledge the validity of the mimetic theory in the broad sense, but then to say 'so what?' The contribution of Christians and Christian institutions to the 'slaughter bench of history' has been so immense, and improvement negligible by comparison – surely any allegedly emancipatory insights in the Gospel narratives have been nullified.

Lucien Scubla likewise questions Girard's radical claims concerning the uniqueness of Christianity, since his own readings of the New Testament and of pre-Christian religious traditions lead him to assert that 'the devaluation of sacrifice is neither the distinctive attribute of Christianity nor the major theme of Christ's teaching; and that the gospels cannot lay exclusive claim to the revelation of the violent foundations of human society' (Dumouchel, 1988: 161). The notion of a 'formidable rupture' that is posited in *Things Hidden* is simply not borne out by the evidence; Christ seems more concerned to radicalize kinship conventions than notions of sacrifice.[4] Domenach's contribution in the same collection speaks up for the narratives (from Socrates on) which are excluded by the imperialism of the Girardian hypothesis, the 'violence done to history itself, in order to usher in the reign of non-violent love . . . . This history is marked not only by advances in decoding but by moral acts, by spiritual, intellectual and aesthetic inventiveness' (Dumouchel, 1988: 157), an objection that has also been raised against Girard's treatment of non-Christian religions.

Girard insists to the contrary, that the transformation wrought by the Gospel is far from negligible. The history of the West's move away from scapegoating (such as it is), and of our desacralized world, which effortlessly sees through scapegoating processes and makes us instinctive partisans for the victim – this history is the product not of an Enlightenment rationality, banishing the darkness of religious superstition, but of the evangelical impulse itself. It is the Paraclete, the advocate for the defence, at work in history, informing and transforming culture and its institutions, who has effected and continues to effect this stupendous change. We have already examined Girard's audacious reversal of the accepted version of events at the dawn of modernity, set out in the final chapter of *The Scapegoat*, 'History and the Paraclete':

> The scientific spirit cannot come first. It presupposes the
> renunciation of a former preference for the magical causality of

persecution so well defined by the ethnologists. Instead of natural, distant and inaccessible causes, humanity has always preferred causes that are *significant from a social perspective and which permit of corrective intervention* – victims. In order to lead men to the patient exploration of natural causes, men must first be turned away from their victims. This can only be done by showing them that from now on persecutors 'hate without cause' and without any appreciable result.

There have indeed been breakthroughs of this order, as in Greece – but only in the case of exceptional individuals. How is such a miracle to be achieved across whole populations? Only 'the extraordinary combination of intellectual, moral and religious factors found in the Gospel text' can bring about such a 'miracle':

> The invention of science is not the reason that there are no longer witch-hunts, but the fact that there are no longer witch-hunts is the reason that science has been invented. The scientific spirit, like the spirit of enterprise in an economy, is a by-product of the profound action of the Gospel text. The modern Western world has forgotten the revelation in favor of its by-products, making them weapons and instruments of power; and now the process has turned against it. Believing itself a liberator, it discovers its role as a persecutor. (Girard, 1986: 204–5)

A thesis of such breadth defies easy assessment; what it does call for is careful reconstruction of the origins of modernity, perhaps an 'archaeology' in Foucault's sense. To this degree, Girard qualifies as a 'postmodern', as Gerard Loughlin points out (1997: 96–103), and his entire work may be regarded as a plea for one of the voices excluded by modernity – the voice of Christian revelation – to be given a fair hearing. The project that comes closest to Girard's here is John Milbank's phenomenal work, *Theology and Social Theory* (1990), together with the theological project arising from this known as 'Radical Orthodoxy'. Milbank puts forward a detailed critique of Girard's work, which he describes (like his own) as a revival of an Augustinian 'two cities' philosophy of history, centred on the question of sacred violence. However, Milbank contends that Girard fails to move beyond what is effectively a liberal Protestant, 'modernist' position towards a genuinely postmodern theology.

Milbank elsewhere expresses deep reservations about the 'quest for sacrifice', arguing that recent attempts by Girard and others (Walter Burkert, Maurice Bloch, Nancy Jay, Luce Irigaray) merely continue a distorted nineteenth-century obsession: 'Why is it that sacrifice should have exercised such a lure upon Victorian discourses, to the degree that they were "framed" by what they purport to "frame", seduced by the object of their own fascination?' (Milbank, 1996: 31). Their approach presents a fearful temptation for Christians, one which involves 'a confusion of evolutionism (any account of a necessitated history) with typology'. It is this uneasiness which shapes Milbank's appraisal of Girard's 'renewal' of the nineteenth-century quest. Girard is one of those 'modern, enlightened reasoners about sacrifice [who have] found themselves captured by sacrificial reason', thereby substituting themselves for the old priests as the new, scientific priests (Milbank, 1996: 31).

Milbank similarly draws attention to the absence in Girard's theory of a positive alternative to sacred violence, a 'counter-sacrificial practice'. For Milbank, the only reason for attributing a unique significance to Christ is to 'call our attention to, and to reinforce, a discovery in the "shape" of Jesus' life and death, of the type of an exemplary practice which we can imitate and which form the context for our lives together, so that we can call ourselves "the body of Christ"' (Milbank, 1990: 396). He finds Girard wanting because his positivist 'extrinsicism' fails to incorporate 'the imaginative and therefore the practical possibilities of the exemplary narratives'. It should be said that Milbank misreads Girard in important respects, as Fergus Kerr maintains in a detailed defence titled 'Rescuing Girard's Argument?' (Kerr, 1992a). Kerr suggests that their projects are in fact so close together, that Milbank has had to work hard to differentiate them. Girard in turn wonders if Milbank's philosophical approach is best suited to Girard's own direct appeal to the Gospels (Adams, 1993).

2. Girard's God
There is a fundamental and obvious question which needs to be asked about Girard's coherence with theology, namely, what doctrine or image of God is at work here? And if we are discussing Christian theology, then the question includes the compatibility of mimetic theory with an understanding of God as triune and incarnate. There are several aspects to this complicated question, the first of which concerns the problem raised in Chapter 8 on soteriology. We noted there that contemporary thought about salvation faces the challenge of how to avoid falling headlong into the 'ugly ditch' of Christian particularity: how do we make convincing the sequence of description-deficiency-recommendation-remedy (Lowe), in a way

> that makes clear Christ is the unique remedy. But if Christology is articulated in terms of our understanding of the (deficient) human condition, then we risk failing to underscore the uniqueness of

Christ, and we risk underplaying the 'good news' because we have made a 'pact with negativity'.

The question, in effect, is that which confronted Anselm in the twelfth century: why the God-Man?

Critics of Girard express the concern that he falls headlong into the ditch: that there is a vacuum at the centre of his theory where we should find God, or Christ. Hans Urs von Balthasar in particular has offered an extended critique in which his final objection to Girard and Schwager is a profoundly theological one: that this 'dramatic' theology fails to convey anything of the drama which is the life of the triune God. As Schwager is indebted to von Balthasar for the precedent of his *Theo-Drama*, it is worth spending some time with von Balthasar's commentary. This appears in one of his sermons, *You Crown the Year with Your Goodness*, and in volume IV of the *Theo-Drama*: 'The Action'. Von Balthasar commends a recovery of the notion of 'substitution' to express the role of Jesus, since its alternative 'solidarity' is an inadequate summary of the biblical affirmation.

But 'how are we to imagine this substitution?' He turns to Girard, whose endeavours in *La violence et le sacré* and *Des choses cachées* he likens to the systems of Teilhard de Chardin and Karl Rahner, insofar as Girard distils the basis of a total anthropology from an all-embracing Christology. In his attempt to overcome the structuralism of Lévi-Strauss, the dialectic of Hegel and Marx, Heidegger, and above all to supersede psychoanalysis in the name of the Christian revelation, we have 'surely the most dramatic project to be undertaken today in the field of soteriology and in theology generally.' (299) Their approach leads helpfully to the central aspects of a drama of redemption.

Yet von Balthasar has problems with Girard's 'distorted' presentation of the theories of Anselm on sacrifice, and with his claim to a purely scientific approach. He questions Girard's insistent use of the terminology of 'power' and 'violence' to the neglect of 'justice' (especially the justice of God, different from power but never acknowledged as primary by Girard), before voicing his most far-reaching misgivings:

> The dramatic tension between the world and God is so overstretched that the link breaks, rendering impossible a drama that involves the two sides. This is clear from the fact that the self-concealing 'mechanism' eliminates all freedom on man's part. Girard maintains a complete hiatus between naturalism and theology; they are not even linked by an ethics. . . . This raises a question that is crucial in the present context: what takes place on the Cross, according to this theory, if the transferral of the world's

guilt to Jesus is only a psychological unloading (as it was in all ritual sacrifice), and if – on the other hand – the power-less Father-God demands nothing in the nature of an 'atoning sacrifice'?

To put it more concretely: the Church regards the eucharistic celebration as a representation of the 'sacrifice of the Cross', in which Christ has effectively offered himself for mankind; how then can she present and offer Christ's self-surrender to the divine Father if the latter, who is no longer an Old Testament God, has 'no pleasure' in it, since he did not *want* the Cross, and even less *commanded* his Son to accept it? (von Balthasar, 1980: 309–10; original emphasis)

Von Balthasar is concerned that both Girard and Schwager concentrate on the human attitude to the Crucified, remaining silent on God's attitude. Isaiah 53.6 presents us 'inescapably' with a God who either *wills* the burdening of the Servant or *allows* it; their analysis fails to arrive at the real problem, namely the relationship between God's justice and his power (312). A number of von Balthasar's misgivings have indeed been addressed in Girard's subsequent work, but the gulf between the two authors remains: von Balthasar insists upon attributing some level of complicity, therefore violence, to God in the crucifixion (before that, in the Suffering Servant passage from Isaiah) – in short, of understanding God's 'wrath' in terms of his ability to exact retribution, rather than accepting the transvaluation of power/powerlessness that has taken place on the Cross.

A reminder is needed at this point that the Christian understanding of God is a Trinitarian one, and that a proper recovery of a triune doctrine of God is essential for overcoming the 'sado-masochistic' implications of penal substitution, which seem to be very close to the kind of picture von Balthasar is presenting. Of the theologians we have looked at thus far, James Alison has gone some way to describing a 'mimetic' doctrine of the Trinity, which is analogous to the psychological model of Augustine, but also makes better sense of the interpersonal language which the Church has traditionally used to describe God (1998: 48–53). Following Oughourlian, Alison proposes a use of the term 'holon' instead of 'person', to convey better the interdividual reality of the divine, which is then integrated into reconstruction of the doctrines of creation and original sin (186–210). It may also be asked whether part of the function of a robust doctrine of the Trinity is to counter the 'mirror imaging' which Schwager warns about in Anselm's doctrine of the *imago*; Schwager notes that there seems to be no place for the Holy Spirit in Anselm's account of the atonement.

This 'economic' view of the Trinity essayed by Alison may be compared to the contemporary recovery, in theologians such as Jürgen Moltmann, of the 'Crucified God'. It is in the 'kenotic', or self-emptying suffering on the cross, that the reality of God's love for us is expressed and made manifest. For Alison, following Girard, this *kenosis* has a sociological reality. The truth that 'God could come into the world to bring about the new creation only as forgiving victim, as that which was on its way out of being through expulsion' (1998: 210) is a Johannine understanding of the Lamb of God, revealed and glorified in the exact moment of his victimization and expulsion. God has no face other than the face of the immolated victim; all other alleged manifestations of the deity are idolatrous.

3. Girard and gnosticism
The charge of 'gnosticism' has been levelled at Girard in several cases: the tag, to be sure, is profoundly unenlightening and contentious, but the misgivings it seeks to articulate must be addressed. Charles Davis (1989: 321) feels constrained finally to reject Girard's hypothesis on account of its 'gnosticism' and its 'lack of humility':

> Girard puts forward an account of human society that removes society from the sphere of human creativity. Human beings are regarded as incapable of making a society for themselves. They are locked into a mutually destructive violence from which they cannot extricate themselves . . . . I must remark that what he outlines is a gnostic anthropology. Human nature is structurally evil. It is not a question of sin, but of being trapped in a structurally necessary, but destructive, mimesis.

Gillian Rose concurs in her extended comparison of Thomas Mann and Girard, when she declares that the latter evinces 'a Gnostic sociology: creation is evil and the creator God is a malevolent demiurge demanding violent sacrifice, while the Godhead is the god of love'; on this view, humanity is 'not sinful but unenlightened – its fate hitherto depending on ignorance, its future on whether it can take on the truth' (Rose, 1992: 133–52). Girard finds a champion in Rowan Williams, who finds Rose's critique of Girard 'weighty', but not altogether fair to his position (Williams, R., 1995: 21). The 'gnostic' tag appears yet again, when Jean-Marie Domenach speaks of a univocal explanation whose price is human autonomy because it

> submits the individual to a mechanism whose crushing weight brings with it in turn the idealism of the goal and of the techniques assigned to temporal salvation. The great difficulty one encounters in conceiving of an ethics and a politics in the Girardian perspective stems, I think, from being torn between a constraining nature and a remote God – a gulf which can be filled by intellect but not by

action. The gnostic aspect of Girard's thought, so convincing and at times so intoxicating, thus comes at the price of the impossibility of any historical thought or practice, whether personal or collective, in the middle of such a distance. (Dumouchel, 1988: 155)

Paisley Livingston speaks for those commentators who are uncomfortable with the theological dimension of Girard's theory, specifically with what appears to be a problematic fideism in Girard's account of demystification (Dumouchel, 1988: 113–34). From *Des Choses Cachées* onward, Girard is adamant that only a factor external to the cultures erected on the sacrificial mechanism – a divine factor – can expose that mechanism. The agent of demystification is not science, but the Logos immanent in Christ: in this way Girard avoids the paradoxical claim that the mimetic system changed its own rules, because the radical change has its provenance outside the system.

For Livingston, this begs the question as to what kinds of social and/or psychological conditions will render human beings capable of being subject to this divine influence, alternatively of opposing it and clinging to their sacrificial illusions. The search for such conditions rests on the assumption that societies exist as a 'totality'. More fundamentally, 'if we do not accept Girard's notion of a truly divine revelation, how can change be accounted for within his system?' Livingston discerns in Girard (primarily in *Violence and the Sacred*) a second approach which allows for the agent of demystification to be the product of the mimetic system itself. Following Jean Dupuy, he posits the mimetic model as a 'self-organising system' which is not however closed and which can generate real complexity; it is incorrect, and creates unnecessary problems, to posit a *closed* dynamic at the heart of mimetic interaction. The theory of mimesis is an interactive mechanism in which the agents' behaviour is conditioned by their reciprocal anticipations of what the others will do; this gives rise to a variety of communicational frameworks, patterns of interaction and cognitive capacities, which constitute an open-ended history.

All the criticisms recounted above express misgivings about Girard's essentially pessimistic analysis of society which leaves humanity helpless and incapable of emancipatory action. This is a distortion of Girard's thought, and the accusation of 'gnosticism' does not help: fundamental Christian doctrines such as the goodness of creation and free-will are firmly in place in his system, even if he does not stress them. But the gauntlet has been thrown down by too many critics not to be taken seriously.

As we have seen, several commentators have judged that it may simply be too early to assess the lasting impact of Girard's work. This is the logic behind the 'research project' as understood by Imre Lakatos, that it is rational to undertake a research project over the medium term, until it becomes too unwieldy in its accommodation of exceptions, in which case it must be abandoned. For some, of course, we have already reached that point; for its proponents, however, this entrusting of a final verdict on mimetic theory to its success over the medium term gives the theory a reasonably secure 'scientific' status – for the time being.

Epilogue

If there is a 'wait and see' dimension to the overall verdict on mimetic theory, we may ask more confidently about its more immediate theological impact. There can be no doubting the huge influence of René Girard's ideas, not just in the academic disciplines of theology and religious studies, but also for the large numbers of practitioners outside the academy. Pastors, spiritual guides and activists for peace, justice and reconciliation have all found Girard's cluster of insights to be immensely fruitful in their proclamation of the Gospel. If nothing else, he has provided an extraordinarily powerful biblical hermeneutic, which makes new sense out of familiar scriptural texts and sheds a light on some of the more puzzling ones. For Christians who wish to take seriously the problem of religiously inspired violence – this means, not simply to see it as a by-product or accidental effect of religious belief – then Girard has addressed the key questions in an incomparable way.

It may be said that the 'new wave' of interest in Girard's work is not directly related to the theological aspects of his work. Theologically, the shock waves impacted a good 35 years ago, with the publication of *Violence and the Sacred*, and with his critique of sacrificial Christianity in *Things Hidden since the Foundation of the World*. Girard's elevation to the membership of the Académie Française is a recognition of his contribution to French language and culture in general; there are exciting resonances with the neurosciences and with evolutionary theory, suggesting that Girard's account of mimesis and hominization may yet find greater recognition. A significant development is surely the establishment of Imitatio Inc., denoting the adoption of mimetic theory by the powerful and wealthy seeking to initiate global social change. Founded in 2007 by Peter Thiel and Robert Hamerton-Kelly 'as an agent for pressing forward the consequences of René Girard's remarkable breakthrough insight into human behaviour as mimetic', it exists to sponsor an ambitious programme of research, publications and conferences. One of its aims is the provision of primary texts, including 'the canonical Girard'.

This seems a far cry from the young scholar trying to make sense of selected novelists, and finding himself overtaken by the truth of the Gospel. The religious note is still there, but in Girard's recent work, as we have seen, it is one of reiteration around the theme of apocalypse. In his most recent book, Girard finds Carl von Clausewitz, the author of

De la Guerre, to be a rich mine of mimetic insights. Clausewitz is associated with the formula that 'war is the continuation of politics by other means' (he is closer, in other words, to Carl Schmitt's conception of politics than that of Hannah Arendt for whom politics and violence are incompatible). It has been suggested by Robert Hamerton-Kelly that this book represents a 'fourth wave' of Girard's mimetic theory: after his literary, social anthropological and biblical 'phases', this latest work is historical in its approach (since Girard was after all trained up as a historian, this may be appropriate). The book opens with an exasperated account from Girard of how the truth of the New Testament's apocalyptic passages is steadfastly ignored, even by Christians, despite the fact that they are an accurate record of the crisis we are undergoing.

Clausewitz is important because he writes of the phenomenon of 'la montée aux extrêmes' – escalation – in an unfinished treatise which was to be read by military theorists all over Europe, though primarily as a source of military strategy. It is necessary to read Clausewitz more deeply, in fact to read his and after that read other misunderstood or neglected texts, the apocalyptic passages of the New Testament. In each case, we are confronting our own reluctance in the face of the truths they contain. Clausewitz himself recoils from the irrational reality which he suddenly comes across (Girard, 2007b: 14), hence the difficult title of the book: 'achever' implies to achieve or complete Clausewitz, which also means to go beyond him and recover the unacknowledged religious implications of his work.

On one level, there is nothing new about Girard's task here: he is, once again, 'reading' authors for the mimetic insights which they contain, sometimes in spite of themselves. In this sense, Carl von Clausewitz joins Dostoyevsky and Shakespeare in the Girardian canon. There is much more here, however, to suggest an intensification, a sharpening of focus. The idea that *De la Guerre* might be read alongside or in tandem with the scriptures is striking: it is as if Girard is doing whatever he can to get us to look at these texts and take them seriously. The apocalyptic theme has appeared before, for example, in the essay in *A Theatre of Envy* on 'Hamlet's Dull Revenge'(Girard, 1991), when Girard asks us if we would feel the same way about Hamlet's 'indecisiveness' if we envisage the Prince with his hand hovering over the nuclear button. In these recent writings of Girard, the threat of global violence now has centre stage, and what has made the difference is 9/11 and the return of archaic religious violence in the form of militant Islam. The world finds itself in a vicious cycle of escalation, with no apparent prospect of escape. It is a world whose uncertainties are so agonizing that we even find ourselves thinking with nostalgia about the 'security' of the Cold War and its Mutually Assured Destruction.

Epilogue

This strikingly sombre note in Girard's recent work, therefore, is certainly unsettling, though a glance back at his previous work suggests that this apocalyptic tone has never been entirely absent. Girard's faith – the faith which he rediscovered on the train between Baltimore and Philadelphia – has always been resistant to the opiate of false consolation. 'It is important for us to recover something in which we can believe; but there must be no cheating' (1987a: 442). Such a recovery means rejecting the nineteenth-century masters of suspicion, as well as the new Puritanism, which would deprive us not of sexuality 'but of something we need even more – meaning. Man cannot live on bread and sexuality.' This 'castration of the signified . . . desiccates every text and spreads the most deadening boredom even in the newest situations' (1987a: 442).

And yet this place of desiccation is also the place of hope. At the conclusion of a previous work on Girard (Kirwan, 2004), I found myself drawn to the conclusion of *Things Hidden*, where he quotes at length from Ezekiel 37. As a place to finish the present work it seems to be even more apt. The prophet tells of the valley of death and dry bones, symbols for Girard of the intellectual despair he has been condemning. And yet: 'I always cherished the hope that meaning and life were one'. Just as Girard describes his method in the humblest terms possible – 'I can only approach texts and institutions, and relating them to one another seems to me to throw light in every direction', so our task in the valley is a relatively straightforward one: to resuscitate meaning, by relating the texts (the bones) to one another, 'without exception'. Girard's latest surprising conjunction of an unfinished treatise on war by Carl von Clausewitz and the apocalyptic passages from the Gospels should not in fact surprise us after all. These too simply await the breath of the Spirit, as recorded in Ezek. 37.10: 'So I prophesied as he commanded me and the breath came into them, and they lived, and stood upon their feet in exceedingly great host.'

Notes

Chapter 1 Introduction: 'The man on the train'

1. For René Girard's conversion experience, see Michel Treguer (Girard, 1994: 180–95), and *The Girard Reader* (Girard, 1996: 283–86).
2. COV&R Conference, May 31–June 2, Antwerp: 'The Place of Girard's Mimetic Theory in the History of Philosophy'.
3. Vanheeswijck draws attention to the comparative study of Girard and Derrida by Andrew McKenna, *Violence and Difference* (McKenna, 1992).
4. Taylor and Vattimo were in attendance at the Antwerp conference. Another philosopher who should be mentioned here is Paul Ricoeur, who has similarly addressed a COV&R conference and spoken appreciatively of Girard's work.
5. 'An Interview with René Girard' (pp. 199–229). The interview first appeared in *Diacritics* 8 (1978): 31–54.
6. In 1966, Girard was one of the organizers of an international colloquium at Johns Hopkins University, 'The Languages of Criticism and the Sciences of Man'. The colloquium was to be a significant moment for the arrival of critical theory in the United States; Girard found the work of Derrida congenial at this time, though later they diverge.

Chapter 2 René Girard: Life and work

1. A complete bibliography of Literature on the Mimetic Theory, edited by Dietmar Regensburger, can be found under 'Girard-Dokumentation', Institut für Dogmatik, Innsbruck: www.uibk.ac.at/theol/cover/mimetic_theory_biblio.html, accessed 15 August 2008.
2. The proceedings of the annual Colloquium are normally published in *Contagion*; COV&R also produces a bi-annual Bulletin. Information about COV&R can be found at http://uibk.ac.at/theol/cover/, accessed 15 August 2008.
3. French originals in 1978 and 2004 respectively.

Chapter 3 The mimetic theory of René Girard

1. www.uibk.ac.at/theol/cover/girard_le_monde_interview.html, accessed 15 August 2008.

2. See Scott and Cavanaugh 2004: 1 for the similarity of politics and religion: 'both are concerned with the production of metaphysical images around which communities are organised'.
3. See Chapter 9 for further discussion by Girard of 9/11 and its implications.
4. Hamerton-Kelly, 1992: 1–5, 44.
5. See Paul Ricoeur, *Freud and Philosophy* (Ricoeur, 1970).

Chapter 4 The Innsbruck connection: Dramatic theology

1. 'The Son of God and the World's Sin' is the final article included in *Der wunderbare Tausch* (1986: 273–312). Balthasar's critique of Girard and Schwager will be examined in Chapter 12.
2. *Jesus im Heilsdrama* (English version, *Jesus and the Drama of Salvation*: Schwager, 1999). For a concise summary of the Theo-Drama, see Schwager's essay 'Christology' in Scott, P., and Cavanaugh, W. T. (eds), *Blackwell Companion to Political Theology*, 2004, pp. 341–62.
3. *Dramatische Erlösungslehre: Ein Symposon* (Niediadomski and Palaver, 1992).
4. The other contributors to the symposium examine the possibility of a dramatic soteriology in relation to Old and New Testament studies, including an essay from Klaus Koch on martyrdom in the book of Daniel, systematic comparisons with von Balthasar and Karl Rahner, perspectives from communicative action theory and narrative soteriology, and a study of salvation in the light of the *conquistadores* in South America.
5. J. Niewiadomski and W. Palaver (eds), *Vom Fluch und Segen der Sündenböcke: Raymund Schwager zum 60. Geburtstag*. Kulturverlag, Thaur-Wien-Munchen, 1995.
6. The *Festschrift* includes essays on Girard and Karl Rahner, Christian anti-Semitism, Augustine on original sin, a reading of St Paul as political theology, and studies of film and poetic inspiration. A second *Festschrift* followed in 2003, 'Dramatic Theology in Conversation' (Niewiadomski and Wandinger (eds), 2003). This volume contains essays on 'dramatic correlation as a method for theology', reflections and clarifications upon themes of sin and violence, and exegesis of passages in Luke and Romans.

Chapter 5 A theological 'anthropophany'

1. Alison, 1998: 42, quoting Milbank, 1990: 222–3.

Chapter 6 The drama of salvation

1. Schwager, 1986. These articles were published originally in *Zeitschrift für Katholishe Theologie* but always conceived as an integral whole.

2. Walter Lowe, 2003, 'Christ and Salvation' in *The Cambridge Companion to Postmodern Theology*. Cambridge UP, Cambridge, pp. 235–51.
3. Lowe refers to the crisis of 'relevance' and 'identity' as set out by Jürgen Moltmann in *The Crucified God*; it can also be seen as one of the defining differences between the contrasting approaches of Karl Rahner and Karl Barth.
4. The document is composed by Christian W. Troll, a German Jesuit working in the area of Christian-Muslim relations: www.answers-to-muslims.com, accessed 24 May 2008.
5. The theme is famously argued for by Gustav Aulen in 1931, in his study *Christus Victor* though scholarly consensus now is that he overstates the case for the 'Christus Victor' motif as the predominant model of the atonement. Scriptural and patristic references would include Col. 2.14–15, Irenaeus, *Contra Heresias* and Ignatius of Antioch's *Epistle to the Romans*.

Chapter 7 'Painting pictures on clouds': The metaphors of atonement

1. For the justice theme, see Gunton, 1988: 83–113.
2. The relevant section of the interview with Rebecca Adams concerning Girard's change of mind on sacrifice is reproduced in James Williams (ed.), *The Girard Reader*. Crossroad, New York, 1996.
3. The original title of Paul Ricoeur's classic study *The Rule of Metaphor* is *La métaphore vive* ('the metaphor lives').

Chapter 8 Girard and the Bible

1. Henri de Lubac, *Exegese Medievale*; Paul Claudel, *Introduction au livre de Ruth*, 19–121; Auerbach's essay on 'Figura' in *Scenes from the Drama of European Literature*, pp. 11–76) 1973 [1938]: 11–76.
2. Raymund Schwager considers the discussion of identity in terms of the multiple *personae* in all four of the Servant Songs: the 'dialogue' between God, the Servant and the people resembles the interchange between characters and Chorus in a Greek drama. He suggests there are three speakers and four perspectives in the Songs: in Isa. 42.1–4, God speaks; in Isa. 49.1–6, it is the Servant, and again in Isa. 50.4–9; in the final song, Isa. 52.13 – 53.12, we have God, then the people (Schwager, 1987, 1999).
3. K. Koch: 'Suhne und Sündevergebung um die Wende von der exilischen zur nachexilischen Zeit', *Evangelishe Theologie* 26 (1966), 237.
4. For this discussion, see Walter Brueggemann, 1985a and 1985b.
5. B. S. Childs, 1979, *Introduction to the Old Testament as Scripture*. Fortress Press, Philadelpia; Norman K. Gottwald, 1979, *The Tribes of Yahweh*. Orbis, New York.
6. John Dawson's study of Origen (via Daniel Boyarin, Hans Frei and Erich Auerbach) commends figural reading as 'the principal site of the tension between past and future' (Dawson, 2002).

Chapter 9 Political theology

1. See Davis, Milbank and Zizek (eds), 2005; de Vries and Sullivan (eds), 2006.
2. The fruits of an interdisciplinary conference in New York in 1989 were published as *Violence and the Sacred in the Modern World* (Juergensmeyer, 1992).
3. Paisley Livingston (ed.), *Disorder and Order*. Anna Libri, Saratoga, CA, 1984.
4. Luther, Martin, 2005 [1523], pp. 436–7.
5. The distinction has for Schmitt a theological basis: he quotes Genesis 3.15 (Eve and the serpent) and Genesis 11.9 (the Tower of Babel) to prove that God wills enmity and division in his creation.
6. Robert Doran (ed.), (2008), 'Cultural Theory after 9/11: Terror, Religion, Media', *SubStance: A Review of Theory and Literary Criticism*, issue 115, 37(1).

Chapter 10 Views from the South

1. G. W. F. Hegel, *Phenomenology of Spirit*, chapter IV A, 'Independence and Dependence [Unselbständigkeit] of Self-Consciousness: Lordship and Bondage'; see also Alexandre Kojève's Introduction to the Reading of Hegel (1947).
2. Fanon, Frantz (1967), *Black Skin, White Masks*. Grove Press: New York, 62.
3. I am working from the German translation rather than the Portuguese original: *Götzenbilder und Opfer*, Assmann, 1996 [1991], 285–6.
4. Decker, Rainer, 2004, *Hexen, Magie Mythen und die Wahrheit*. Though dealing specifically with the European witch-craze and its aftermath, especially in Germany, Deckler draws explicit parallel with contemporary events in northern South Africa and the Congo (p. 7).
5. By Henry Wasswa, The Associated Press: www.histarch.uiuc.edu/harper/congo200.html, accessed 15 August 2008.
6. For further applications of mimetic theory to African contexts, see Simonse (1992), Farris in Federschmitt et al. (eds), 1998; Girard's own analysis of a Venda myth (Girard, 1993b), and Munyaneza's case study of Ruanda (Munyaneza, 2001).

Chapter 11 Girard and the religions

1. The papers, responses and plenary discussions were recorded in *Contagion* 9, Spring 2002, with an Introduction and Epilogue by Robert J. Daly, of Boston College and the principal organizer of the Colloquium.
2. In 2002, it was Goodhart's turn to host the COV&R Colloquium, at the University of Purdue Indiana, with the specific theme of 'Judaism and Christianity', including engagement with scholars such as Bruce Chilton and Michael Fishbane.
3. See Goodhart: 'the insight about scapegoats is absolutely central to human culture ... the way in which mimesis opens itself into a scapegoating process seems to be ineluctably human. We are hard wired for that. So, regardless of religion, we have to respond' (2002: 149).

Chapter 12   Girard and the theologians

1. In 'Ethnological Lie and Mythical Truth' (since retracted to some extent), Hayden White thinks that the Girard of *La Violence et le Sacré* is recommending the scapegoating mechanism as a way of ordering society, and charges him with Nazi sympathies (White, 1978), while the critiques of Sarah Kofman (1987) and Toril Moi (1982) judge Girard's concentration on the theme of (largely) male configurations of violence to be an indicator of his misogyny; as he wryly points out (Golsan, 1993: 145), 'if there ever was case of damned if you do, damned if you don't, here it is'.
2. Davis, 1989: 327 (original emphasis); Andrew Lascaris (1989) has responded to Davis' strictures.
3. Alison, 1996a. He asserts that, contrary to the charge of totalitarian thinking, 'his very small understanding of the triangular and imitative nature of desire, which can never properly be understood except in as far as the student allows him or herself to be chewed over by it, is something far more like St. Thérèse's "Little Way" than yet another straitjacket'.
4. On the question of sacrifice in the New Testament, we may note two respondents to Robert Daly's 1997 paper, Paul Duff (1997) and Bruce Chilton (1997). They argue that Daly (and by implication Girard) overstress the anti-sacrificial trajectory of primitive Christianity. Chilton stresses the dangers of 'scapegoating sacrifice', and insists that '[t]he denial of sacrifice is the last bulwark, and perhaps the strongest, of Christian exceptionalism'.

Bibliography

An extensive bibliography of Literature on the Mimetic Theory, edited by Dietmar Regensburger, can be found under 'Girard-Dokumentation', Institut für Dogmatik, Innsbruck: www.uibk.ac.at/theol/cover/mimetic_theory_biblio.html, accessed 15 August 2008.

Works of René Girard

Girard, R., 1962, *Proust: A Collection of Critical Essays*. Edited, with Introduction by René Girard. Prentice-Hall, New York [Reprinted: Greenwood Press, Westport, CT, 1977].
— 1965, *Deceit, Desire and the Novel: Self and Other in Literary Structure*. Johns Hopkins UP, Baltimore (*Mensonge romantique et vérité romanesque*. Grasset, Paris, 1961).
— 1976, *Critique dans un souterrain*. L'age d'homme, Lausanne.
— 1977, *Violence and the Sacred*. Johns Hopkins UP, Baltimore; Athlone, London (*La Violence et le Sacré*, Grasset, Paris, 1972).
— 1978, *'To double business bound': Essays on Literature, Mimesis and Anthropology*. Johns Hopkins UP, Baltimore; Athlone, London.
— 1986, *The Scapegoat*. Johns Hopkins UP, Baltimore; Athlone, London (*Le Bouc émissaire*. Grasset, Paris, 1982).
— 1987a, *Things Hidden since the Foundation of the World*. Research undertaken in collaboration with Jean-Michel Oughourlian and Guy Lefort, Stanford UP, Stanford, CA (*Des Choses cachées depuis la fondation du monde*. Grasset, Paris, 1978).
— 1987b, *Job: The Victim of His People*. Athlone, London (*La Route Antique des hommes pervers; Essais sur Job*. Grasset, Paris, 1985).
— 1988, 'The Founding Murder in the Philosophy of Nietzsche' in Dumouchel, P. (ed.), *Violence and Truth*. Athlone Press, London, pp. 227–46.
— 1989, 'Theory and Its Terrors' in Kavanaugh, T. M. (ed.), *The Limits of Theory*. Stanford UP, Stanford, CA, pp. 225–54.
— 1990, 'Innovation and Repetition', *SubStance*, issue 62/63, 19(2/3), 7–20.
— 1991, *A Theatre of Envy: William Shakespeare*. Oxford UP [Reprinted: Gracewing Press, England, 2000].
— 1993a, 'A Conversation with René Girard' in Adams, R. (ed.), 1993.

Bibliography

Girard, R., 1993b, 'A Venda Myth Analyzed' in Golsan, R. J. (ed.), *René Girard and Myth: An Introduction*. Garland Publishing, Inc., New York and London, pp. 151–79.

— 1994, *Quand ces choses commenceront . . . Entretiens avec Michel Treguer*. arléa, Paris. (*Wenn al das beginnt . . . ein Gesprach mit Michel Treguer*. Lit Verlag, Munster, 1997).

— 1996, 'The Anthropology of the Cross: A Conversation with René Girard' in Williams, J. (ed.), *The Girard Reader*. Crossroad, New York, pp. 262–88.

— 1997a, *Resurrection from the Underground: Feodor Dostoevsky*. Crossroad, New York (*Dostoievski: Du double a l'unité*. Plon, Paris, 1963).

— 1997b, 'Der Sündenbock hat ausgedient', *Der Speigel*, 25 August 1997, pp. 112–15.

— 2001a, *I See Satan Fall like Lightning*. Orbis, Maryknoll, NY (*Je vois Satan tomber comme l'éclair*. Grasset, Paris, 1999).

— 2001b, 'What we are witnessing is mimetic rivalry on a planetary scale', *Le Monde* (6 November 2001) at: www.uibk.ac.at/theol/cover/girard_le_monde_interview.html, accessed 15 August 2008.

— 2001c, *Celui par qui le scandale arrive*. Desclée de Brouwer, Paris.

— 2007a, *Evolution and Conversion*. T&T Clark Continuum, London (*Les origines de la culture*, 2004. Desclée de Brouwer, Paris).

— 2007b, *Achever Clausewitz*. Carnets Nord, Paris.

— 2007c, 'The Evangelical Subversion of Myth' in Hamerton-Kelly, R. (ed.), 2007, pp. 29–50.

— 2008, 'Interview with René Girard' (by Robert Doran), *SubStance*, issue 115, 37(1), 20–32.

Secondary literature

Adams, R. (ed.), 1993, 'A Conversation with René Girard: Interview by Rebecca Adams', *Religion and Literature* 25.2 (special edition).

Afsaruddin, A., 2006, 'Competing Perspectives on *Jihad* and "Martyrdom" in Early Islamic Sources', in Wicker, B. (ed.), 2006, pp. 15–31.

Alison, J., 1996a, 'Girard's Breakthrough', *The Tablet*, 29 June, 848–9.

— 1996b, *Raising Abel: The Recovery of the Eschatological Imagination*. Crossroads, New York.

— 1998, *The Joy of Being Wrong: Original Sin through Easter Eyes*. Crossroads, New York.

— 2001, *Faith beyond Resentment: Fragments Catholic and Gay*. DLT, London.

— 2003, *On Being Liked*. DLT, London.

Anselm of Canterbury [1998], *The Major Works*. Oxford UP, Oxford.

Assman, H. (ed.), 1991, *Sobre idolos y sacrifios: René Girard con teologos de la liberacion*. Coleccion Economia-teologia. San José, Costa Rica: Editorial Departmento Ecumenico de Investigacones, Petrópolis (*Götzenbilder und Opfer: René Girard im Gespräch mit der Befreiungstheologie*. Lit Verlag, Thaur, 1996).

Auerbach, E., 1953 [1945], *Mimesis: The Representation of Reality in Western Literature*. Princeton UP, New Jersey.

Bibliography

— 1974 [1938], *Figura. Scenes from the Drama of European Literature*. Peter Smith, Gloucester.
Aulen, G., 1970 [1931], *Christus Victor: An Historical Study of the Three Main Types of the Idea of the Atonement*, trans. Herbert, A. G. SPCK, London.
Austen, J., 1999, 'Review of Peter Geshiere, *The Modernity of Witchcraft: Politics and the Occult in Postcolonial Africa*', *Journal of Social History* 33 (Fall), 198–9.
Bailie, G., 1995, *Violence Unveiled: Humanity at the Crossroads*. Crossroads, New York.
von Balthasar, H. U., 1994 [1980], *Theo-Drama: Theological Dramatic Theory* IV: 'The Action'. Ignatius Press, San Francisco. (*Theodramatik: Dritte Band* 'Die Handlung'. Johannes Verlag, Einsiedeln).
Bandera, C., 1994, *The Sacred Game: The Role of the Sacred in the Genesis of Modern Literature*. Pennsylvania State UP, University Park, PA.
Barker, M., 2003, *The Great High Priest: The Temple Roots of Christian Liturgy*. T&T Clark, London.
Bell, D. Jr, 1992, *Liberation Theology after the End of History*. Routledge, London.
van Binsbergen, W., 'Witchcraft in modern Africa as virtualised boundary conditions of the kinship order': www.shikanda.net/african_religion/witch.htm, accessed 15 August 2008.
Bongmba, E. K., 2001, *African Witchcraft and Otherness: A Philosophical and Theological Critique of Intersubjective Relations*. SUNY, New York.
Brueggemann, W., 1985a, 'A Shape for Old Testament Theology, I: Structure Legitimation', *Catholic Biblical Quarterly* 47, 28–46.
— 1985b, 'A Shape for Old Testament Theology II: Embrace of Pain', *Catholic Biblical Quarterly* 47, 395–415.
Bureau, R., 1988a, 'A Gabonese Myth' in Dumouchel, P. (ed.), *Violence and Truth. On the Work of René Girard*. Athlone Press, London, pp. 27–43.
— 1988b, 'Maitres et disciples dans les religions africaines', *Studia Missionalia* 37, 337–61.
Calasso, R., 1994, *The Ruin of Kasch*, trans. Weaver, W., and Sartarelli, S. Belnap Press of Harvard UP, Cambridge, MA.
Cavanaugh, W. T., 1995, '"A Fire Strong Enough to Consume the House": The Wars of Religion and the Rise of the State', *Modern Theology* 11.4, October 1995, 397–420.
Chauvet, L.-M., 1995, *Symbol and Sacrament: A Sacramental Reinterpretation of Christian Existence*. Liturgical Press, Collegeville, MN.
Chilton, B., 1992, *The Temple of Jesus. His Sacrificial Program within a Cultural History of Sacrifice*. Pennsylvania State University Press, University Park, PA.
— 1997, 'Sacrificial Mimesis', *Religion* 27, 225–30.
Cormack, M., 2002, *Sacrificing the Self: Perspectives on Martyrdom and Religion*. Oxford UP, Oxford.
Daly, R., 1978, *The Origins of the Christian Doctrine of Sacrifice*. Fortress Press, Philadelphia, PA.
— 1990, 'Sacrifice' in Fink, P. (ed.), *New Dictionary of Sacramental Worship*. Gill and Macmillan, Dublin, pp. 1135–7.
— 1997, 'Is Christianity Sacrificial or Anti-Sacrificial?', *Religion* 27, 231–43.

Bibliography

Daly, R., 'Violence and Institution in Christianity', *Contagion* (Spring 2002), 4–33.

Davis, C., 1989, 'Sacrifice and Violence: New Perspectives in the Theory of Religion from René Girard', *New Blackfriars* 70, 311–28.

Davis, C., Milbank, J., and Zizek S. (eds), 2005, *Theology and the Political*. Duke UP, London, 2005.

Dawson, J. D., 2002, *Christian Figural Reading and the Fashioning of Identity*. University of California Press, Berkeley, CA.

Decker, R., 2004, *Hexen: Magie, Mythen und die Wahrheit*. Primus Verlag, Darmstadt, Germany.

Detienne, M., 2006, 'The Gods of Politics in Early Greek Cities', in de Vries and Sullivan (eds), 2006, pp. 91–101.

Domenach, J-M., 1988, 'Voyage to the End of the Sciences of Man', in Dumouchel, P. (ed.), 1988, pp. 152–9.

Duff, P., 1997, 'The Sacrificial Character of Earliest Christianity: A Response to Robert J. Daly's "Is Christianity Sacrificial or Anti-Sacrificial?"', *Religion* 27, 245–8.

Dumouchel, P. (ed.), 1988, *Violence and Truth: On the work of René Girard*. Athlone, London. (*Violence et Vérité: autour de René Girard: Proceedings of Colloque de Cerisy on R. Girard*, Grasset, Paris, 1985).

Eagleton, T., 2005, *Holy Terror*. Oxford UP, Oxford.

Fanon, F., 1963, *The Wretched of the Earth*. Penguin, Harmondsworth, London.

Farris, J. R., 1998, 'Choosing Our Victims: Reflections on the Theory of René Girard and the Theology of Power' in Federschmidt et al. (eds), 1998, pp. 29–32.

Federschmidt, K. H., Atkins, U., and Temme, K. (eds), 1998, *Violence and Sacrifice: Cultural, Anthropological and Theological Aspects Taken from Five Continents*. Intercultural Pastoral Care and Counseling 4. SIPCC, Düsseldorf.

Fiddes, P. S., 1989, *Past Event and Present Salvation*. Darton, Longmann and Todd, London.

Fleming, C., 2004, *René Girard: Violence and Mimesis*. Polity Press, Cambridge.

Ford, D., 2006, *Self and Salvation*. Cambridge UP, Cambridge.

Fraser, G., 2001, *Christianity and Violence: Girard, Nietzsche, Anselm, Tutu*. Darton, Longman and Todd, London.

Frei, H. W., 1974, *The Eclipse of Biblical Narrative: A Study in Eighteenth and Nineteenth Century Hermeneutics*. Yale UP, New Haven, CT.

Galvin, J. P., 1982, 'Jesus as Scapegoat? *Violence and the Sacred* in the Theology of Raymund Schwager', *The Thomist* 46, 173–94.

— 1989, 'The Marvellous Exchange: Raymund Schwager's Interpretation of the History of Soteriology', *The Thomist* 53, 675–91.

— 1992, 'Zur dramatischen Erlösungslehre Raymund Schwagers: Fragen aus der Sicht Karl Rahners' in Niewiadomski and Palaver (eds), 1992, pp. 157–64.

Gauchet, M., 1997, *The Disenchantment of the World: A Political History of Religion*. Princeton UP, Princeton, NJ.

Geschiere, P., 1997, *The Modernity of Witchcraft: Politics and the Occult in Postcolonial Africa*. University of Virginia Press, Charlottesville, VA.

Bibliography

Golsan, R. J. (ed.), 1993, *René Girard and Myth: An Introduction*. Garland Publishing Inc., New York and London.
Goodhart, S., 1988, '"I am Joseph": René Girard and the Prophetic Law' in Dumouchel, P. (ed.), 1988, pp. 53–74.
— 1996, *Sacrificing Commentary*. Johns Hopkins UP, Baltimore, MD.
— 2002, 'Discussion summary', *Contagion* 9 (Spring), 149.
Gunton, C. E., 1988, *The Actuality of Atonement: A Study of Metaphor, Rationality and the Christian Tradition*. T&T Clark, Edinburgh.
Hamerton-Kelly, R. (ed.), 1987, *Violent Origins: Walter Burkert, René Girard, and Jonathan Z. Smith on Ritual Killing and Cultural Formation*. Stanford UP, Stanford, CA.
— 1992, *Sacred Violence: Paul's Hermeneutic of the Cross*. Fortress Press, Minneapolis.
— 1994, *The Gospel and the Sacred; the Politics of Violence in Mark*, foreword by René Girard. Fortress Press, Minneapolis.
— (ed.), 2007, *Politics and Apocalypse*. Michigan State UP, East Lansing, MI.
Heim, S. M., 2006, *Saved from Sacrifice: A Theology of the Cross*. Eerdmans, Grand Rapids, MI and Cambridge.
Hobbes, T., 1991 [1651], *Leviathan*. Cambridge Texts in the History of Political Thought. University Press, Cambridge.
Irigaray, L., 1986, 'Les femmes, le sacré, l'argent', *Critique* 42, 372–83.
Jasper, D., 1998, 'Literary Readings of the Bible' in Barton, J. (ed.), *Cambridge Companion to Biblical Interpretation*. Cambridge UP, Cambridge, pp. 21–34.
Jay, N., 1992, *Through Your Generations Forever. Sacrifice, Religion and Paternity*. University Press, Chicago, IL.
Juergensmeyer, M. (ed.), 1992, *Violence and the Sacred in the Modern World*. Frank Cass & Co, London.
— 2000, *Terror in the Mind of God*. University of California Press.
Juilland, A. (ed.), 1986, *To Honor René Girard*. Presented on the occasion of his sixtieth birthday by colleagues, students and friends. Stanford French and Italian Studies 34; Anma Libri, Palo Alto, CA.
Keenan, D. K., 2003, 'The Sacrifice of the Eucharist', *Heythrop Journal* 44.2, 182–204.
— 2005, *The Question of Sacrifice*. Indiana UP, Bloomington and Indianapolis.
Kerr, F., 1986, *Theology after Wittgenstein*. Blackwell, Oxford.
— 1992a, 'Revealing the Scapegoat Mechanism: Christianity after Girard' in M. McGhee (ed.), *Philosophy, Religion and the Spiritual Life*. University Press, Cambridge, pp. 161–175.
— 1992b, 'Rescuing Girard's argument?', *Modern Theology* 8.4, October 1992, 385–399.
Kierkegaard, S., 1983 [1845], *Fear and Trembling/Repetition*. Princeton UP, Princeton, NJ.
Kirwan, M., 2004, *Discovering Girard*. Darton, Longman and Todd, London.
Kofman, S., 1987, 'The Narcissistic Woman: Freud and Girard', in Moi, T. (ed.), *French Feminist Thought: A Reader*. Blackwell, Oxford, pp. 210–26.
Lakatos, I., 1970, 'Falsification and the Methodology of Scientific Research Programmes' in Lakatos, I., and Musgrave, A. (ed.) *Criticism and the Growth of Knowledge*. Cambridge UP, Cambridge, 91–196.

Bibliography

Lascaris, A., 1989, 'Charles Davis versus René Girard', *New Blackfriars* 70(831), 416–22.
Lefebure, L. D., 1996, 'Mimesis, Violence and Socially Engaged Buddhism: Overture to a Dialogue', *Contagion* 3 (Spring 1996), 122–40.
Loughlin, G., 1997, 'René Girard: Introduction' in Ward, G. (ed.), *The Postmodern God, a Theological Reader*. Blackwell, Oxford, pp. 96–103.
Lowe, W., 2003, 'Christ and Salvation' in Vanhoozer, K. (ed.), 2003, pp. 235–251.
Luther, M., 2005 [1523], 'Temporal Authority: To What Extent It Should Be Obeyed' in Timothy F. L. (ed.), *Basic Theological Writings* (2nd edition). Fortress Press, Augsburg, pp. 429–59.
Mack, B., 1985, 'The Innocent Transgressor: Jesus in Early Christian Myth and History', *Semeia* 33, 135–65.
— 1987, 'Introduction: Religion and Ritual' in Hamerton-Kelly, R. (ed.), *Violent Origins: Walter Burkert, René Girard and Jonathan Z. Smith on Ritual Killing and Cultural Formation*. Stanford UP, Stanford, pp. 1–73.
McKenna, A. J. (ed.), 1985, 'René Girard and Biblical Studies', *Semeia* 33; Introduction, pp. 1–11.
— 1992, *Violence and Difference: Girard, Derrida and Deconstruction*. University of Illinois Press, Urbana, IL and Chicago, IL.
— 2002, 'Scandal, Resentment, Idolatry: The Underground Psychology of Terrorism'. *Anthropoetics* 8(1) (Spring/Summer 2002), posted 1 June, 2002. www.anthropoetics.ucla.edu/ap0801/resent.htm, accessed 15 August 2008.
Mandunu, J. K., 1992, *Das 'Kindoki' im Licht der Sündenbocktheologie: Versuch einer christlichen Bewältigung des Hexenglaubens in Schwarz-Afrika*. Studien zur interkulturellen Geschichte des Christentums 85. Peter Lang, Frankfurt a.M. u.a.
Melberg, A., 1995, *Theories of Mimesis*. Cambridge UP, Cambridge.
Milbank, J., 1990, *Theology and Social Theory: Beyond Secular Reason*. Blackwell, Oxford.
— 1996, 'Stories of Sacrifice: From Wellhausen to Girard', *Modern Theology* 12, 27–56.
Moi, T., 1982, 'The Missing Mother: The Oedipal Rivalries of René Girard', *Diacritics* 12, 21–31.
Moltmann, J., 1994, 'Covenant or Leviathan? Political Theology for Modern Times', *Scottish Journal of Theology* 47(1), 19–41.
Munyaneza, M., 2001, 'Violence as Institution in African Religious Experience: A Casse Study of Rwanda', *Contagion* 8 (Spring 2001), 39–68.
Niewiadomski, J., and Palaver, W. (eds), 1992, *Dramatische Erlösungslehre: Ein Symposion*. Innsbrucker Theologische Studien 38. Tyrolia, Innsbruck.
— (eds), 1995, *Vom Fluch und Segen der Sündenböcke: Raymund Schwager zum 60. Geburtstag*. Kulturverlag, Thaur.
Niewiadomski, J., and Wandinger, N. (eds), 2003, *Dramatische Theologie im Gespräch: zum 65. Geburtstag von Raymund Schwager*. Lit Verlag, Munster.
North, R., 1985, 'Violence and the Bible: The Girard Connection. *Catholic Biblical Quarterly* 47, 1–27.
Nowak, S., 1994, 'The Girardian Theory and Feminism: Critique and Appropriation', *Contagion* (Spring 1994), 19–29.

Bibliography

Oughourlian, J. M., 1991, *The Puppet of Desire*. Stanford UP, Stanford, CA (*Un Mime Nommé Desir*, Grasset, Paris, 1982).

Palaver, W., 1992, 'A Girardian Reading of Schmitt's Political Theology', *Telos* 93, 43–68.

—— 1995, 'Hobbes and the Katēchon: The Secularization of Sacrificial Christianity', *Contagion* 2 (Spring 1995), 37–54.

—— 1996, 'Schmitt on *Nomos* and Space', *Telos* 106 (Winter 1996), 105–27.

—— 2003, *René Girards mimetische Theorie*. Lit Verlag, Munster.

Petrella, I. (ed.), 2005, *Latin American Liberation Theology: The Next Generation*. Orbis, New York.

Potolsky, M., 2006, *Mimesis*. Routledge, New York and London.

Quessnell, Q., 1990, 'Grace' in Komonchak, J., Collins, M., and Lane, D. (eds), *New Dictionary of Theology*. Gill and Macmillan, Dublin, pp. 437–50.

Rahner, K., 1978, *Foundations of Christian Faith: An Introduction to the Idea of Christianity*. Crossroad, New York.

Rapoport, D., 2002, 'The Four Waves of Rebel Terror and September 11', *Anthropoetics* 8(1) (Spring/Summer 2002), posted 1 June, 2002. www.anthropoetics.ucla.edu/apo801/terror.htm, accessed 19/02/2006.

Regensburger, D. (ed.), 2002, Colloquium on Violence and Religion (COV&R) critical commentaries and articles on 'Terrorism, Mimetic Rivalry and War' at www.uibk.ac.at/theol/cover/war_against_terrorism.html, accessed 15 August 2008.

Ricoeur, P., 1970, *Freud and Philosophy: An Essay on Interpretation*. Yale UP, New Haven, CT.

Rike, J., 1996, 'The Cycle of Violence and Feminist Constructions of Selfhood', *Contagion* 3 (Spring 1996), 21–42.

Rose, G., 1992, *The Broken Middle: Out of Our Ancient Society*. Blackwell, Oxford.

St Augustine [1972], *City of God*. Penguin, Harmondsworth, London.

Scheler, M., 1998 [1915], *Ressentiment* (Marquette University Press, Milwaukee, WI.

de Schrijver, G. (ed.), 1998, *Liberation Theologies on Shifting Grounds: A Clash of Socio-economic and Cultural Paradigms*. University Press, Leuven.

Schwager, R., 1978 (1987), *Brauchen wir ein Sündenbock?; Gewalt und Erlösung in den biblischen Schriften*. Kosel, München (*Must There be Scapegoats?: Violence and Redemption in the Bible*. Harper & Row, San Francisco, CA).

—— 1985, 'Christ's death and the prophetic critique of sacrifice' in McKenna, A. J. (ed.), 1985, pp. 109–23.

—— 1986, *Der Wunderbare Tausch: Zur Geschichte und Deutung der Erlösungslehre*. Kosel, München.

—— 1987, 'Imiter et Suivre', *Christus* 133, 5–18.

—— 1988, 'The Theology of the Wrath of God', in Dumouchel, P. (ed.), 1988, pp. 44–52.

—— 1992, 'Rückblick auf das Symposion', in Niewiadomski and Palaver (eds), 1992, 339–84.

—— 1995, 'Redemption through Sin? Dramatic as opposed to Dialectic Interpretation', unpublished paper delivered at *Colloqium on Violence and Religion*, Loyola, Chicago, June 1995.

Bibliography

Schwager, R., 1996, *Jesus im Heilsdrama: Entwurf einer biblischen Erlösungslehre*. Tyrolia, Innsbruck (*Jesus and the Drama of Salvation*. Crossroads, New York, 1999).

Schwager, R., and Niewiadomski, J., 1996, 'Dramatische Theologie als Forschungsprogramm', *ZKTh* 118, 317–44.

— 2003, *Religion erzeugt Gewalt: Einspruch!* Lit Verlag, Munster.

Schweiker, W., 1989, 'Sacrifice, Interpretation and the Sacred: The Importance of Gadamer and Girard for Religious Studies', *Journal of American Academy of Religion* 55/4, 788–810.

— 1990, *Mimetic Reflections: A Study in Hermeneutics, Theology, and Ethics*. Fordham UP, New York.

Scott, P., and Cavanaugh, W. T. (eds), 2004, *Blackwell Companion to Political Theology*. Blackwell, Oxford.

Scubla, L., 1988, 'The Christianity of Rene Girard and the Nature of Religion', in Dumouchel, P. (ed.), 1988, pp. 160–78.

Simonse, S., 1992, *Kings of Disaster: Dualism, Centralism and the Scapegoat King in the Southeastern Sudan* (Studies in Human Society V). Leiden, New York: E. J. Brill.

Sobrino, J., 2001 [1999], *Christ the Liberator: A View from the Victims*. Orbis, New York.

Stark, R., 2004, *For the Glory of God: How Monotheism Led to Reformations, Science, Witch-Hunts, and the End of Slavery*. Princeton UP, Princeton, NJ.

Swanson, T. D., 1994, 'An Ungodly Resemblance: Colonial Violence and Inca Analogies to Christianity' in Smith, T. H., and Wallace, M. I. (eds), *Curing Violence*. Forum Fascicles 3. Polebridge Press, Sonoma, CA, pp. 121–36.

Swartley, W. M. (ed.), 2000, *Violence Renounced: René Girard, Biblical Studies and Peacemaking*. Pandora Press US, Telford, PA.

Taylor, C., 1989, *Sources of the Self: The Making of the Modern Identity*. Cambridge UP, Cambridge.

Taylor, S. J., 2006, 'Save Us from Being Saved: Girard's Critical Soteriology', *Contagion: Journal of Violence, Mimesis and Culture* 12–13, 21–30.

Vanhoozer, K., 1997, 'Anthropology' in Gunton, C. (ed.), *Cambridge Companion to Christian Doctrine*. Cambridge UP, Cambridge, pp. 158–88.

Vanhoozer, K. (ed.), 2003, *The Cambridge Companion to Postmodern Theology*. Cambridge UP, Cambridge.

de Vries H., and Sullivan, L. E. (eds), 2006, *Political Theologies: Public Religions in a Post-Secular World*. Fordham UP, New York.

Wallace, M., 1989, 'Postmodern Biblicism: The Challenge of René Girard for Contemporary Theology', *Modern Theology* 5, 309–25.

White, H., 1978, 'Ethnological "Lie" and Mythical "Truth"', *Diacritics* 8.1 (Spring 1978).

Wicker, B. (ed.), 2006, *Witnesses to Faith? Martyrdom in Christianity and Islam*. Ashgate Publishing, Aldershot, England.

Williams, J., 1988, 'The Innocent Victim: René Girard on Violence, Sacrifice and the Sacred', *Religious Studies Review* 14.4, 320–6.

— 1991, *The Bible, Violence and the Sacred: Liberation from the Myth of Sanctioned Violence*. Harper Collins, San Francisco.

Bibliography

— 1996 (ed.), *The Girard Reader*. Crossroads, New York, including interview with René Girard, pp. 263–88.
Williams, R., 1995, 'Between Politics and Metaphysics; Reflections in the Wake of Gillian Rose', *Modern Theology* 11(1), 3–22.
Wink, W., 1992, *Engaging the Powers*. Fortress Press, Minneapolis.

Index

Abel 82, 83
Académie Française 1, 143
Adams, R. 76, 147
Aeschylus, *Eumenides* 94
Alison, J. 46, 50, 54, 60, 68, 103, 132, 134, 147, 150
　on the Trinity 138–9
Anselm of Canterbury 60–5, 67, 69
Anspach, M. 95
anthropology, theological 45–56
'anthropophany' 45, 55
apocalypse and apocalyptic 99–101, 102–5, 143–4
Arendt, H. 101–2, 144
Assmann, H. 149
Auerbach, E., on Mimesis 9, 10–11, 19, 87, 91
　see also Figura, figural interpretation
Augustine 78, 96, 136
Aulen, G., and 'Christus Victor', 70, 147

Bailie, G. 81
Balthasar, H. U. von
　on Karl Rahner 49
　on Schwager and Girard 138–9
　and 'Theo-Drama' 9, 12, 36, 55, 59, 132, 147
Barker, M. 75
Barth, K. 48–50, 69, 115
Benedict XVI 93

Bible, biblical revelation 27, 31, 81–92
Bin Laden, O. 23
Binsbergen, W. van 112–14
Boston COV&R (on Mimetic Theory and Religions) 120, 123–30
Braque, G 15
Brueggemann, W. 54, 89–92, 148
Buddhism and mimetic theory 126–7
Butler, J. 93

Calasso, R. 74–5
Camus, A. 6, 8, 13, 16
capitalism 24, 116
Cavanaugh, W. T. 97
Cervantes, M. de 1, 3, 15, 23–4
Chardin, T. de 43
Chauvet, L.-M. 75, 77–8
Childs, B. S. 89, 90, 92, 148
Chilton, B. 75, 150
Christ, Christianity 1–2, 3, 14, 18, 21, 38–9, 120
　opposition to Jesus 83–4
Claudel, P. 87, 148
Clausewitz, C. 16, 143–5
Colloquium on Violence and Religion (COV&R) 120, 123–30, 132, 146, 149
conversion, and René Girard 2, 3, 12, 15, 129, 146

161

Index

see also novel, and 'novelistic conversion'

Daly, R. 76, 77, 123, 132, 150
Dante 16
Darwin, C. 18, 20–1
Davis, C. 133, 150
Dawkins, R. 22–3
Dawson, J. D. 148
Deleuze, G. 16, 116
Derrida, J. 7, 8, 16
Descartes, R. 48
Detienne, M. 93-4, 98
Dionysus 27
Domenach, J.-M. 133, 135, 140
Dostoyevsky, F. 1, 3, 4
  Brothers Karamazov 8, 15
Dramatic Theology 31, 36–44, 147
  see also Schwager, R
Duff, P. 150
Dumouchel, P. 35, 121, 132

Eliot, T. S. 45
Europe, imitation of (Fanon) 107–8
Evans-Prichard, E. 20
existentialism 45

Fanon, F., *The Wretched of the Earth* 106–8, 115, 149
Figura, figural interpretation 11, 19, 87–8, 91, 131
Fleming, C. 26, 30, 32, 132
Ford, D. 65, 70, 79
Foucault, M. 7, 8, 136
Freud, S. 24, 99
  and Oedipus Complex 26, 60
  Totem and Taboo 26
Frye, N., and 'New Criticism' 6, 14

Galvin, J. P. 37, 55

Rahnerian critique of Girard 66–7
Genesis, Book of 45, 82, 85–6
Girard, R. N.
  on the 'apocalyptic feeling' 99–101, 103
  on the Bible 81–6, 87
  comparison with Anselm 61–5
  comparison to Fanon 106, 115–16
  conversion experience 1–4, 121
  early life and career 13–17
  on hope for meaning 145
  on Islamist terrorism 22–3, 129–30
  and liberation theology 109, 116
  mimetic theory of 20–32
  on non-Christian religions 127–8
  on the Paraclete 118, 135–6
  philosopher or literary critic 5–9
  relationship to Raymund Schwager 33–4, 41
  on sacrifice 33, 76, 79
  on violence in the modern world 94–6
  on witchcraft 118–19
Gnosticism, and Girard 140–2
Goodhart, S. 81, 123–4, 149
Gottwald, N. 89, 90, 92, 148
grace, doctrine of 51–3
Gunton, C. 73, 148

Habermas, J. 22, 93, 133
Hamerton-Kelly, R. 28–9, 30–1, 63–4, 81, 102–5, 130, 134, 143–4
Hegel, G. W. F. 6–7, 24, 107, 115, 149
Heidegger, M. 7
Heim, S. M. 67

Index

Heraclitus 84–5
Hinduism, and mimetic theory 125–6
Hobbes, T. *Leviathan*, 24, 35, 95–6, 97, 102
Holy Spirit *see* Paraclete
Holy Week 2, 121–3
'hominization' 50–1, 81
Hugo, V. 16

Ignatius of Loyola 58–66
Imitatio.org 143
Innsbruck 31, 33, 133, 146
Islam 79, 95, 103
 and mimetic theory 124–5, 129–31

Job 16, 73
John, Gospel of 35–45, 140
 Johannine *logos* 84–6
John of the Cross 58–9, 66
Joyce, J. 13
Judaism, and mimetic theory 123–4
Juergensmeyer, M. 94–6, 149

Kahane, M. 95
Kant, I. 48
Katēchon 96, 102
 see also Schmitt, C. and Hobbes, T.
Keenan, D. K. 77
Kerr, F. 132, 137
Kierkegaard, S. *Repetition*, 4, 9–10
Kirwan, M. 145
Kojève, A. (on Hegel) 6–7, 107

Lacan, J. 16
Lakatos, I., and research programmes 32, 42–3, 142
Lefebure, L. D. 126–7

Lefort, G. 17, 50
Lévi-Strauss, C. 8, 16, 26
liberation theology *see* political and liberation theologies
literary theory 4, 5–6, 7–8
Livingston, P. 141, 149
Lonergan, B. 129
Loughlin, G. 136
Lowe, W. 59–60, 129, 137–8, 148
Lubac, H. de 87, 148
Luther, M. 69, 96–7, 149

Machaut, G. de, *Judgement of the Kings of Navarre* 28
Mack, B. 81, 94, 134
Mandunu, J. K. 114–15
Marcion 57
Maritain, J. 103
martyrdom 79, 131
 and testimony 99
Marx, K. 99
McKenna, A. 35, 81
Melberg, A. on mimesis 10
Metz, J. B. 104
Milbank, J. 53, 132, 136–7, 149
mimesis 10, 12, 14, 24, 25
mimetic theory 28–30
 as a 'hermeneutic of suspicion' 30
 scientific status of 8–29
Molière 8
Moltmann, J. 104, 148
Moreau, J. 15
myth 28

Newton, I. 20–1
Nietzsche, F. 8, 16, 24
Niewiadomski, J. 41, 42
North, R. 81, 86–7
novel, and 'novelistic conversion' 2, 3, 28

Oedipus 26–7

Index

Oughourlian, J. M. 17, 21, 50–1

Palaver, W. 41, 42, 98–9
'Paraclete' 40, 135
Paul 74, 96
philosophy, 5, 26
    and René Girard 6–7, 146
Picasso, P. 15
Plato 4, 12
political and liberation
    theologies 31, 40–56, 93–105,
    106–10, 116–17
Potolsky, M., on mimesis, 11
Proust, M. 1, 4
The Past Remembered 13, 15, 24

Quessnell, Q. 52

Rahner, K. 31, 33, 43–4, 47–50,
    53–6, 59, 66–7
Rapoport, D. 95
religions, and mimetic
    theory 120–31
Ricoeur, P. 133, 146, 147, 148
Rose, G. 140
Rousseau, J.-J., *Emile* 56

sacrifice, and 'sacrificial
    mechanism' 18–19, 26–7,
    75–9, 80, 136–7
Sartre, J.-P. 6, 106
Satan, victory over 70–3, 80
scapegoat, scapegoating 25–6,
    135–6
Schmitt, C. 97–9, 102
    on 'Friend or Foe' distinction
    98, 149
    see also Katēchon
Schwager, R. 31, 33
    on Anselm of Canterbury 62
    Dramatic Theology 37–41, 55,
    81, 132–3, 147, 148

    on imitation and discipleship
    34–5
    on metaphors of salvation 72
    on scriptures 86–7
    on 'wrath of God' 35
Schweiker, W. 132
Scott and Cavanaugh 93, 147
Scubla, L. 135
Second World War 14–15
September 11th, and 'War on
    Terror' 22–3, 95, 102–3, 144
Shakespeare, W. 8–9, 14, 16, 24
    Hamlet 144
    Julius Caesar 8
    A Midsummer Night's Dream 13
    Winter's Tale 8–9, 13
Simonse, S. 114–15, 149
Sobrino, J. 116
Sölle, D. 104
Soteriology (doctrine of salvation)
    39, 57–69, 137–40
Stark, R.
Stendhal 1, 3
Strauss, L. 103
Suffering Servant (Isaiah
    40–55) 27–34, 82–3, 88, 92,
    120, 123, 148
supersessionism 130–1

Taylor, C. 7, 146
Taylor, S. 67–8
theology 1, 5, 33
    as 'Queen of the Sciences' 5–6
Thiel, P. 103, 105, 143
Tocqueville, A. de 24
Troll, C., on 'Christian Answers to
    Muslim Questions' 65–6, 148

Vanheeswijck, G., on Girard and
    Philosophy 6–7, 146
Vanhoozer, K. 45
Vattimo, G. 7, 146

Index

vineyard, parable of the 37–8
Voegelin, E. 103
Vries, H. 93–4

Wagner, R. 16
Wallace, M. 81
White, H. 150

Whitehead, A. N. 7
Williams, J. 15–16, 81, 132, 147
Williams, R. 93, 99, 132, 140
witchcraft, witchcraze 106
   in Africa 110–15, 117–19

Zizek, S. 93, 149